WITHDRAWN

2-13

THE EAST-WEST CENTER, established in Hawaii by the United States Congress in 1960, is a national educational institution with multinational programs. Its purpose is to promote better relations and understanding among the nations and peoples of Asia, the Pacific area, and the United States through their cooperative participation in research, study, and training activities.

Fundamental to the achievement of the Center's purpose is the cooperative discovery and application of knowledge, and the interchange of knowledge, information, ideas, and beliefs in an intercultural atmosphere of academic freedom. In Center programs, theory and practice are combined to help current and future leaders generate, test, and share knowledge about important world problems of mutual concern to people in both East and West.

Each year about 1500 scholars, leaders, public officials, mid-level and upper-level managers, and graduate students come to the Center to work and study together in programs concerned with seeking alternative approaches and solutions to common problems. For each participant from the United States, two come from the Asian/Pacific area. An international, interdisciplinary, professional staff provides the framework, content, and continuity for programs and for cooperative relationships with universities and other institutions in the Center's area of operations.

Center programs are conducted by the East-West Communication Institute, the East-West Culture Learning Institute, the East-West Food Institute, the East-West Population Institute, and the East-West Technology and Development Institute. Each year the Center also awards a limited number of Open Grants for graduate degree education and research by scholars and authorities in areas not encompassed by the problem-oriented institutes.

The East-West Center is governed by the autonomous board of a public, nonprofit educational corporation—the Center for Cultural and Technical Interchange between East and West, Inc.—established by special act of the Hawaii State Legislature. The Board of Governors is composed of distinguished individuals from the United States and countries of Asia and the Pacific area. The United States Congress provides basic funding for Center programs and for a variety of scholarships, fellowships, internships, and other awards. Because of the cooperative nature of Center programs, financial support and cost-sharing arrangements also are provided by Asian and Pacific governments, regional agencies, private enterprise, and foundations.

The Center is located in Honolulu, Hawaii, on 21 acres of land adjacent to the University of Hawaii's Manoa campus. Through cooperative arrangements with the University of Hawaii, the Center has access to University degree programs, libraries, computer center, and the like.

THE EAST-WEST CULTURE LEARNING INSTITUTE seeks to develop more effective methods of helping persons from different cultures to understand other cultures as well as their own. In particular, the Institute is concerned with ways and means by which cultures may come in contact with each other for the mutual benefit of persons in those cultures while individual and national identities are maintained. For program purposes, it conducts cooperative research, study, and training in four main areas: cultural identity, language in culture, cultures in contact, and thought and expression in culture learning.

COUNSELING ACROSS CULTURES

Counseling across Cultures

Edited by
Paul Pedersen, Walter J. Lonner,
and Juris G. Draguns

A Culture Learning Institute Monograph
EAST-WEST CENTER 禾
The University Press of Hawaii
Honolulu

Library of Congress Cataloging in Publication Data

Main entry under title:

Counseling across cultures.

(East-West Center. A Culture Learning Institute
monograph)
"Some of the papers . . . were delivered at a sym-
posium for the 1973 Annual Meeting of the American
Psychological Association in Montreal, Canada . . .
sponsored by the Society for the Psychological
Study of Social Issues."
Includes bibliographies and index.
1. Counseling—Congresses. 2. Psychiatry,
Transcultural—Congresses. I. Pedersen, Paul,
1936–   II. Lonner, Walter J.   III. Draguns,
Juris, 1932–   IV. Society for the Psychological
Study of Social Issues. V. Series.
[DNLM: 1. Counseling. 2. Cross-cultural com-
parison. BF637.C6 C855]
BF637.C6C63   616.8'914   75-37892
ISBN 0-8248-0381-7

Contents

Preface

Counseling is increasingly becoming an intercultural enterprise as modern populations become more consciously aware of their pluralistic composition and as those same populations compete for limited resources. Counselors who force their own notions of healthy and normal onto persons who do not share the counselor's value assumptions have, through cultural naiveté, cognitive rigidity, or misunderstanding, become tools of their own dominant political, social, or economic value systems. It is dangerous, at best, for me to assume that I know better than you what is good for you. Just as the notion of individual differences has influenced counseling theory, in the same way we are beginning to appreciate the implications of groups that have their own individuality that distinguishes them from other clusters in our society.

It might be useful to illustrate the pervasiveness of cultural differences in counseling relationships through an example of how differences in cultural values might affect the counseling interview. First, consider the four basic aspects in counseling where cultural values might intrude. The most obvious is the culture of the counselor, which has socialized him to accept certain assumptions as being beyond debate. Second is the culture of the client, who likewise has been trained to accept certain assumptions about reality. Third are the frequently neglected assumptions inherent in the counseling problem itself, which may derive from a culture quite different from that of either the counselor or counselee. Finally, there is the culture of the environment in which the counseling is occurring, and this environment will impose its own restrictions and opportunities on the counseling relationship. We might, in the extreme instance, find ourselves working with a client from another culture, on a problem relating to a third culture, in the environment of a fourth culture. Each participating culture will impose its own demands on what constitutes a satisfactory solution to the counseling interaction.

It would be foolish for a counselor to ignore the culturally biased assumptions he or she brings into counseling, even though, having been made aware of them, he or she may choose to continue to use them. The purpose of this book is not so much the elimination of cultural bias in the process of counseling—if, indeed, that could or even should be done—but rather to help counselors become more aware of the cultural biases that surround them and affect all of their interpersonal behavior. If after surveying the issues we discuss, the reader chooses not to modify his or her own value assumptions, then that is the reader's prerogative, even though these assumptions may be contrary to those of the authors. If a counselor chooses to be monocultural, let him or her at least be deliberately and intentionally monocultural and not be deluded accidently by his or her own cultural encapsulation.

Some of the papers in this book were delivered at a symposium for the 1973 annual meeting of the American Psychological Association in Montreal, Canada. The symposium was sponsored by the Society for the Psychological Study of Social Issues, which is Division 9 of the American Psychological Association. Persons with specialized skills in intercultural communications were invited to join the symposium to discuss the influence of cultural values on the counseling process. In the initial invitation to prepare a program, a number of questions were suggested as the foci for discussion. What are the ways in which cultural differences between a counselor and a counselee affect counseling? How serious is the implicit cultural bias among counselors and counselor training programs? What are the indigenous alternatives to counseling in non-Western cultures? How can a counselor evaluate his own implicit cultural bias? How could counselors be better trained to work in a multicultural population? How do psychological problems vary with the culture of the clients? Why do some methods work better than others with persons from other cultures who are being counseled? What can we learn from other cultures that will sharpen our own skills as counselors? Is the counseling process itself—as a product of Westernized, developed cultures—culturally encapsulated?

Counseling is increasingly matching partners from different cultures, either between nationality groups, ethnic groups, or groups that define their roles as being culturally differentiated. Consequently, counselors need to be aware of culture-specific aspects in the counseling process and in their particular counseling style so that they can deal more skillfully with the culture variable. This book brings together mental health professionals who share an interest in intercultural counseling and whose presentations provide the basis for a better understanding of the ways in which culture influences counseling.

The following chapters combine efforts of psychologists, psychiatrists, and communications specialists who share an interest in providing mental health services to a multicultural population. Draguns begins the first chapter by surveying the issues under discussion throughout the book. In chapter 2, Pedersen reviews the literature relevant to the focus of this volume, and describes the process of counseling across international, intranational, and culturally defined role groups. Next, Vontress, in chapter 3, explores the implications of how racial and ethnic diversity complicates the process of establishing a counseling relationship within (or across) different American ethnic populations. Trimble, in chapter 4, describes the more frequent errors committed by Caucasians who are working with Native American Indian clients. Chapter 5 by Alexander, Workneh, Klein, and Miller discusses findings of clinical research on the foreign student from the point of view of the therapist as well as from that of the student and the implications of cultural differences for appropriate psychiatric intervention. Stewart's chapter 6 on cultural sensitivities describes how differences and similarities of cultural predispositions impinge upon communication, particularly in a helping relationship. In chapter 7, David describes intercultural adjustment in terms of cultural reinforcers and aversive stimuli and emphasizes desensitization and counterconditioning procedures for bridging cultural differences in counseling. Sundberg's chapter 8 introduces variables related to evaluating the effectiveness of intercultural counseling in terms of accurate communications, appropriate intervention, and the sponsoring of realistic relationship expectations. Lonner's chapter 9 discusses the use and misuse of psychological tests that have been developed in one culture being used in another culture. Wohl's chapter 10 looks at the clinical applications of intercultural psychotherapy. Wintrob's chapter 11 applies many of the problems discussed to his own personal experiences.

The chapters divide themselves into three foci of emphasis. The issues are surveyed by Draguns' discussion of the principal themes in the other chapters. Pedersen reviews the accumulated counseling literature, and Wintrob looks at the challenges of counseling from his own point of view as a practicing psychiatrist. Their intent is to provide a context for understanding intercultural counseling processes. The second focus, represented by Stewart, David, Sundberg, Lonner, and Wohl, relates to the methods used in intercultural counseling. Their intent is to apply counseling and communication theories to the problems of cultural differences in a series of approaches that might be applied to the practice of intercultural counseling. The third focus, as expressed by Vontress, Alexander, and Trimble, relates to a discussion of target populations that bring their own value presuppositions into the counseling relationship. The objective of these three authors is to demonstrate both the variation of cultural values among target populations and the differentiation within each population.

The overall function of this book should be to motivate readers toward exploring the materials, techniques, ideas, and populations mentioned by the authors as resources by which an individual may increase an understanding of his or her own culture as well as that of others. Ultimately, the reader will learn best about a particular target population from direct contact with its members and not from books or expert advice. The authors of this book hope that it will encourage readers to examine their own cultures and the alternatives to them as they relate to a better understanding of counseling as a deeply complex, interpersonal relationship.

Paul Pedersen
Walter J. Lonner
Juris G. Draguns

1 Counseling across Cultures: Common Themes and Distinct Approaches

JURIS G. DRAGUNS

CAN COUNSELORS BE MORE SENSITIVE TO CULTURAL DIFFERENCES?

In the first chapter of this volume, Dr. Juris Draguns cites five overlapping themes that recur in various forms throughout the remaining chapters. First is the categorization of values into culture-specific and culture-general aspects—a theme shared by much of the literature on intercultural topics. A second theme contrasts the subjective emphasis on relationships with the objective emphasis on technique as being two parallel avenues leading toward effective intercultural counseling. A third theme is that of the bilaterality of the client-counselor relationship; involved are an exchange of learning and benefits to both partners and a mutualistic rather than a hierarchical view of the counseling process. A fourth theme discusses the issue of whether a counselor can and/or should change the client's values in any particular direction. The final theme that Draguns highlights is that of the orientation of all the articles toward the future—toward improving the quality of intercultural counseling in multicultural populations.

Draguns goes on to review the various chapters, and here he raises questions with each of the authors and examines the implications of their various suggestions. This chapter thereby provides the essence of a continuing discussion among the authors about the issues involved in intercultural counseling.

The parameters of intercultural counseling are not yet so clearly defined that they distinguish this discipline, by issues or topics, from surrounding disciplines. Primary contributors to the literature have credentials in a variety of related fields, which allow them to contribute insights to intercultural problems from their own various perspectives. At worst, this diffuseness has led to confusion and disorganization of resources; at best, it has provided an exciting frontier for counselors who are seeking to break out of their own Eurocentric encapsulation. Draguns, by contributing to this collection, seeks to prevent counselors from accepting blindly both the encapsulated cultural bias of counseling and the arguments critical of that bias.

1

The advantage of an edited multiauthor volume lies in its diversity of outlook and content; its pitfall lies in the lack of integration of its heterogeneous components. This chapter has been written to enhance the former and to counteract the latter potentiality inherent in the chapters that follow. To this end, I will first seek to articulate the commonalities detectable despite the very different approaches and themes of the several contributors. Once this is done, I will focus attention on the distinctive features of their papers. In the process, I will take the opportunity to bring my own point of view to bear upon the issues discussed and will not refrain from registering occasional disagreements with my fellow contributors.

FIVE COMMON THEMES

The reader will note in the following chapters at least five themes that are of common interest to all the authors.

The Emic-Etic Distinction

First, the emic-etic distinction, although explicitly referred to by only Lonner, Sundberg, and Stewart, appears implicitly to suffuse all of the papers. The terms *etic* (culturally generalized) and *emic* (culturally specific) were coined by the linguist Pike (1954). They pertain to the two contrasting frames of reference used when one is describing and analyzing cultural phenomena: emic refers to the viewing of data in terms indigenous or unique to the culture in question, and etic, to viewing them in light of categories and concepts external to the culture but universal in their applicability. The emic-etic dichotomy, descriptive of looking at a culture from the inside or from the outside, has come into widespread use in recent writings in intercultural psychology. Price-Williams (1974) has provided a particularly useful analysis of the problems and complexities inherent in relying upon either of these two outlooks; Triandis, Malpass, and Davidson (1973) have reviewed the use of these two approaches in recent intercultural research; and Berry (1969) has outlined a rather detailed technique of switching from one frame of reference to the other in the course of intercultural investigation.

All of the authors, therefore, are involved in the struggle to separate the humanly universal and the culturally particular elements of experience as these factors enter into the counselor-counselee relationship when the two participants to this transaction come from different cultures. David and Stewart, in their two very different chapters, grounded in social learning and cognitive theories respectively, have worked to bring a general theoretical framework to bear upon the understanding and/or control of the intercultural counseling situation, which is a pronouncedly etic, or generalized, undertaking. Vontress, Trimble, and Lonner, as well as, to some extent, Alexander, Workneh, Klein, and Miller, are concerned with the cultural specificity of the counselee's perspective, expectation, and experience. All of them caution the actual or prospective counselors who operate across the culture gulf against "counseling as usual" and point to particular stumbling blocks, traceable to the counselor's and/or the counselee's experience. Their concerns legitimately can be described as emic, or culture-specific. Worth highlighting in this connection is the caveat embedded in the papers by Alexander et al., as well as that by Trimble, against imputing psychopathological and psychodynamic meanings to obstructions in the counseling process with a client culturally different from oneself. To these authors, such a tendency appears to be a particularly ominous example of what recently has been called the "pseudoetic" orientation in intercultural psychology (Triandis et al., 1973); the counselor's culture-bound experience is assumed implicitly to be an adequate base to guide and interpret the behavior of individuals socialized in other cultural contexts.

Of the several authors, Trimble has gone farthest toward the emic polarity in urging understanding and sensitivity to the very marked differences among the Indian cultures in their value orientations and in their actual or potential reflections in the counseling experience. It is commonly recognized, of course, that the emic and etic orientations are equally valid and complementary, and it is my hope that this compendium will initiate thought and stimulate work toward the integration of these two perspectives. The crucial thing is to recognize these orientations for what they are; practical and conceptual pitfalls appear only when the etic orientation is mistaken for the emic or vice versa. In any intercultural work, basic or applied, the investigator, to quote the terminology of the French psychiatrist Benoit (1964), is subject to both centrifugal and centripetal pull. Thus, any formulations in intercultural psychology must allow room both for the etic and the emic, or the centripetal and centrifugal, forces that impinge upon each of us as members of the human species existing in a culturally specific context.

Relationship versus Technique

The second shared theme pertains to the relative importance of relationship and technique in intercultural counseling. Alexander et al. in particular, but also Trimble and Vontress, have accumulated convincing instances and have presented generalizations that point to the cultural relativity of many of the mainstream American or Western counseling techniques and of their underlying assumptions. From a somewhat different point of view, Lonner has highlighted the limitations and pitfalls of relying upon test instruments and situations as though they were an interculturally constant yardstick. An important theme of Stewart's paper is that of how deeply the American culture-bound assumptions are embedded in the counseling experience. The issue that these observations bring to the fore is basic to the nature of the counseling process, whether it is applied from within the counselor's cultural frame of reference or outside of it.

What, indeed, is the essence of counseling? If the type of counseling, nature of the relationship, techniques employed, or environmental manipulation are artificially extricated, which of them will survive in a culturally different milieu? Implicitly or explicitly, Sundberg, Trimble, Vontress, Alexander et al., Wohl, and Wintrob address themselves to this issue. The common thread that runs through their treatments of this topic stresses flexibility of technique, importance of personal sensitivity, and openness to direct and active intervention. A general précis might read thusly: be prepared to adapt your techniques (e.g., general activity level, mode of verbal intervention, content of remarks, tone of voice) to the cultural background of the client; communicate acceptance of and respect for the client in terms that are intelligible and meaningful within his or her cultural frame of reference; and be open to the possibility of more direct intervention in the life of the client than the traditional ethos of the counseling profession would dictate or permit. Thus, the nature of the relationship would appear to be the interculturally most robust ingredient of the counseling situation, provided that the counselor is aware of such countertransference implications as Vontress and Wintrob describe. In this, a parallel may be discerned with the recent concerns in the research literature on psychotherapy (e.g., Strupp, 1970) that stress the weight of nonspecific factors in the psychotherapeutic process.

Yet, this is not to imply that the techniques employed are not important. On the basis of their clinical experience, Vontress, Trimble, and Alexander et al. provide a host of specific and practically useful points of immediate relevance to the intercultural counselor: what to do, what to avoid, how to communicate across a variety of cultural gulfs. Sundberg, who deals with the same subject matter on a more abstract and general plane, asks what principles should govern the counselor's acts and expectations when counseling across a cultural barrier. Finally, intercultural counseling, to judge from the accounts of Trimble, Vontress, Alexander et al., and Wintrob in particular, is not for the chair- or office-bound counselor who restricts his or her work to verbal interchange with clients at specified places and times. Stewart and Sundberg remind us of the culturally specific background of verbal, time-bound counseling, whereas Trimble and Vontress confront us with the challenges of dealing with counselees who will not talk, keep appointments, or, generally, "play the game" of the highly abstract, stylized counseling interaction that has been rather widely accepted in certain restricted segments of the American and other Western societies. Being a part of the counselee's social relationships, or even acting as a catalyst in their formation may be an important part of counseling according to Alexander et al.

A special place in the context of the relationship-versus-technique dilemma is occupied by the application of behavior modification, a theme of central concern in David's presentation. On the one hand, one could argue that the laws of learning are universal and, hence, applicable regardless of variations of the cultural milieu. On the other hand, the point could be advanced that the explicit social control of behavior through behavior modification by an expert is open to a variety of culturally patterned interpretations that could influence the degree and nature of its acceptability. In this volume, Alexander et al. have shared their observations and experiences that point to the limitations of behavior modification techniques when applied to students from abroad who are attending American universities. David, however, has convincingly made a case in his chapter, as well as elsewhere (Brein & David, 1971), for the use of the behavior modification orientation in preparing the prospective American traveler for life in a different country. The question remains open as to what extent these techniques can be utilized in ameliorating the problems of both temporary and permanent immigrants to the United States. It might be added that already a promising start within the behavior modification framework has been made (David & King, 1973).

The Bilaterality of the Client-Counselor Relationship

The third concern reflected in the several contributions to this volume is that which deals with the degree to which the counseling experience is a bilateral learning process, affecting both the counselor and the counselee. David's chapter, explicitly couched in learning theory, focuses upon the streamlining and disciplining of the culture learning process by the counselee. Wintrob and Wohl have been candid in revealing what they learned when they plunged into the intercultural personal contacts that counseling outside of one's own social milieu entailed. Other writers, Trimble in particular, emphasize the potential value of the counseling process as an avenue for learning the "subjective culture" of the counselee (Triandis et al., 1973) by the counselor. Indeed, it is my belief, expressed at greater length elsewhere (Draguns, 1975), that counseling and psycho-therapy situations across cultures are destined to play as important a role in the emergent formulations of intercultural psychology as that which psychotherapy has historically played in the development of theories of personality and of psychopathology. When the cultural gap between the counselor and the counselee is bridged, the subjective experience communicated in the counseling process becomes a window through which one can glimpse the other's culture with its shared frame of reference—its subjective world. This perspective is difficult, perhaps impossible, to obtain except through the self-disclosure for which counseling and psychotherapy provide a setting and an opportunity. Of course none of the foregoing statements are meant to imply that the counselor directly or bumptiously should indulge his intercultural curiosity at the expense of the counselee's effort and time. It is the counselee's problems and goals that must be paramount.

The Autoplastic-Alloplastic Dilemma

The fourth shared problem focuses upon the goals of counseling in relation to cultural experience. Vexliard (1968), a French social psychologist, has articulated the distinction between autoplastic and alloplastic modes of adaptation; the former involves accommodating oneself to the givens of a social setting and structure, and the latter involves shaping the external reality to suit one's needs. Applied to the counseling situation, this dichotomy boils down to the question: How much should the counselee be helped to adapt to a given reality and how much should he be encouraged to shape and change that same reality? Historically, counseling with persons not native to the United States has been markedly autoplastic in orientation. Even in this area, the question of overadaptation to the host country as a result of an excessively autoplastic inclination or program has been raised (Brislin & Van Buren, 1974). Even more markedly has the counseling of visibly different and/or socially disadvantaged American minority groups, as represented in this book by Drs. Vontress and Trimble, taken an autoplastic bias, although recently the counseling situation has been seen as one of the avenues of emancipation and liberation—a way of freeing the individual to restructure the situation that brought him or her into counseling in the first place. The theme of autoplasticity-alloplasticity as a professional, ethical, and political dilemma for the intercultural counselor is a central one in Wohl's chapter. In their extremes—notably unrepresented in this volume—the alloplastic bias degenerates into revolutionary rhetoric and bombast, and the autoplastic bias, into the jargon and scholasticism of the most rigid variants of the medical model as misapplied on the social scene. The alloplastic mode refers any personal problem to its putative social and political causes and the autoplastic traces it to personal pathology. Wohl, in his review of pioneering contributions to intercultural psychotherapy, provides particularly glaring examples of acceptance of the social situation as being immutable; from the vantage point of the current political and social climate, examples of such an orientation by the therapist would no doubt strike many readers as being reactionary politically and rigid clinically. I would add, however, that a similar lopsidedness results if solutions to personal problems are sought exclusively in institutional or social change, for such broad changes are neither within the counselor's nor the counselee's power to execute. More significant in a conceptual sense is the fact that we do not have any kind of reliable empirical data that would permit us even to envisage a social setting that would be immunized against the kinds of problems that spark the need for counseling or therapy. Steering clear of these two extremes, each counselor who has a culture gap to overcome must help the counselee both to act upon other people, objects, and situations, and to be acted upon—to accommodate to the ambient situation. The counselor should realize that each counselee, whether an immigrant or a member of a minority group, has a different formula for combining the elements of autoplastic and alloplastic adaptation.

The Australian social psychologist R. Taft (1966) has identified a spectrum of adaptive modes including encapsulation in the community of one's compatriots, a headlong plunge into the social world of the host culture, or integration of the elements of host and original culture patterns into a complex web of personal behavior and experience. No doubt this general scheme is applicable, albeit probably with variations, to other types of culturally distinct counselees. The point is that where the counselee stands on the issue of adaptation to the host or majority culture is of great moment in the counseling process. To the extent that the counselee is conflict-torn on this issue—a situation typically found in intercultural counseling—the goal of counseling must be to help him find his own best solution to the dilemma of how to combine the familiar and the strange, the old and the new, into his own life.

Futuristic Thinking among Intercultural Workers

It is striking to what extent the thinking of all the authors is pointed to the future. To be sure, all of the chapters rest on a sound clinical and research base, but it would be fair to say that, in the current state of our under-standing of intercultural counseling, hypotheses prevail over findings, formulations over substance. Although Sundberg has organized his chapter specifically around a number of research hypotheses, the other authors refer often to work needed and problems to be solved.

THE ROLE OF PSYCHOLOGICAL TESTS IN INTERCULTURAL COUNSELING

Turning to this remaining objective, we will first concentrate on Lonner's contribution, which deals with a rather specialized problem: the role of psychological tests in intercultural counseling. Lonner's thesis may be summarized by saying that cultural factors intervene at all stages of testing a client from another culture, these factors including the norms of the test, the subjective definition of the test-taking situation, and the sets that shape the client's response to particular test items. Lonner feels that a test gives a poor representation of a person, expecially of an individual from another culture (even though, to append my opinion, it may still be a useful one). Whether any useful application of psychological tests can be salvaged in the intercultural context depends on the assumptions on which the use of the tests rests. In the traditional psychometric sense, a test is constructed to reveal a miniature sample of individually characteristic behavior that stands in a known relationship to significant parameters of real-life performance. It is from this conception of the test that Lonner proceeds and, within its scope, there is indeed no solution to the problem of validation with many of the culturally deviant clients. For, as Lonner rightly points out, the client may not be comparable either to his or her culture's or subculture's norms nor to those of the American middle-class mainstream. There is, however, a more flexible, open-ended view of psychological tests, especially those applicable within the field of personality (Fulkerson, 1965; Schneidman, 1964). Within this framework, a test is viewed simply as an additional avenue of communication beyond the direct and open elicitation of self-related information. On such a basis, there remains a distinct, if modest, place for tests in the intercultural counseling process, provided that the tests are used both sparingly and flexibly. Vontress's critical, although not nihilistic, treatment of tests in his chapter would appear to be consonant with this position. What is imperative in such cases is that assumptions and goals of testing be made explicit and that important safeguards be observed. In particular, the test should never be interpreted mechanically or automatically in the light of its available culture-bound norms when it is used with a culturally atypical client. Moreover, it should not be used by itself to arrive at decisions affecting the client's life, but only to provide additional information for understanding the client's outlook and experience.

Worth a brief mention is a minor point concerning the scope and role of response sets in intercultural testing. Lonner proceeds from the assumption that there exists a far-reaching, culturally mediated parallel between the way an individual will react to a given test and the way he or she will react to a specific situation in "real" life. For example, individuals from some of the traditional cultures of the Far East often are reluctant to voice disagreements in interpersonal situations; therefore, they may exhibit a bias toward acquiescence when taking true-false personality inventories. The fragments of evidence we now have concerning intercultural comparisons of response sets (Iwasaki, Okuno, & Cowen, 1965; Iwasaki & Zax, 1969; Zax & Takahashi, 1967a, 1967b) argue for putting more emphasis on instrument-specific and situation-specific response sets, a view that has been in ascendancy in the mainstream of the response-set literature over the last few years (e.g., Block, 1965; Rorer, 1965). Very recently, however, Chun, Campbell, & Yoo (1974) have provided some empirical support for Lonner's expectations of the relationship between the extremity of response style and general cultural characteristics. Specifically, Koreans were found to be significantly less given to outspoken item-endorsement than are Americans. Thus, my skepticism concerning the cultural stability of written response styles should itself be taken skeptically.

None of the foregoing argues against the heuristic value of investigating possible parallels between culturally inculcated styles of self-presentation and social response on the one hand and test-taking tendencies on the other. The only point on which Lonner and I would differ would be that of the extent of such parallels.

The Sympathy-Empathy Distinction

To turn to Stewart's challenging and innovative argument, I am both impressed and fascinated with the potential usefulness of the sympathy-empathy distinction, which goes far beyond intercultural counseling, as well as with the proposition that Americans establish relationships on the basis of similarities of experience and outlook rather than on differences. Stewart's formulations are based on impressive interdisciplinary scholarship that brings forth converging evidence from several fields of inquiry. Nonetheless, one must be skeptical of these far-reaching formulations. Byrne's research, which Stewart cites, seemed to highlight the intercultural generality of adjustment in terms of similarity and shared experience, which would suggest that Stewart's argument at this point is heuristic and, as such, is well worth taking seriously. The questions remain as to what extent Americans exhibit a bias toward similarity and how much do they do so when compared with other cultures. These questions should be answered by systematic empirical comparisons across cultures, and their results could then be brought to bear upon the concerns and realities of the counseling situation.

Preparing the Individual for a New Culture

David's paper leaves little room for doubt that the systematic application of the social-learning theory to the task of preparing individuals for new cultural milieus is an undertaking both of practical and conceptual significance. Such an undertaking overcomes the limitations of the atheoretical practical empiricism in which so many intercultural counselors operate and which dominates the intercultural counseling literature. A practical consideration is the preventive, orthopsychiatric aspect of David's project. Alexander et al. have reminded us that immigrants are reluctant to seek help except at rather advanced stages of entanglement with personal and situational problems. The procedures that David has outlined might fill the gap between specific aversive experiences and the general feeling of helplessness in the face of an alien cultural setting and might be utilized as means of preclinical and subclinical intervention. However, three questions do occur which David's presentation stimulates but does not answer. (1) Can the entire reality of the counseling process be fitted into the social learning framework, that is, can the sympathy-empathy distinction, so articulately brought out by Stewart, be reformulated in social-learning terms? (2) What is the role of individual differences and social fluctuations within David's model? David appears to emphasize the unity of the culture to be entered and the similarities among the potential entrants. Yet, we know that people seek a new cultural experience for a variety of reasons and do anticipate a multitude of distinct reinforcements. They may encounter danger, however, when they are inculcated with expectations of homogeneity in the culture to be encountered, especially in one as pluralistic as that of the United States. (3) Finally, is the concentrated learning experience based on social learning principles bilaterally applicable, i.e., to persons coming to the United States as well as to Americans going abroad? Alexander et al. have shared their experiences with the limitations of behavior modification techniques when such techniques were applied to their foreign student clients. Although David does allude in this book to his successful experiences in applying social learning theory to "cushioning" the aversive first-contact experiences of immigrants, we must realize that teaching techniques in intercultural counseling will not be universally applicable. Rather, we must ask ourselves what techniques to apply with whom.

CULTURAL STEREOTYPING

Trimble's contribution to this book highlights the Scylla and Charybdis of intercultural counseling. On the one hand is the practice and attitude of "counseling as usual," with the counselor oblivious to the cultural background of the client; on the other hand and equally destructive is the penchant for seeing the counselee as a caricature—American Indian, ghetto Black—and thereby overlooking his or her individuality. The step from cultural sensitivity to cultural stereotyping is as short as it is ominous. Ideally, in the practice of counseling and psychotherapy it is the individual who is in focus, not his race or culture. Cultural factors alone do not provide the answers to the dilemmas that a counselor faces. Trimble is to be commended for his demonstration of the close relationship that exists between research findings and counseling practice and for alerting counselors to the dangers of looking at a different cultural reality from afar, from a distance, for example, at which all the distinct Indian cultures appear alike. And yet it can be maintained that the search for empirically demonstrable commonalities across Indian tribes is a legitimate undertaking. After all, whatever the differences among the many Indian nations and tribes, for the past two or three hundred years they have been exposed to somewhat similar social stresses and pressures. But the existence of these common factors must not lead the counselor into a mindless and unreflective use of them in the counseling process.

Somewhat similar problems are discussed, although in a different context, by Alexander et al. in their paper that focuses on the heterogeneous pool of students from many lands that one encounters at an American university. We are indebted to these researchers for their sensitive clinical analysis of the psychological situation in which these students, some of them beset by cumulative problems, find themselves. The challenge here is in distinguishing two types of problems: those which arose because the counselee is a foreign student in an American academic setting and those which have their roots in his or her own culture or origin. For example, Alexander et al. have stated that group therapy tends to be counterproductive with foreign students. Is this true because the student is an alien living in an unfamiliar culture or because he has received specific cultural training in interpersonal decorum and self-disclosure? Alexander et al. rather sharply distinguish also between personal problems and psychopathology, attributing cultural plasticity to the former and worldwide uniformity to the latter. On the basis of empirical research and a recent review (Draguns, 1973) I am as dubious of the bases of this distinction as I am of the statement that schizophrenia is interculturally constant and that the effect of a rejecting mother may be as pathogenic in Addis Ababa as it is in New York. The issue surrounding cultural influences in defining psychological disturbance over the entire range of its severity is an open one, yet data seem to be pointing to the generalization that psychological disorders are influenced by adverse cultural shaping.

CHARACTERISTICS NEEDED BY THE INTERCULTURAL COUNSELOR

Vontress's contribution deals with a question that is adumbrated in Pedersen's chapter: Can an American mainstream middle-class counselor

effectively work with minority-group counselees? Pedersen cites a number
of authorities who have answered this question in the negative. The care
and detail that Vontress devotes to alerting the potential practitioner
about the hazards of his culturally limited mode of operation when
applied to Black, Indian, Hispanic, and Appalachian clients is testimony
to his conviction that these obstacles are difficult but not impossible to
overcome. To be sure, what it does take to overcome them is the kind
of valuable, techinque-oriented information that Vontress copiously
provides. However, what is equally indispensable is the fact that the
counselor must be prepared to learn, change, and shift his accustomed
mode of operation. What kind of a person is best equipped for embarking
upon this type of venture? Recent work highlights the characteristic of
being open to experience (Fitzgerald, 1966), and the old construct of
tolerance for ambiguity has been rediscovered in its potential relevance
for the counseling situation (Gruberg, 1969). Whether or not these
characteristics are relevant remains to be empirically demonstrated;
conceptually, however, the identification of such characteristics would
seem to be the first step toward finding persons who would be adept and
comfortable when interacting personally with clients from different
cultural milieus.

PROBLEMS OF COUNTERTRANSFERENCE

Vontress's treatment of the issue of countertransference anticipates the
major theme of Wintrob's chapter—that of the counselor's subjective
experience when working with a culturally different client. Of the several
authors represented in this volume, Wintrob has probably gone farthest
in a cultural sense, although not necessarily a geographic one, to provide
clinical services outside of his culture. His account, refreshing in its
immediacy and subjectivity, brings to the fore a variable factor found in
intercultural counseling that is anticipated by Wohl and skirted in the
remainder of the chapters—the impact of intercultural therapy or counseling upon the person providing such service. Psychotherapy and
counseling are personally demanding tasks. The encounter with a new
culture is a stressful experience, even under the most fortunate circumstances. The two sources of stress, the therapeutic and the cultural,
interact geometrically and their impact is vividly described in Wintrob's
account. Yet, the result of these stresses may be enriching and rewarding,
productive of growth and benefit to the counselor as well as to the counselee. If we learn about ourselves through being juxtaposed with others,
then this learning process becomes all the more poignant and intense in
the atmosphere of personal and emotional give-and-take found in counseling and psychotherapy, and becomes especially so when these skills are

tried out beyond one's own cultural domain. Although the most intense of Wintrob's personal intercultural challenges have come from Liberia, he indicates in his chapter that their relevance was not exhausted in the face of seemingly minor cultural variations, such as those encountered by a Canadian professional in training in a United States metropolis or by a psychiatrist in Connecticut, facing clients who reject his rational-scientific explanatory framework. This brings up a point that is also of relevance in Pedersen's chapter: what are the limits of culture as a meaningful variable in the counseling situation? Superficially, the concept of culture in this situation has an esoteric ring. It conjures images of people who, like Wintrob, have gone far from their home base to form helpful relationships with persons different in language, way of life, and outlook. More searchingly, however, such a situation describes only the extremes of culture-contact in the counseling situation. One might venture to say that it is a rare counselor or psychotherapist who, in the pluralistic society of the United States, has not had to bridge a cultural gulf. There is much to be learned from perceptive subjective accounts of such experiences.

THE WORKABILITY OF INTERCULTURAL PSYCHOTHERAPY

If Wintrob's contribution marks the subjective personal extreme of this volume, Sundberg's chapter characterizes the objective, abstract-theoretical end of the continuum. He has compiled a list of hypotheses, based on intracultural and intercultural research evidence. Of interest in this connection are two themes: the presence or absence of counselor-counselee compatibility in a number of characteristics and the client's "degrees of freedom"—the range of the choices open to him in changing himself or his environment. The former parameter determines the effectiveness of counseling procedures; the latter sets the limits to their relevance. To elaborate, there is a triadic relationship of counselor–counselee–culture to consider in deciding whether or not counseling will work or whether, indeed, it is even worth trying. The relationship of counseling to the personality of the client and to the actual range of choices available to the client in changing him- or herself or the ambient environment has not received enough attention in the literature, although there are a few sources that allude to the importance of these considerations (Draguns, 1975; Prince, 1969). In this volume, the problem of the client's choices is discussed by Wohl. A typology of cultures based on their members' openness to counseling and on their amenability toward different types of counseling remains to be constructed. The kind of comparative research that Sundberg suggests at the end of his chapter is a step in this direction, although it might be expanded if the differing counselor as well as the counselee cultures were systematically varied. On the most general plane, Sundberg's message implies the use of the counseling process to learn about cultures and the use of intercultural research to optimize the effectiveness of counseling.

Wohl's paper has points of contact with Wintrob's in content and with Sundberg's in orientation. As in Wintrob's work, its point of departure is the emotionally taxing experience of attempting to render therapeutic service in a locale where the therapist's own cultural experience is but an uncertain and misleading guide. The resulting frustrations lead Wohl to examine what is basic and what is peripheral in psychotherapy and to fit cultural characteristics to the modes of psychotherapy practiced, an issue central to Sundberg's concern. Wohl's conclusions as to the workability of intercultural psychotherapy are cautiously pessimistic; such a contact holds promise only if the right mixture of therapist, client, and cultural characteristics obtains. Wohl, in a careful culling of the pertinent literature, has found that extant works are almost exclusively written in the form of subjective, personal accounts based on case studies. It would appear that the time has come to go beyond this clinical documentation in order to vary systematically the triad of therapist, client, and culture, with the aim eventually of establishing the parameters of successful therapeutic intervention. Wohl rather sharply differentiates subcultural variations among clients sharing the same political structure and physical habitat from intercultural differences in the specific and restricted sense of the term, i.e., in milieus both socially and geographically removed. Yet, his conclusion that intercultural therapy in the narrow sense of the term is both difficult and possible is curiously parallel to that of Vontress.

The themes discussed are broadly consonant with some of Pedersen's statements regarding the current state of intercultural counseling literature. His survey suggests that the boundaries between studies on intercultural counseling and the more basic research on behavior across cultures are flexible and blurred. He also brings to light the fact that the field of intercultural counseling overall and the special foci of activity within it have a sizeable store of recorded experience and conceptualization. Unlike his predecessor of two or more decades ago, the present-day practitioner of intercultural counseling does not have to start from scratch. However, the amount of work reviewed by Pedersen, impressive as it may be, is not complete. Of necessity, his survey has centered on the concerns and activities of counselors in the United States and on the groups that they serve. Recent years have seen a worldwide expansion of this field of activity so that even my own very casual and unsystematic perusal of the international literature has turned up references on the adaptation problems of Middle Eastern students in Pakistan (Zaidi, 1975), West Indian migrants to London (Kiev, 1964), southern Italian workers in

Switzerland (Risso & Böker, 1964), and Peruvian Indians settling in Lima (Seguin, 1962). All of this suggests that intercultural counseling is one of the answers to the problems produced by the unprecedented mobility of our times. Voluntarily or involuntarily, more people are now changing their domiciles across boundaries and oceans; self-contained cultural groups, little disturbed by the cultural mainstream, have a hard time preserving their preferred isolation; long-submerged minorities voice their needs and problems in the process of striving to establish a workable relationship with the majority culture. Individuals who have been scarred and bruised in these encounters or who fear such injuries reach out across the various man-made barriers to be heard and understood. The response to this need is the challenge and concern of intercultural counseling.

REFERENCES

Benoit, G. Qu'est-ce que la psychiatrie transculturelle? *Information Psychiatrique*, 1964, *40*, 592–637.

Berry, J. W. On cross-cultural comparability. *International Journal of Psychology*, 1969, *5*, 119–128.

Block, J. *The challenge of response sets*. New York: Appleton-Century-Crofts, 1965.

Brein, M., & David, K. H. Intercultural communication and the adjustment of the sojourner. *Psychological Bulletin*, 1971, *76*, 215–230.

Brislin, R. W., & Van Buren, H. Can they go home again? *Exchange*, 1974, *9*, 19–24.

Chun, K. T., Campbell, J. B., & Yoo, J. H. Extreme response style in cross-cultural research: A reminder. *Journal of Cross-Cultural Psychology*, 1974, *5*, 465–480.

David, K. H., & King, W. L. Review and analysis of problems of recent immigrants in Hawaii. JSAS *Catalog of Selected Documents in Psychology*, 1971, *3*: 46. (Ms. No. 349) ·

Draguns, J. G. Comparison of psychopathology across cultures: Issues, findings, directions. *Journal of Cross-Cultural Psychology*, 1973, *4*, 9–47.

Draguns, J. G. Resocialization into culture: The complexities of taking a worldwide view of psychotherapy. In R. W. Brislin, S. Bochner, & W. J. Lonner (Eds.), *Cross-cultural perspectives on learning*. New York: John Wiley & Sons, Halsted, 1975.

Fitzgerald, E.T. Measurement of openness to experience: A study of regression at the service of the ego. *Journal of Personality and Social Psychology*, 1966, *4*, 655–663.

Fulkerson, S. Some implications of the new cognitive theory for projective tests. *Journal of Consulting Psychology*, 1965, *29*, 191–197.

Gruberg, R. A significant counselor personality characteristic: Tolerance for ambiguity. *Counselor Education and Supervision*, 1969, *8*(2), 119–124.

Iwasaki, S., Okuno, S., & Cowen, E. L. The social desirability of trait-descriptive terms: Sex and cultural differences based on a Japanese arts college sample. *Tohoku Psychologica Folia*, 1965, *24*, 56–64.

Iwasaki, S., & Zax, M. Personality dimensions and extreme response tendency. *Psychological Reports*, 1969, *25*, 31–34.

Kiev, A. Psychotherapeutic aspects of Pentecostal sects among West Indian immigrants to England. *British Journal of Sociology*, 1964, *15*, 129–138.

Pike, K. L. *Language in relation to a unified theory of the structure of human behavior*. Part 1: Preliminary edition. Summer Institute of Linguistics, 1954.

Price-Williams, D. Psychological experiment and anthropology: The problem of categories. *Ethos*, 1974, *2*, 95–114.

Prince, R. Psychotherapy and the chronically poor. In J. C. Finney (Ed.), *Culture change, mental health, and poverty*. Lexington: University of Kentucky Press, 1969.

Risso, M., & Böker, W. Verhexungswahn: Ein Beitrag zum Veständnis der Wahnwahrnehmungen süditalienischer Arbeiter in der Schweiz. *Bibliotheca Psychiatrica Neurologica*, 1964, *124*.

Rorer, L. G. The great response-style myth. *Psychological Bulletin*, 1965, *63*, 129–148.

Schneidman, E. S. Projective techniques. In B. B. Wolman (Ed.), *Handbook of clinical psychology*. New York: McGraw-Hill, 1964.

Seguin, C. A. (Ed.). *Psiquiatria y sociedad: Estudios sobre la realidad peruana*. Lima: Universidad Nacional Mayor de San Marcos, 1962.

Strupp, H. H. Specific or nonspecific factors in psychotherapy and the problem of control. *Archives of General Psychiatry*, 1970, *23*, 393–401.

Taft, R. *From stranger to citizen*. London: Tavistock, 1966.

Triandis, H. C., Malpass, R. S., & Davidson, A. R. Psychology and culture. *Annual Review of Psychology*, 1973, *24*, 355–378.

Vexliard, A. Tempérament et modalités d'adaptation. *Bulletin de Psychologie*, 1968, *21*, 1–15.

Zaidi, S. M. H. Adjustment problems of foreign Muslim students in Pakistan. In R. W. Brislin, S. Bochner, & W. J. Lonner (Eds.), *Cross-cultural perspectives on learning*. New York: John Wiley & Sons, Halsted, 1975.

Zax, M., & Takahashi, S. Response styles among Japanese and American children. *Japanese Psychological Research*, 1967, *9*, 58–61. (a)

Zax, M., & Takahashi, S. Cultural influences on response style: Comparison of Japanese and American college students. *Journal of Social Psychology*, 1967, *71*, 3–10. (b)

2 The Field of Intercultural Counseling

PAUL PEDERSEN

WHY SHOULD COUNSELORS BE INTERESTED IN CULTURAL DIFFERENCES?

In the following chapter, Dr. Paul Pedersen reviews the literature from a variety of disciplines sensitive to the role of differentiated cultural values in the counseling process. In intercultural research generally, there are hundreds of articles, dozens of books, and several journals that focus tangentially on the problems of helping individuals from other cultures, and there exist at least six professional societies attempting to coordinate resources. This chapter introduces literature dealing with the variety of alternatives in counseling clients from other cultures.

Counseling, in the context of this chapter, refers to a broad range of interpersonal relationships in which persons are seeking help on problems involving psychological stress of some sort. Culture is likewise broadly defined to include special populations that share the same world view or tend to make the same assumptions about their environment. Counseling often occurs in a context that is already divided by international, ethnic, and socially defined roles. Special populations have their own characteristic points of view, or subjective cultures. It is possible to specify both "favorable" and "unfavorable" conditions for counselors seeking to work with clients who have a different point of view. Counselors who are unwilling or unable to accommodate to the cultural differences between themselves and their clients may be described as "encapsulated" and are likely to encounter greater resistance from their clients. This chapter discusses the danger of a "self-reference criterion," where one judges others as though they were exactly like one's self; and it discusses the advantage of assisting clients from other cultures, whose cultures frequently have their own unique ways of maintaining mental health. The chapter closes by mentioning a conference sponsored by the American Psychological Association in Vail, Colorado, during autumn of 1973. That conference recommended that counselors working with clients from other cultures recognize an ethical obligation to accommodate the client's culture in their counseling.

   This chapter reviews the field of intercultural counseling and examines the ways
in which a monocultural bias has influenced counseling psychology, disregarding
the values of a pluralistic society. As the reader considers the points of view discussed
in this chapter, he or she should consider also the counseling environment from the
client's point of view and should be aware of the specialized resistance that might be
encountered with a client from another culture. The reader also will doubtlessly
notice that some of the literature cited is outside the area of counseling psychology
and draws upon work in other disciplines such as anthropology, social work, and
related social sciences that share a concern for clients from other cultures.

The counselors' recognition of intercultural differences results in their
implicit acceptance of disagreement in the definition of normal, healthy
behavior. Culturally encapsulated counselors assume that a counselor can
deal with clients from other cultures without a modification in the style of
counseling. Evidence of cultural encapsulation is presented in the literature
about counseling style, outcomes of counseling, problems of clients, and
the training of counselors, with the basic assumption following the
Euro-American definition of counseling as a professional activity.
Increased competition for limited resources at the international level
(between countries), at the national level (between ethnic groups), and at
the personal level (between role groups) requires that we attend to cultural
group differences just as we would to individual differences in the delivery
of mental health services.
   An intercultural description of counseling contains three levels of
analysis in the definition of cultural differences. At the first and most
obvious level, international differences between persons from different
countries provide a variety of cultural points of view. We expect persons
from other countries to be somehow different and we are more accepting
of their differences, even though we may disagree with their point of view.
At a second level, we are being sensitized to intercultural differences
between underrepresented ethnic groups who have their own independent
heritage, all contrary to "mainstream" national values; such groups are
to be found within almost every country of the world. The various ethnic
groups are more immediately and obviously competing for limited
resources in ways that encourage culturally identifiable strategies by which
these groups define and identify themselves. At the third and most subtle
level, there is a differentiation of roles, independent of nationality or
ethnicity, toward systems that resemble cultures, in creating unique value
systems according to sex role, life style, or social status. Work in social
psychology has documented that we are least accepting of differences
between ourselves and persons who, according to our expectations,
"should" be more like us. We are more likely to stereotype them as
deviants from our own culture than as legitimate members of an alterna-

tive counterculture. To the extent that we demand conformity to our own value system at the international, national, or personal level, so much are we likely to be intolerant of differences. In the following review of the literature, intercultural counseling will be described at these three levels of analysis.

CULTURAL SYSTEMS AND MENTAL HEALTH SERVICES

Until fairly recently, the interrelationship between culture and personality has been systematically studied more often by anthropologists than by psychologists. The literature is polarized into two opposing ways of looking at personality in relation to culture. One position takes the view that there is a fixed state of mental health whose observation is obscured by cultural distortions and which relates cultural behaviors to some universal, or etic, definition of acceptable behavior. This position assumes that there is a single and universal definition of mental health, whatever the individual's origin. A contrasting position views intercultural differences as clues to divergent attitudes, values, and assumptions that differentiate one culture from another in a relativist, or emic, framework. In the second alternative each sociocultural context defines its own norms of mental health.

Anthropologists have tended to take a relativist position when classifying and interpreting behavior. Typically, they have identified unusual behavior as being unique to each culture, allowing multiple notions of acceptable behavior to coexist with one another in the intercultural situation, and have examined each culture as a separate configuration (Sears, 1970). Psychologists, on the other hand, have tended to link social characteristics and psychological phenomena, while giving only minimum attention to the different intercultural values. Draguns and Phillips (1972) claim that only with the recent emergence of social psychiatry as a discipline have systematic observations been applied to the study of the influence of social and cultural factors upon psychopathological systems. The interface between psychology and anthropology has been dealt with more extensively by Edgerton (1974) and Price-Williams (1974).

In addition to anthropology and psychology, psychiatry has produced the most systematic literature in which conditions of mental health are described in a way that will accommodate both the universal and relativist view (Caudill & Lin, 1969; Fromm, 1955; Kaplan, 1961; Lebra, 1974; Opler, 1959; Pedersen, 1974). Psychiatry has tended to emphasize indepth study of "culture-bound" disorders, those unique to isolated areas of the world, from the point of view of the medical (biochemical, neurophysiological, and physiological) models. The common assumption that cultural factors condition the basic form and structure of problems makes this literature valuable and relevant to counseling. The overlapping categories of anthropological psychiatry, ethnopsychiatry, transcultural psychiatry, and/or intercultural psychiatry demonstrate an interdisciplinary coverage shared by psychiatry, social sciences, and public health that lacks coordination and often is confusing to persons interested in intercultural counseling.

Each culture structures the behavior and shapes the attitudes of its members in ways that both contribute to individual stress and help the individual reconcile stress. Some of the more obvious ways that cultures might contribute to individual problems might be through adverse child-rearing practices, imposing unrealistic rules or restrictions on individual behavior, rewarding deviant behavior with prestigious roles, perpetuating genetic weaknesses through intrafamilial marriage patterns, allowing improper hygiene or nutrition habits. or otherwise limiting an individual's choices.

Kiev (1969) cited studies demonstrating that culturally institutionalized factors have an important role in influencing established behavior. The internal systems of social control were discussed in the context of shame and guilt resulting from internalized cultural values. Guilt was described as the internalized conscience, which prevents deviation from cultural norms and enforces conformity. Shame is less dependent on internalized norms and depends on real or projected power by others in the community to punish deviation from the cultural norms.

How does an individual come to do what he "ought" to do in preserving his own cultural system? Weidman (1965) has described these control mechanisms as supporting the development of a superego constellation of internalized pressures, which are more effective in some cultures than in others. Naroll (1969) has described societies where rules or practices involve rupture of, or strain on, social ties in ways that suggest that the society rather than the individual is "sick." Soddy (1962) and Kupferer and Fitzgerald (1971) have reviewed literature on mental disorder and cultural differences. Cultural identity is not always a barrier to intercultural counseling and may serve as a resource for maintaining mental health. Giordano (1973) summarized the literature on how ethnicity involves a conscious and unconscious process that fulfills a deep psychological need for security, identity, and a sense of historical continuity. This support system is implemented, for example, through the family and other affinity units in the cultural community.

Hollingshead and Redlich (1958) and Torrey (1972) have presented evidence showing how professional mental health services are class-bound, relating the expectancy and type of psychiatric disorder to an individual's position in society's class structure. Clients from different social classes were given different treatments and diagnoses. Low-income persons were less likely to be in therapy, or, if they were, they remained in therapy for shorter periods of time, even though similar symptoms were described as being more severe. Likewise, low-income persons were treated by less experienced staff and were treated with short-term somatic therapies generally considered to be less valuable. Norms for adjustment were defined according to the middle-class values favoring conformity, thrift, respectability, control of emotions, and future orientation.

There has been some confusion in the literature between social class differences and racial affiliation as they influence adjustment. Menacker (1971) and Sweeney (1971) have discussed guidance for persons from a low-income environment, emphasizing that years of neglect, even benign neglect, are not eradicated by a few hours of counseling. A low-income population must be viewed within the total context of its unique home and community environment. Gordon and Smith (1971) likewise have maintained that the guidance specialist should be concerned with changing the environment as well as with changing the student being counseled. There is a danger that the counselor will stereotype a low-income client, disregarding his individuality. This tendency is particularly dangerous when the counselor comes from an upper- or middle-class background. Carkhuff and Pierce (1967) concluded that patient-counselor *similarity* produces *greater* self-exploration by the client, and patient-counselor *dissimilarity* results in *less* self-exploration.

In an attempt to deal appropriately with cultural differences, Flaugher, Campbell, and Pike (1969) concluded that closer attention must be given to the underlying assumptions of predictive studies, recognizing that unperceived and uncontrolled combinations of influences on these assumptions may determine results as fully as the predictive measures being evaluated. Freeberg (1969), for example, described many of these "unspecific biases" in the use of tests. Lonner discusses this question more fully in chapter 9 of this volume. In the academic setting, where achievement is most frequently measured by the ability to write well and to do well in written tests, the cultural loading of measurement criteria is most immediately obvious. Freeberg, in attempting to isolate these "unspecific biases" in the use of tests, found that (1) the format is entirely verbal at a relatively high reading level without pictorial information being supplied when the syntax of expression and impression is bound to be culturally loaded; (2) the content is often culturally biased, favoring middle-class concepts, language, or experiences that frequently tend to be foreign and unrelated to contrast-culture activities; (3) most of the formal measures are lengthy, contributing to distractibility and poor test-taking motivation; (4) oral presentation is seldom used, although performance of disadvantaged youth on intellectual ability measures has been found to be superior in certain respects when oral presentation is utilized; (5) tests are designed to be administered to large, highly structured groups in which the disadvantaged youth is not likely to seek clarification or assistance where appropriate; (6) tight time restrictions are themselves detrimental to noncompetitive individuals who have not become "test-wise" through previous practice in test-taking.

Gardner Lindzey (1961) considered the extent to which Western tests such as the Rorschach and Thematic Apperception Test, in which interpretive procedures are based on Euro-American norms, have been useful in providing information about persons from other cultures. Spain (1972) has discussed the more recent contributions. Cronbach's and Drenth's (1972) edited volume, which resulted from a conference on mental tests and cultural adaptation, addresses the question of whether tests should be used to adapt people individually and collectively to the presently dominant model of Western industrial society rather than to uncover human potentialities in their own non-Western cultures. Brislin, Lonner, and Thorndike (1973) have provided the most recent and comprehensive review of interculturally viable tests and inventories, along with data from intercultural validation of these instruments.

THE CULTURALLY ENCAPSULATED COUNSELOR

We are experiencing a revolution in the field of guidance and counseling against established and entrenched values (Cook, 1971). Jaffe (1973) has presented a strong argument for demystifying therapy by removing the authoritarian, moralistic, and pseudoetic components of counseling without denying the skills and authoritative practice. A reduction of the status gap between client and counselor may be a necessary prerequisite for developing noncoercive therapy relationships. Agel (1971, 1973) has become an advocate of radicalism, propounding a "Manifesto of the Radical Therapist," with a focus on changing the system rather than merely treating "dissatisfied" individuals. Agel (1973) takes the revolutionary position that psychological repression is just another aspect of the general oppression of a capitalistic system.

As the counselor works with persons belonging to a life style different from his own for any length of time, he participates in and contributes to a process of acculturation by himself and his clients. The counselor may assist his client to choose cultural assimilation, where the dominant culture enforces its adoption, integration, and where its "best" elements are incorporated; or adaptation, where the individual or group accommodates to the dominant environment. The counselor who is himself undergoing acculturation must first recognize those characteristics of his own style of behavior, attitudes, beliefs, and personal assumptions that will allow him to experience another culture as a means of learning about that culture. Otherwise, the therapist may substitute his own "self reference" criteria of desired social effectiveness for alternative criteria more appropriate to the client's environment (Kanfer & Phillips, 1970). Bloombaum, Yamamoto, and James (1968) have described ways in which psychotherapists are culturally conditioned in their responses. Rotenberg (1974) described how Western definitions of normality and psychological treatment are rooted in the Protestant ethic. Other research reveals how counselors directly or unconsciously condition client responses to suit their own theoretical orientation (Bandura, 1961; Bandura, Lipher, & Miller, 1960; Murray, 1956; Rogers, 1960).

Seward (1970) has provided an early but very useful review of the ways in which classical psychotherapists have been caught up in their own social milieu. Seward's point is that each of the traditional theories of psychotherapy emphasizes the individual as an isolated biosocial unit. These theories do not touch on the complexity of personality development in a plural society in which each person is in a feedback relationship with several cultures at the same time. She also provided useful case studies of patient/therapist encapsulation where "normal" behavior for the patient's subculture group was mistakenly interpreted as pathological.

Wrenn (1962) described encapsulation as a process affecting the counseling profession by substituting symbiotic model stereotypes for the real world, disregarding cultural variations among clients, and dogmatizing a technique-oriented definition of the counseling process. Kagan (1964) and Schwebel (1964) further suggested that counselor education programs may actually be contributing to the encapsulation process by implanting a cultural bias, however implicit, in their curricula. Counselors tend to become "addicted" to one system of cultural values in a dependency that is counterproductive to effective counseling (Morrow, 1972).

Professional encapsulation is a result of basic processes of our life activity (Kagan, 1964; Schwebel, 1964; Wrenn, 1962). (1) We define reality according to a monocultural set of assumptions and stereotypes which then become more important than the real world. (2) We become insensitive to cultural variations among individuals and assume that our views correspond to reality. The assumption that "I know better than they do what is good for them," not surprisingly, is offensive to the target audience. (3) Each of us harbors unreasoned assumptions that we accept without proof. When those assumptions are threatened by an alternative religion, political view, or cultural value, we can easily become fearful or defensive. When the minority culture is perceived as threatening, it quickly becomes an enemy to be opposed and ultimately defeated for the sake of self-preservation. (4) A technique-oriented job definition further contributes toward, and perpetuates, the process of encapsulation. Each relationship is evaluated according to whether or not it contributes toward solving problems rather than helping persons. However, when the counselor seeks to escape encapsulation by blindly accepting the problem as resulting from the client's culture, he only succeeds in absolving himself of any responsibility to interpret the behavior of others as being relevant and meaningful to his own life activity.

Stewart, Danielian, and Festes (1969) have described mainstream American values in five systems of assumptions that express the values that typically guide our thinking about mental health services in the Western world. These five systems are:

1. Self-expression in Western society takes place in an "activity modality" of doing. Activity should result in externalized visible accomplishment. A contrasting "being" orientation, referring to the spontaneous expression of that which is regarded as the given nature of human personality, is given less consideration. The "being-in-becoming" orientation, which stresses experience rather than accomplishment in an existential or situational framework, is less popular. The passive, contemplative, experiencing mode is nonisomorphic to the "American way." Activism is most clearly seen in our mode of problem-solving, and decision-making. Learning is perceived as an active and not a passive process that requires both performance and motivation by the learner if success is to be achieved. The passive student with low motivation is quickly labeled as a "slow learner."
2. Social relationships in Western society emphasize equality and informality. By contrast, many other cultures emphasize inequality, formality, status, and ascription of role. The effect in Western culture, ironically enough, tends to be a competitive depersonalization of friendship relations through pretended impartiality and pseudo-objectivity as contrasted with more personalized interactions elsewhere.
3. Achievement is a prime motivating force. A person *is* what a person *achieves* by objective, visible, and measurable criteria. An emphasis on personal and documented accomplishment is more important than place of birth, family background, heritage, or traditional status. Failure is difficult to accept and is avoided or rationalized as being part of the long-range learning process leading toward eventual accomplishment.
4. The world is viewed as an object to be exploited, or developed, for the material benefit of man. Man is clearly separated from other forms of

nature-life and has a responsibility to control nature rather than to live in harmony with it. Control and exploitation are necessary for progress and are assumed to be necessary for the continued existence of a person or organization. There is an optimistic view of the future that assumes that the possibilities for progress are somehow infinite, as contrasted with the more fatalistic notion elsewhere that that which is good is limited.

5. The rights, value, and importance of an individual's identity are implicit in Western culture. In child-training, socialization, and education, individual achievement and autonomy are encouraged so that children will develop their own opinions, solve their own problems, and have their own possessions. There is a tendency to resist formal authoritative external controls, and a preference for minimal authority in an informal democratic mode which utilizes persuasion rather than coercion, and democratic rather than autocratic decision-making. The self is not easily merged with the collection of individuals we call a group, in which an individual can become lost or lonely.

Some of the research has attempted to relate personal qualities of the counselor to effectiveness in intercultural counseling. We might expect counselors who are open-minded to have less difficulty than would counselors who are more dogmatic. Indeed, Kemp (1962) and Mezzano (1969) did find that open-minded counselors excel in the supportive understanding and self-exploration that are usually associated with counseling effectiveness; whereas Russo, Ketz, and Hudson (1964), Allen (1967), Millikan (1965), and Millikan and Patterson (1967) have discovered that prejudice or factors related to prejudice are associated with less effective counseling (as assessed by counseling supervisors).

In intercultural counseling there is a greater danger of mutual misunderstanding (McFayden & Winokur, 1956), less understanding of the other culture's unique problems (Kincaid, 1969), and a spontaneous hostility that destroys rapport and increases the chances of greater negative transference toward the counselor (Vontress, 1969). Thomas (1962) pointed out the danger of confusing a client's appropriate cultural response with neurotic transference. Middleton (1963), Woods (1958), and Trent (1954) suggested numerous other sources of difficulty for the Caucasian professional who is counseling Blacks. Ignorance of one another's culture contributes to resistance to the goals of counseling. This resistance is usually accompanied by some feelings of hostility, threat, or unwillingness to allow the stranger access to a client's private feelings.

Counselors who are most different from their clients in race and social class or who are not of the same sex have the greatest difficulty effecting constructive changes, whereas helpers who are most similar to their clients in these respects have the greater facility for empathic counseling relationships (Carkhuff & Pierce, 1967). Along the same lines, Mitchell (1970) has suggested that the great majority of Caucasian counselors cannot effect a solution for a Black client since so frequently they are part of the problem. Williams (1970) likewise asserted that the Caucasian mental health worker cannot successfully counsel the "Black psyche." The very notion of counseling is too frequently seen as demeaning, debilitating, patronizing, and dehumanizing (Russel, 1970), particularly when the counselor's implicit or explicit bias is communicated to the contrast-culture client (Ayres, 1970). Stranges and Riccio (1970) likewise found that counselor trainees preferred counselors of the same racial and cultural backgrounds.

There is an assumption throughout the research that intercultural counseling introduces special sources of resistance not present in same-culture counseling relationships. Muliozzi (1972) tested this hypothesis and discovered that Caucasian counselors felt more genuine and empathic with Caucasian than with Black clients; whereas Black clients did not see Caucasian counselors as being less understanding, less genuine, or less unconditional in their regard, although they did *not* feel that Caucasian counselors "liked them as much," this opinion being relative to a sample of Caucasian clients' perceptions on the same measure. Muliozzi (1972) suggested that Caucasian counselors may be unrealistic in their fear of not being accepted by Black clients as therapeutic helping agents. In spite of the barriers discussed by Vontress in chapter 3, there may be instances where Caucasians are in a position that is as good or better than that of their Black colleagues to work with Black clients.

Each cultural group requires a different set of skills, unique areas of emphasis, and specific insights for effective counseling to occur. Szalay and Bryson (1973) have pointed out that each subjective culture has a group-specific cognitive organization. Members of that group behave similarly to the extent that their subjective world views are similar. The more themes on which two groups agree and the greater their agreement, the less will be their psychological distance.

INTERCULTURAL ADJUSTMENT

A group characteristically perceives subjectively the social interpersonal part of its environment (Triandis, Vassiliou, Vassiliou, Tanaka, & Shanmugam, 1972). Elements of this subjective culture include associations, attitudes, beliefs, concepts, evaluations, expectations, memories, opinions, role perceptions, stereotypes, and values. Members of a culture tend to share similar perceptions of these values, and persons who differ in their way of perceiving important elements of the subjective culture tend to dislike each other and to have difficulties in reaching agreements. Similarities, on the other hand, are likely to make it easier for two individuals to be attracted to each other and to work together.

Amir (1969) has demonstrated that merely getting members of different groups together is not enough to produce understanding and harmony. The direction of change depends on whether change occurs under favorable conditions that tend to reduce prejudice, or unfavorable conditions that increase it. Amir's review of the literature of research on intercultural relationships suggested that favorable conditions occur: when there is equal status contact between the members of the various ethnic groups; when the contact is between members of a majority group and higher status members of a minority group; when the social climate is likely to promote intergroup contact; when the contact is intimate rather than casual; when the contact is pleasant or rewarding; and when the members of both groups interact in functionally important activities toward superordinate goals. Unfavorable conditions apply: when the contact situation produces competition between the groups; when the contact is unpleasant or involuntary; when the prestige or status of one group is lowered as a result of the contact; when members of a group perceive themselves as being victims of ethnic "scapegoating"; when one group in the contact has moral standards that are objectionable to the other; and when the minority group members are of lower status in their own community. Unfortunately, intergroup contact typically does not occur under favorable conditions; thus, intercultural prejudice often is increased.

Brein and David (1971) reviewed the literature on intercultural adjustment from the perspective of intercultural communications. If we view counseling as a form of specialized communications, then the cultural barriers that bar accurate communications become extremely important. Barna (1970) cited five barriers to accurate communications across cultures. First, there is the obvious barrier of language differences. Language is much more than learning new sound symbols. Knowing a little of a foreign language may allow one only to make a "fluent fool" of oneself if one is unaware of the implicit meanings behind highly subtle linguistic symbols. Secondly, there is the area of nonverbal communications such as gestures, postures, and other metamessages on which we depend for communications (Ekman, Friesen, & Ellsworth, 1972). It is difficult to recognize the unspoken codes that are utilized so automatically in a given culture that they may not even be consciously recognized by members of that culture. Such codes communicate definite feelings or attitudes which may emphasize, harden, soften, or contradict the spoken messages. The stereotypes that provide structure to the scrambled raw experiences of our own or other cultures are the third barrier of preconceptions. We perceive pretty much what we expect to perceive, screening out whatever does not fit our expectations. The stereotype then has a tendency to become realized through the "self-fulfilling prophecy" of the communicator. A fourth deterrent is a tendency to evaluate what others say or do as being either good or bad for us. Evaluation frequently interferes with understanding the other person's point of view of himself; it leads the counselor into the trap of communicating that "I know better than you what you should do." Stewart's distinction between empathy and sympathy in chapter 6 elaborates on this theme. A fifth barrier is the typically high level of anxiety that is particularly obvious in intercultural encounters where neither person is certain what is expected of him or her. This phenomenon is dealt with more extensively in the literature about culture shock.

The term "culture shock" was first introduced by Kalvero Oberg (1958) to describe the anxiety that results from the loss of one's sense of when to do what and how. Hall (1959) defined culture shock as the removal or distortion of many of the familiar cues one encounters at home and the substitution for them of other cues that are strange. Oberg (1958) described several stages in the process of culture shock. In the first, or incubation, stage the sojourner may feel genuinely euphoric about the exciting new culture around him. This is followed by a second stage in which the individual must deal with crises that have resulted from normal daily activities; such activities suddenly seem to present insurmountable difficulties and generate in the individual a hostility toward those around him for being "unreasonable." The sojourner is making a psychological transition from his own back-home values and the host-culture values. If this transition is not completed, the sojourner is likely to experience extreme dissatisfaction with his host-culture environment. In the third stage the sojourner begins to understand his host culture and to regain his own normal sense of humor, psychological balance, and sense of well being. The fourth stage occurs when the sojourner begins to accept his host culture as offering both positive and negative alternatives. The fifth and final stage occurs when the sojourner returns home and experiences reverse culture shock in his readjustment.

The conflict between a sojourner's expectations and his actual experiences can be summarized by four stages of adjustment. The first stage of fascination is followed by a second stage of hostility against the host culture, followed by a third stage of adjustment, and a fourth stage of genuine biculturalism where the sojourner is able to act in accord with host-culture norms. Having experienced culture shock in one culture does not prevent an individual from experiencing culture shock in the future, although it may provide the sojourner with some insights into why he feels as he does (Foster, 1965). Through culture shock, the sojourner learns the specific ways in which other persons from other cultures are influenced in their behavior and how he or she is likewise influenced by his or her own culture.

COUNSELING SPECIAL POPULATIONS

The coincidence of various racial groups and economic classes in our society has favored a Caucasian middle class over "minority" populations. Counselors, in working with members of these subcultures, have occasionally been accused by them of maintaining or protecting the status quo. Counseling with these special populations requires a sensitivity to the issues of economic imbalance. There has been an implicit assumption by Caucasian middle-class society that other cultures do not advance themselves because of the "deficit hypothesis"—an assumption that a lower-economic-class community is disorganized and that the disorganization presents itself in various forms of deficit. Cole and Bruner (1972), who have discussed this point of view, see the deficit hypothesis as a distortion. One widely assumed source of deficit is lack of mothering. Children in less affluent families are assumed to lack adequate parental attention, following the stereotype which implies illegitimacy and the phenomenon of the "absent father." The mother is assumed to be less occupied with rearing her family, with less time to develop a warm supporting relationship, and giving less guidance to her children in establishing their goals. A second characteristic of the deficit hypothesis is that children growing up in that environment lack a seldom-defined "early stimulation," the absence of which is thought to result in lower test scores and poorer academic performance later in life. The implication is that lower-economic-class communities are somehow not only different in their cultural values but inferior by comparison to middle-class communities, although few counselors would admit to making that assumption.

Most of the literature cited earlier relates to counseling relationships between American Black clients and Caucasian counselors, which have attracted more attention than other examples of intercultural counseling. Vontress, in 1971 and in this book (chapter 3), summarizes the problem as being one of impaired rapport, with some intercultural relationships being more difficult in counseling than others. Vontress (1969) described ways that a counselor's cultural attitudes can destroy counseling rapport by inhibiting empathy, ignoring significant aspects of a client's background, misunderstanding a client's language, or unknowingly dealing

jects. Torrey (1970, 1972) identified the expectations of
ast-culture clients and the personal qualities of a counselor
ly related to the healthy change, accurate empathy, and
warmth and genuineness that are essential to effective
care. Pine (1972) provided one of the best reviews of the
counseling minorities in the United States, with an emphasis
on ___ ucasian differences.

The problems specific to the Chicano, or Mexican-American, community are probably best described by Torrey (1970), who contends that
Westernized systems of mental health care services can be described as
being largely irrelevant to the needs of the Mexican-American population
that he studied. First, problems of transportation, family responsibilities,
and cost factors make those services relatively inaccessible to low-income
populations. Second, Mexican-Americans typically were required to use
English, which was not their first language. Third, the services were
perceived as being class-bound, with better service being provided to the
more affluent and powerful clients. Fourth, the services were perceived
as being culture-bound, guided by middle-class, Anglo-Caucasian values
in the defining of problems as well as of solutions. Fifth, the services were
perceived as protecting the status-quo point of view. Sixth and finally,
the services were considered to be less effective than those provided by
traditional healers such as the *curanderos*, who are readily available to
each local population. Madsen (1969), Pollack and Menacker (1971),
Clark (1959), Karno and Edgerton (1969), Aguilar (1972), and Morales
(1970, pp. 257–262) have provided additional examples of the problems
confronting the Mexican-American and of his resources for coping with
them. Wagner and Haug (1971) have produced what may be the best
comprehensive basic text of edited articles on the problems of adjustment
among Chicanos.

Native-American Indian culture presents its own unique requirements
for effective counseling. When counseling Native American Indian youth,
the counselor is likely to be confronted by passively nonverbal clients
who listen and absorb knowledge selectively. A counselor who expects
counselees to verbalize their feelings is not likely to have much success
with Native American clients. The Native American is more likely to
withdraw and, using the advice he has received, work out the problems
by himself. The Native American is very conscious of having to make his
own decisions and is likely to resist being pushed in a particular direction
by persons seeking to motivate him or her. Bryde (1971), in an insightful
treatment of Native American students, found one of the chief problems
to be the rapid turnover of counselors. Some kind of ongoing relationship
is required if counseling is to be effective. Saslow and Harrover (1968)

have gone so far as to say that school experiences tend to inhibit rather than to facilitate the Native American's psychosocial adjustment because of the culturally insensitive counselors and teachers to be found in the schools.

The Native American Indian community shares many of the problems facing other contrast-cultures in American society. There are unique values present in each tribal group of Native Americans that make a tremendous difference in how Native Americans perceive one another. At the same time, Native Americans are attempting to develop a universal Native American culture. Trimble discusses these two tendencies in chapter 4 of this volume. The Native American Indian's value orientation is different from the dominant culture in many specific ways. Sprang (1965) discussed six specific ways that value orientations differ. (1) There is a "present" orientation that deemphasizes the future. (2) The lack of time consciousness devalues punctuality and places little importance on meeting tight schedules. (3) The giving of material goods is valued higher than the accumulation of them. Persons who accumulate wealth may be feared or rejected by other members of the tribe. (4) Respect for age is valued to the point of sometimes being a handicap for young educated leaders seeking to bring about innovative change. (5) Cooperation and working together in noncompetitive ways are the accepted means of attaining goals. (6) Harmony with nature, accepting the world rather than changing it, is highly valued as a life style.

Until fairly recently, Asian-Americans have not received much attention or recognition as requiring special insights and skills for effective mental health support services. Sue and Kirk (1972) have described how Chinese-American students produce test results different from the larger population. Sue and Sue (1972) and Sue (1973) have described the following options as being those open to Asian-Americans: traditionalism (resulting in problems of guilt, shame, and lack of openness), marginalism (resulting in problems of independence and self-hate), and Asian-Americanism (resulting in problems of racism). Fantl (1959) has described the problems of a Chinese family, and Kitano (1969) has described problems of Japanese-Americans.

Foreign students in the United States constitute a population with its own special requirements for counseling services. Tan (1967) has written an excellent review of studies, showing how foreign students perceive counselors as authority figures, advice-givers, and sources of information, with some more than others viewing counselors as being authoritarian. Selltiz, Christ, Havel, and Cook (1963), in their study of 300 students from many countries at 34 colleges in the United States, showed that about 70 percent of these students only infrequently or rarely formed close friendships or mixed socially with Americans. Even though about 50 percent of the students did indicate that they spent much of their free time with Americans, another 50 percent indicated that they never spoke with Americans as they would with a close friend from home. Goldson, Suchman, and Williams (1956) credited the absence of intimate foreign student-host relationships to the cultural distance between these two groups, with Europeans interacting more intimately and with greater satisfaction with American hosts than do Asians. Studies by Bennett, Passin, and McKnight (1958) among Japanese students, by Lambert and Bressler (1956) among Indians, and by Sewell and Davidson (1956) among Scandinavians suggest that the greater difference in customs, values, and life styles between Asians and Westerners creates barriers to communication.

A functional acculturation by the foreign students requires that they develop new skills in both formal classroom and off-campus peer relationships. In their off-campus relationships, the foreign students preserve their own identity and protect themselves against the "foreign" culture in a variety of ways. Although the quality of a foreign student's interaction with his hosts has been described by Gezi (1965) as a very significant factor in the student's adjustment, other research by Klein, Alexander, Tseng, Miller, Yeh, and Chu (1971), elaborated in chapter 5, suggests that psychologists overestimate the value of person-to-person contact between visitors and hosts and underestimate the importance of maintaining relationships with the visitor's conationals. Herman and Schild (1961) and, more recently, Antler (1970) also have concluded that harmonious interaction with fellow countrymen is of greater importance to a non-American's adjustment than is interaction with Americans. Torrey, Van Rheenan, and Katchadourian (1970) pointed out that academic pressures rather than cultural frustrations complicate adjustment to the unique aspects of a university community.

Research among Chinese students at the University of Wisconsin (Chu et al., 1971) demonstrated three implications of depending on countrymen for support. (1) International students associate mostly with fellow nationals because warm, intimate, dependent, personally satisfying contacts are almost exclusively limited to members in their conational group; (2) their relationships with host country nationals rarely go beyond superficial pleasantries; (3) they become rather discouraged about any prospects for deep intercultural friendships and do not expect such friendships to develop. The result is almost a "paranoid" attitude toward Americans, which tends to increase over time. Chu, Yeh, Klein, Alexander, and Miller (1971) concluded that the Chinese students returned home with a considerably less favorable impression of the United States than they had had before they came to this country.

Arkoff, Thaver, and Elking (1966) pointed out the reasons why counselors can expect difficulty in working with foreign students. In the first place, the students from another culture are less likely to be familiar with the kinds of counseling resources available to them on an American university campus. Second, foreign students probably have relied on other sources of psychological support back home, sources such as family teachers, leaders in the community, or peers, which are not easily available to them in the host community. Third, there may well be a greater toleration of eccentric or deviant patterns of behavior—by American culturally defined standards of normality—in the students' home countries. Fourth, foreign students are less likely to define a situation of internal conflict as a culture-related problem, requiring their initiative in obtaining outside assistance, but more as an internal adjustment they should work out by themselves. Fifth, the foreign student may expect counselors to be more authoritarian—giving advice that recommends or demands specific behaviors in a parent-surrogate role—than most American counselors would find comfortable. Arkoff, Thaver, and Elking (1966) further found a sample of Asian students strongly accepting those very coping techniques of increasing will power, avoiding morbidity, and thinking pleasant thoughts, which American psychologists and students in the sample strongly rejected as being simplistic!

INDIGENOUS MENTAL HEALTH CARE SYSTEMS

Watts's (1961) Oriental prescription as providing a "way of liberation" resembles the processes of liberation described by Jung, self-actualization described by Maslow, functional autonomy described by Allport, and/or creative selfhood described by Adler. Although Watts was a Westerner writing about Asia, he did make a point valuable to Western psychologists. The person is viewed as a participant in the social game that is based on conventional rules and that defines boundaries between the individual—an ego—and his or her environment—a hostile and alien world. Watts went on to say that the duty of the therapist is to involve the participant in a "counter-game" that restores a unifying perspective of ego and environment and that results in the liberation of the person. The skills required of a counselor in many ways parallel the insights resulting from Zen training (Leung, 1973). A counselor working with a client in a crisis must be able to empathize or understand what is happening to the client and at the same time concentrate on outside factors relevant to the client's problem. Whereas Western psychology has studied the psyche or mind as a clinical entity, Eastern cultures have regarded mind and matter, soul and body, as being interdependent. Numerous materials on Eastern thought and culture have been written by Asians themselves from the point of view of Asian culture and religion.

Oriental religious training shares some similar goals with counselor education in our culture. Fromm, Suzuki, and Martino (1960) described some of these similarities, as did Watts (1961) and Pande (1968). Kiev (1964) compiled an edited volume of articles in which a wide range of cultures are described and in which it is shown how mental health services are maintained outside the strictly defined field of counseling. Berger (1962) has written of an interesting adaptation of Zen's "no-thought" to counseling, a technique in which the mind can function on its own, free of established forms and practices. The object of Zen-influenced counseling is to separate abstractions in the form of case descriptions, diagnoses, or test results from the total reality of a counselee as a person.

Sinclair (1967) described the sequence of indigenous healing rituals in New Guinea where first, at the impact of a crisis, the victim becomes fearful and anxious. Second, a cause of the misfortune is sought through divination in the supernatural. Third, the responsibility for the crisis is transferred to a supernatural agency so that the personal anxiety that threatens the psychological equilibrium becomes identified as the enemy. There are numerous other examples of societies, in addition to those in New Guinea, where the supernatural is seen to contain many hostile forces capable of acting upon the individual (Weidman, 1969; Weidman & Sussex, 1971; Yap, 1969). Wittkower and Weidman (1969) described the psychologically integrative function of magic in which something that is ill-defined, anxiety-arousing, and disruptive is given a name.

It is educational to compare counseling processes as we know them in the West with functionally similar experiences in other cultures (Torrey, 1972). Both therapists and indigenous healers use the process of "naming" in their treatment. An attempt is made to identify the unknown element of illness by giving it a name. The therapist must know the right name to treat a destructive behavior appropriately. The effect of treatment either by Western therapists or by indigenous healers is to lessen the ambiguity of the crisis and to identify a "cause" that will allow the crisis to be explained in the culturally normal order of things. Both systems depend on the culturally determined personal qualities and credibility of the therapist to establish rapport with the individual seeking help. Without the cooperation of the person seeking help, both types of healers recognize themselves as operating under severe and sometimes impossible handicaps. Some kind of a coalition between the help-giver and the help-receiver must be nurtured if an effective relationship is to be developed. Both systems depend on the client's expectation that he or she will get better as a result of working within this relationship. By demonstrating his own legitimacy and effectiveness as a help-giver, a counselor can often raise a client's expectations. Demonstrations of prestige and status are used for this purpose as are expensive equipment and elaborate ceremony. The magical techniques of divination have a functional purpose in much the same way as training and certification of skill serve to display a counselor's credentials in the community. Any counselor who has tried to function in a nonaccepting culture recognizes the importance of his first being accepted in his role as help-giver. There are few techniques used in Western therapy that are not also found to some degree in other cultures, but there are techniques practiced in other cultures that are only rarely used by Western psychotherapists.

CONCLUSIONS

Torrey (1972) concluded that sufficient evidence exists from inter-cultural studies of counseling and psychotherapy to raise many questions about our system of selecting, training, and certifying therapists. Stranges and Riccio (1970) found that counselor trainees preferred counselees of the same racial and cultural background. It appears that professional psychologists currently are being trained toward the ultimate goal of serving the psychological needs of the middle class to which they belong (Gordon, 1965). Lewis and Locke (1969) have pointed out specific exam-ples of racism in the training of counselors, whereas Vontress (1969) has called for more preservice and in-service training designed to help coun-selors examine their attitudes toward the culturally different by exposing them consciously and directly to the clients from other cultures. There is increasing evidence from professional psychologists that the trained counselor is not prepared to deal with individuals who come from different racial, ethnic, or socioeconomic groups whose values, attitudes, and general life styles are different from and threatening to his own (Padilla, Boxley, and Wagner, 1972).

Some training programs are emerging (Carkhuff & Banks, 1970) that enable trainees to improve their skills in communication across culture, class, race, sex, and generational differences. The desegregation of schools more than any other single factor has given impetus to the intercultural training of counselors through a variety of models (Chenault, 1968; Lewis & Lewis, 1970; Pulvino & Perrone, 1973; Triandis, 1975).

The American Psychological Association sponsored a conference on patterns and levels of professional training at Vail, Colorado, in July 1973. One of the recommendations of that conference was that the counseling of persons of culturally diverse backgrounds by persons who are not trained or competent to work with such groups should be regarded as unethical. Training and continuing education coursework on the special needs of different religious and of different racial, ethnic, sexual, and economic groups was recommended for all professional psychologists. It is apparent that cultural sensitivity and awareness will play an increasingly important role in the training of counselors.

REFERENCES

Agel, J. *The radical therapist*. New York: Ballantine Books, 1971.

Agel, J. *Rough times*. New York: Ballantine Books, 1973.

Aguilar, I. Initial contacts with Mexican-American families. *Social Work*, 1972, *17*(3), 66–70.

Allen, T. W. Effectiveness of counselor training as a function of psychological openness. *Journal of Counseling Psychology*, 1967, *14*, 35–40.

Amir, Y. Contact hypothesis in ethnic relations. *Psychological Bulletin*, 1969, *71*(5), 319–342.

Antler, L. Correlates of home and host family acquaintanceship among foreign medical residents in the United States. *Journal of Social Psychology*, 1970, *80*, 49–57.

Arkoff, A., Thaver, F., & Elking, L. Mental health and counseling ideas of Asian and American students. *Journal of Counseling Psychology*, 1966, *13*(2), 219–228.

Ayres, C. *The disadvantaged: An analysis of factors affecting the counselor relationship*. Paper read at the Minnesota Personnel and Guidance Association Mid-Winter Conference, Minneapolis, Minnesota, February 1970.

Bandura, A. Psychotherapy as a learning process. *Psychological Bulletin*, 1961, *58*, 143–159.

Bandura, A., Lipher, P., & Miller, P. Psychotherapists approach avoidance reactions to patients' expressions of hostility. *Journal of Consulting Psychology*, 1960, *24*, 1–8.

Barna, L. M. Stumbling blocks in interpersonal intercultural communications. In D. Hoopes (Ed.), *Readings in Intercultural Communications* (Vol. 1). Pittsburgh: University of Pittsburgh Intercultural Communication Network of the Regional Council for International Education, 1970.

Bennett, J. W., Passin, H., & McKnight, R. K. *In search of identity: The Japanese overseas scholar in America and Japan*. Minneapolis: University of Minnesota Press, 1958.

Berger, E. M. Zen Buddhism, general psychology and counseling psychology. *Journal of Counseling Psychology*, 1962, *9*(2), 122–127.

Bloombaum, M., Yamamoto, J., & James, Q. Cultural stereotyping among psychotherapists. *Journal of Consulting and Clinical Psychology*, 1968, *32*(1), 99.

Brein, M., & David K. H. Intercultural communication and the adjustment of the sojourner. *Psychological Bulletin*, 1971, *76*, 215–230.

Brislin, R. W., Lonner, W. J., & Thorndike, R. M. *Cross-cultural research methods*. New York: John Wiley & Sons, 1973.

Bryde, J. F. *Indian students and guidance*. Boston: Houghton Mifflin Co., 1971.

Carkhuff, R. R., & Banks, G. Training as a preferred mode of facilitating relations between races and generations. *Journal of Counseling Psychology*, 1970, *17*, 413–418.

Carkhuff, R. R., & Pierce, R. Differential effects of therapist race and social class upon patient depth of self-exploration in the initial clinical interview. *Journal of Consulting Psychology*, 1967, *31*(6), 632–634.

Caudill, W., & Lin, Tsung-yi (Eds.). *Mental health research in Asia and the Pacific*. Honolulu: East-West Center Press, 1969.

Chenault, J. A. Proposed model for a humanistic counselor education program. *Counselor Education and Supervision*, 1968, *8*(1), 4–11.

Chu, H. M., Yeh, E. K., Klein, M. H., Alexander, A. A., & Miller, M. H. A study of Chinese students' adjustment in the U.S.A. *Acta Psychologica Taiwanica*, March 1971 (No. 13).

Clark, M. (Ed.). *Health in the Mexican-American culture*. Berkeley and Los Angeles: University of California Press, 1959.

Cole, M., & Bruner, J. S. Cultural differences and inferences about psychological processes. *American Psychologist*, 1972, *26*, 867–876.

Cook, D. R. (Ed.). *Guidance for education in revolution*. Boston: Allyn & Bacon, 1971.

Cronbach, L. J., & Drenth, P. J. D. *Mental tests and cultural adaption*. The Hague: Mouton, 1972.

Draguns, J., & Phillips, L. *Culture and psychopathology: The quest for a relationship*. Morristown, New Jersey: General Learning Corporation, 1972.

Edgerton, R. B. Cross-cultural psychology and psychological anthropology: One paradigm or two. *Reviews in Anthropology* 1974, *1*, 52–65.

Ekman, P., Friesen, W., and Ellsworth, P. *Emotion in the human face*. New York: Pergamon Press, 1972.

Fantl, B. Cultural factors in family diagnosis of a Chinese family. *International Journal of Social Psychiatry*, 1959, *5*, 27–32.

Flaugher, R. L., Campbell, J. T., & Pike, L. W. Prediction of job performance for Negro and white medical technicians. *Research Bulletin*, Princeton, New Jersey: Educational Testing Service, April 1969.

Foster, R. J. *Examples of cross-cultural problems encountered by Americans working overseas: An instructor's handbook*. Alexandria, Virginia: Human Resources Research Office, 1965.

Freeberg, N. E. Assessment of disadvantaged adolescents: A different approach to research and evaluation measures. *Research Bulletin*, Princeton, New Jersey: Educational Testing Service, May 1969.

Fromm, E. *The sane society*. New York: Holt, Rinehart & Winston, 1955.

Fromm, E., Suzuki, D. T., & Martino, R. *Zen Buddhism and psychoanalysis*. New York: Harper & Row, 1960.

Gezi, K. I. Factors associated with student adjustment in cross-cultural contact. *California Journal of Educational Research*, 1965, *16*(3), 129–236.

Giordano, J. *Ethnicity and mental health: Research and recommendations*. New York: National Project on Ethnic America of the American Jewish Committee, 1973.

Goldson, R. K., Suchman, E. A., & Williams, R. M. Factors associated with the development of cross-cultural social interaction. *The Journal of Social Issues*, 1956, *12*, 26–32.

Gordon, E. W., & Smith, P. M. The guidance specialist and the disadvantaged student. In D. R. Cook (Ed.), *Guidance for education in revolution*. Boston: Allyn & Bacon, 1971.

Gordon J. Project cause: The federal anti-poverty program and some implications of sub-professional training. *American Psychologist*, 1965, *20*, 333–343.

Hall, E. T. *The silent language*. New York: Doubleday & Co., 1959.

Herman, S. N., & Schild, E. O. The stranger group in a cross-cultural situation. *Sociometry*, 1961, *24*, 165–176.

Hollingshead, A. B., & Redlich, R. C. *Social class and mental illness*. New York: John Wiley & Sons, 1958.

Jaffe, D. A counseling institution in an oppressive environment. *The Journal of Humanistic Psychology*, *13*(4) 1973, 25–46.

Kagan, N. Three dimensions of counselor encapsulation. *Journal of Counseling Psychology*, 1964, *11*(4), 361–365.

Kanfer, F. H., & Phillips, J. S. *Learning foundations of behavior therapy*. New York: John Wiley & Sons, 1970.

Kaplan, B. (Ed.). *Studying personality cross-culturally*. New York: Harper & Row, 1961.

Karno, M., & Edgerton, R. B. Perception of mental illness in a Mexican-American community. *Archives of General Psychiatry*, 1969, *20*, 233–238.

Kemp, C. Influence of dogmatism on the training of counselors. *Journal of Counseling Psychology*, 1962, *9*, 155–157.

Kiev, A. (Ed.). *Magic, faith and healing: Studies in primitive psychiatry today*. New York: Free Press of Glencoe, 1964.

Kiev, A. Transcultural psychiatry: Research problems and perspectives. In S. C. Plog & R. B. Edgerton (Eds.), *Changing perspectives in mental health*. New York: Holt, Rinehart & Winston, 1969.

Kincaid, M. Identity and therapy in the Black community. *Personnel and Guidance Journal*, 1969, *47*(9), 884–890.

Kitano, H. H. Japanese-American mental illness. In S. C. Plog & R. B. Edgerton (Eds.), *Changing perspectives in mental illness*. New York: Holt, Rinehart & Winston, 1969.

Klein, M. H., Alexander, A. A., Tseng, K.-H., Miller, M. H., Yeh, E.-K., and Chu, H.-M. *Foreign students in a big university: Subculture within a subculture*. Mimeographed, 1971.

Kupferer, J. H., & Fitzgerald, T. K. *Culture, society and guidance*. Boston: Houghton Mifflin Co., 1971.

Lambert, R. D., & Bressler, M. *Indian students on an American campus*. Minneapolis: University of Minnesota Press, 1956.

Lebra, W. P. (Ed.). *Transcultural research in mental health* (Vol. II of Mental Health Research in Asia and the Pacific). Honolulu: The University Press of Hawaii, An East-West Center Book, 1972.

Leung, P. Comparative effects of training in external and internal concentration on two counseling behaviors. *Journal of Counseling Psychology*, 1973, *20*(3), 227–234.

Lewis, M. D., & Lewis, J. A. Relevant training for relevant roles: A model for educating inner-city counselors. *Counselor Education and Supervision*, 1970, *10*(1), 31–38.

Lewis, S. O., & Locke, D. Racism encountered in counseling. *Counselor Education and Supervision*, 1969, *9*(1), 49–60.

Lindzey, G. *Projective techniques and cross-cultural research*. New York: Appleton-Century-Crofts, 1961.

Madsen, W. Mexican-Americans and Anglo-Americans: A comparative study of mental health in Texas. In S. C. Plog & R. Edgerton (Eds.), *Changing perspectives in mental illness*. New York: Holt, Rinehart & Winston, 1969.

McFayden, M., & Winokur, G. Cross-cultural psychotherapy. *Journal of Nervous and Mental Disorders*, 1956, *123*, 369–374.

Menacker, J. *Urban poor students and guidance*. Boston: Houghton Mifflin Co., 1971.

Mezzano, J. A note on dogmatism and counselor effectiveness. *Counselor Education and Supervision*, 1969, *9*(1), 64–65.

Middleton, R. Alienation, race and education. *American Sociological Review*, 1963, *28*, 973–977.

Millikan, R. L. Prejudice and counseling effectiveness. *Personnel and Guidance Journal*, 1965, *43*, 710–712.

Millikan, R. L., & Patterson, J. J. Relationship of dogmatism and prejudice to counseling effectiveness. *Counselor Education and Supervision*, 1967, *6*, 125–129.

Mitchell, H. The Black experience in higher education. *The Counseling Psychologist*, 1970, *2*, 30–36.

Morales, A. The impact of class discrimination and white racism in the mental health of Mexican-Americans. In N. N. Wagner & M. Haug (Eds.), *Chicanos: Social and psychological perspectives.* St. Louis: C. V. Mosby Co., 1970.

Morrow, D. L. Cultural addiction. *Journal of Rehabilitation*, 1972, *38*(3), 30–32.

Muliozzi, A. D. *Inter-racial counseling: Does it work*? Paper presented at the American Personnel and Guidance Association meeting, Chicago, 1972.

Murray, E. The content analysis method of study psychotherapy. *Psychological Monographs*, 1956, *70* (Whole No. 420).

Naroll, R. Cultural determinants and the concept of the sick society. In S. C. Plog & R. B. Edgerton (Eds.), *Changing perspectives in mental illness.* New York: Holt, Rinehart & Winston, 1969.

Oberg, K. Cultural shock and the problem of adjustment to new cultural environments. In D. Hoopes (Ed.), *Readings in intercultural communications.* Pittsburgh: Pittsburgh Intercultural Communications Network of the Regional Council for International Education, 1972.

Opler, M. K. The cultural backgrounds of mental health. In M. K. Opler (Ed.), *Culture and mental health.* New York: Macmillan Co., 1959.

Padilla, E., Boxley, R., & Wagner, N. *The desegregation of clinical psychology training.* Mimeographed, 1972.

Pande, S. K. The mystique of 'Western' psychotherapy: An Eastern interpretation. *Journal of Nervous and Mental Disorders*, 1968, *146*, 425–432.

Pedersen, P. *Cross-cultural counseling: Readings in intercultural communications* (Vol. 4). Pittsburgh: The Intercultural Communication Network of the Regional Council for International Education, 1974.

Pine, G. J. Counseling minority groups: A review of the literature. *Counseling and Values*, 1972, *17*(1), 35–44.

Pollack, E., & Menacker, J. *Spanish-speaking students and guidance.* Boston: Houghton Mifflin Co., 1971.

Price-Williams, D. R. Psychological experiment and anthropology: The problem of categories. *Ethos*, 1974, *2*(2), 95–114.

Pulvino, D. J., & Perrone, P. A. A model for retooling school counselors. *Counselor Education and Supervision*, 1973, *12*(4), 308–313.

Rogers, J. Operant conditioning in a quasi-therapy setting. *Journal of Abnormal and Social Psychology*, 1960, *60*, 247–252.

Rotenberg, M. The Protestant ethic versus Western people-changing sciences. In J. L. M. Dawson & W. Lonner (Eds.), *Readings in cross-cultural psychology.* Hong Kong: University of Hong Kong Press, 1974.

Russel, R. D. Black perspective of guidance. *The Personnel and Guidance Journal*, 1970, *48*, 721–729.

Russo, R. J., Ketz, J. W., & Hudson, G. Are good counselors open-minded? *Counselor Education and Supervision*, 1964, *3*(2), 74–77.

Saslow, H. L., & Harrover, M. J. Research on psychological adjustment of Indian youth. *American Journal of Psychiatry*, 1968, *125*(2).

Schwebel, M. Ideology and counselor encapsulation. *Journal of Counseling Psychology*, 1964, *11*(4), 366–369.

Sears, R. R. Transcultural variables and conceptual equivalence. In I. Al-Issa & W. Dennis (Eds.), *Cross-cultural studies of behavior.* New York: Holt, Rinehart & Winston, 1970.

Selltiz, C. J., Christ, R., Havel, J., & Cook, S. W. *Attitudes and social relations of foreign students in the United States.* Minneapolis: University of Minnesota Press, 1963.

Seward, G. *Clinical studies in cultural conflict.* New York: Ronald Press Co., 1970.

Sewell, W. H., & Davidson, O. M. The adjustment of Scandinavian students. *Journal of Social Issues*, 1956, *12*(1), 9–19.

Sinclair, A. *Field and clinical survey report of the mental health of the indigenes of the Territory of Papua and New Guinea*. Port Moresby: Government Publication, 1967.

Soddy, K. (Ed.). *Cross-cultural studies in mental health*. Chicago: Quadrangle Books, 1962.

Spain, D. H. On the use of projective techniques for psychological anthropology. In F. L. K. Hsu (Ed.), *Psychological anthropology*. Cambridge, Massachusetts: Schenkman Publishing Co., 1972.

Sprang, A. Counseling the Indian. *Journal of American Indian Education*, October 1965, 10–18.

Stewart, E. C., Danielian, J., & Festes, R. J. *Simulating intercultural communication through role playing* (HumRRO Tech. Rep. 69–7). Alexandria, Virginia: Human Resources Research Organization, May 1969.

Stranges, R., & Riccio, A. A counselee preference for counselors: Some implications for counselor education. *Counselor Education and Supervision*, 1970, *10*, 39–46.

Sue, D. W., & Kirk, B. A. Psychological characteristics of Chinese-American students. *Journal of Counseling Psychology*, 1972, *19*, 471–478.

Sue, D. W., & Sue, S. Counseling Chinese-Americans. *Personnel and Guidance Journal*, 1972, *50*, 637–645.

Sue, S. Training of Third World students to function as counselors. *Journal of Counseling Psychology*, 1973, *20*(1), 73–78.

Sweeney, T. J. *Rural poor students and guidance*. Boston: Houghton Mifflin Co., 1971.

Szalay, L. B., & Bryson, J. A. Measurement of psychocultural distance: A comparison of American Blacks and whites. *Journal of Personality and Social Psychology*, 1973, *26*, 166–171.

Tan, H. Intercultural study of counseling expectancies. *Journal of Counseling Psychology*, 1967, *41*(2), 122–130.

Thomas, A. Pseudo-transference reactions due to cultural stereotyping. *American Journal of Orthopsychiatry*, 1962, *32*, 894–900.

Torrey, E. F. *The irrelevancy of traditional mental health services for urban Mexican-Americans*. Paper presented at the American Orthopsychiatric Association, San Francisco, California, March 23–26, 1970.

Torrey, E. F. *The mind game: Witchdoctors and psychiatrists*. New York: Emerson Hall, 1972.

Torrey, E. F., Van Rheenan, F. J., and Katchadourian, H. A. Problems of foreign students: An overview. *Journal of the American College Health Association*, 1970, *19*, 83–86.

Trent, R. D. The color of the investigator as a variable in experimental research with Negro subjects. *Journal of Social Psychology*, 1954, *40*, 281–287.

Triandis, H. C. Culture training, cognitive complexity and interpersonal attitudes. In R. W. Brislin, S. Bochner, & W. J. Lonner (Eds.), *Cross-cultural perspectives on learning*. New York: John Wiley & Sons, Halsted, 1975.

Triandis, H. C., Vassiliou, V., Vassiliou, G., Tanaka, Y., & Shanmugam, A. V. *The analysis of subjective culture*. New York: John Wiley & Sons, 1972.

Vontress, C. E. Cultural barriers in the counseling relationship. *Personnel and Guidance Journal*, 1969, *48*, 11–17.

Vontress, C. E. *Counseling Negroes*. Boston: Houghton Mifflin Co., 1971.

Wagner, N. N., & Haug, M. J. *Chicanos, social and psychological perspectives*. St. Louis: C. V. Mosby Co., 1971.

Watts, A. W. *Psychotherapy East and West*. New York: Mentor Press, 1961.

Weidman, H. H. *Shame and guilt: A reformulation of the problem.* Paper presented at the meeting of the American Anthropological Association, Denver, Colorado, November 1965.

Weidman, H. H. The self-concept as a crucial link between social sciences and psychiatric theory. *Transcultural Psychiatry Research Review*, 1969, *6*, 113–116.

Weidman, H. H., & Sussex, J. N. Cultural values and ego functioning in relation to the typical culture-bound reactive syndromes. *International Journal of Social Psychiatry*, 1971, *17*(2), 83–100.

Williams, R. L. Black pride, academic relevance, and individual achievement. *The Counseling Psychologist*, 1970, *2*, 18–22.

Wittkower, E. D., & Weidman, H. H. Magic, witchcraft and sorcery in relation to mental health and mental disorder. *Social Psychiatry*, 1969, *8*, 169–184.

Woods, F. J. Cultural conditioning in mental health. *Social Casework*, 1958, *39*, 327–333.

Wrenn, G. C. The culturally encapsulated counselor. *Harvard Educational Review*, 1962, *32*(4), 444–449.

Yap, P. M. The culture-bound reactive syndromes. In W. Caudill & T.-y. Lin (Eds.), *Mental health research in Asia and the Pacific.* Honolulu: East-West Center Press, 1969.

Racial and Ethnic Barriers in ɔunseling

CLEMMONT E. VONTRESS

SHOULD A COUNSELOR FROM ONE CULTURE WORK WITH A CLIENT FROM ANOTHER?

Dr. Clemmont Vontress brings to this volume the perspective of a black psychologist who is frequently quoted and widely published on topics of counseling persons from other cultures. Some of his publications have already been discussed in Pedersen's review of the literature on intercultural counseling in the second chapter. In discussing the barriers encountered in counseling, Vontress contributes insights based on his work at George Washington University. Cultural diversity has been a valuable heritage of our national ideology. In human terms, however, the immigrant or minority populations have been pressured to assimilate to the dominant culture. The purpose of this chapter is to show that racial-ethnic differences have trapped both the counselor and client between the world as it is and as it should be.

The cultural bias implicit in counseling services available to racial and ethnic minorities combines with the client's cultural resistance to encumber his or her ability to communicate. Because many diagnostic skills are invalidated, attempts to identify preventive and remediative measures are often destroyed, and the benefits of counselor intervention are nullified. Differences in racial and ethnic background and socioeconomic status together with language difficulties and other factors interact to create problems in establishing rapport. More than usual attention should be paid to structuring the relationship, especially when the special population is typically suspicious of outsiders and when socialization patterns in that group encourage structured solutions.

Transference is commonplace in therapeutic encounters and may be positive or negative, conscious or unconscious. It is especially likely that transference will occur in counseling minorities when those minorities have had negative experiences with "mainstream" Americans. Countertransference is also a relationship barrier when counselors are unable to see themselves as they are perceived by some clients—products of a society seen as racist. Minority-group clients quickly pick up the racial implications of verbal and nonverbal behavior and they react negatively. Linguistic or paralinguistic differences in expression constitute another impediment because they too are culturally shaped. The more a special population is set apart physically and psychologically from the dominant group, the more the counselor is apt to experience language difficulties when attempting to communicate with its members. Several psychosocial factors, such as reserve in self-disclosure, self-rejection, machismo, personalism, poor attending behavior, and modesty, constitute barriers for the culturally provincial counselor.

The diagnosing of culturally different clients is difficult because diagnostic tools, whether standardized or unstandardized, psychometric or impressionistic, are often culture-specific and, therefore, generally invalid for assessing minorities. Recurring problems among deprived subcultural groups in this country are economic disability, educational bankruptcy, and negative self-perception. Therapeutic intervention is especially difficult, because the problems the clients bring to counseling are almost always externally caused, directly or indirectly. An approach to counselor training involving additional and innovative cognitive and affective experiences is recommended in order to help counselors overcome cultural barriers.

Vontress provides specific guidelines, which one can accept, reject, or debate, emphasizing that intercultural counseling is a complex process of interaction with its own specialized prerequisites. The problems are similar to those found in any effective counseling relationship but the solutions to those problems might be very different for each culture. He provides suggestions which can be tried, tested, and evaluated according to their effectiveness. This chapter moves from the generalized view of the "field and focus" toward a more specific application of intercultural counseling theory. Vontress highlights the continuing theme of attending to the client as a total person in all of his or her needs in a particular context or environment, one defined largely by the client's cultural values rather than those of the counselor.

The racial and ethnic diversity of people in the United States has never been denied. Early observers characterized the nation as a "melting pot," a folksy concept that suggested that culturally different citizens eventually would lose the distinct identities separating them. The concept aptly described many assimilation-oriented immigrants, who were so committed to becoming "real Americans" that their social and cultural interests, identities, and allegiances lay predominantly in the host society rather than in the ethnic community or in the old country. The least assimilation-oriented immigrants confined themselves to their ethnic enclaves, spoke their languages proudly, worshipped in their own way, and in general kept alive ethnic subcultures.

As racial and ethnic enclaves grew and became more obvious and often annoying to the dominant cultural group, the concept "cultural pluralism" developed a special appeal for Americans verbally committed to the ideals of democracy and tolerance (Zintz, 1969, p. 40). The term implied cooperation between majority and minority; it suggested mutual respect, appreciation, and acceptance of cultural differences; and it inferred that minorities would not have to fear repression or obliteration of their heritages. Cultural pluralism was put to a severe test during the great push for civil rights in the fifties and sixties, when the largest and most severely excluded minority in the United States, Americans of African descent, expressed as never before great pride in their racial and ethnic heritage and demanded equal rights. Concurrently and subsequently other racial and ethnic groups—American Indians, persons of Spanish heritage, and Jewish Americans—declared aloud their identities while simultaneously decrying the inequalities inflicted upon them by the dominant-group Americans. Their voices and the cries of Black Power announced to all that the United States comprises many subcultures, from which constituent minorities acquire language patterns, customs, values, and world views that are often foreign to members of the dominant cultural group. The demands for equal rights caused a variety of reactions from mainstream Americans. These ranged from humanitarian concern to overt anger and hostility toward the minorities for upsetting the social status quo.

The social phenomenon just described reflects the fact that when human groups exist apart for whatever reason, they, in time, develop different language habits and nuances, personalities, perceptions of themselves and others, and values and norms that guide their behavior. They become culturally different. The differences, in turn, become reasons for exclusion by those in power. In the United States, racial and ethnic minorities are excluded from equal opportunity to the degree that they are different from the dominant group. In the case of blacks, primary exclusion variables are color of skin, curl of hair, and slave heritage. These are genetically transmitted; that is, if one or both parents have the characteristics, the offspring will have them also, at least to some extent. Although "slave heritage" is not a biological trait, the fact that one's forebears were slaves is a historical fact. Because of the dominant group's intense reactions to real and imagined differences, primary variables, singly or interactively, eventuate into numerous potent secondary exclusionary forces, such as differences in language, values, education, income, housing, general culture, and lifestyle. These are the excuses often given by dominant-group Americans for excluding minorities, since one is less apt to condemn oneself as a bigot than one would if one admitted to excluding human beings because of their color, hair texture, or previous servitude—factors over which the excluded have no control.

Indeed, citizens in the American society are separate and unequal; and this fact is evident throughout the social order. Whenever majority and minority group members meet one another, the likelihood of misunder-standing and ill-will is great. Counseling, the largest helping profession in this country, has not gone untouched by the lack of understanding and goodwill between the majority and minorities. As a process, counseling is a psychological interaction involving two or more individuals. One or more of the interactants is considered to be able to help the other person or persons live and function more effectively at the time of the involvement or at some future time. Specifically, the goal of counseling is to assist, directly or indirectly, the recipient or recipients in adjusting to or otherwise negotiating the various environments that influence his or her psycho-logical well-being. To accomplish this goal, the counselor must relate to and communicate with the client, must determine the client's state of adjustment, must decide alone or with him or her the course of action needed to improve the client's current or future situation, and, in addition, should be able to intervene at some level of competency to assist the client.

This chapter focuses on the effects of racial and ethnic factors on the counseling process; i.e., it points out how cultural differences affect the ability of the counselor to relate and communicate with his or her client therapeutically, to discuss problems the counselor may experience in making a diagnosis of the minority-group client, to suggest some diffi-culties inherent in making recommendations to assist minority-group clients, and to consider briefly problems of intervention often encountered in intercultural counseling.

THE RELATIONSHIP

Counseling is a dynamic process where elements shift and gain or lose momentum. The interactants are replaced or increased as other problems become more-or-less demanding of their attention and concern. Even so, I will attempt here to examine various aspects of the counseling relation-ship as it relates to minority-group individuals.

Rapport

As a relationship between two or more individuals, counseling suggests *ipso facto* the establishment of a mutual bond between the interactants. The emotional bridge between the counselor and the counselee is referred to as rapport, a concept that pervades therapeutic literature. Simply defined, rapport connotes a comfortable and unconstrained mutual trust and confidence between two or more persons (Buchheimer & Balogh, 1961, p. 4). In a counseling dyad, it implies positive feelings combined with a spirit of cooperativeness. In therapeutic groups, rapport is the existence of a mutual responsiveness that encourages each member to react immediately, spontaneously, and sympathetically to the sentiments and attitudes of every other member (Hinsie & Campbell, 1960, p. 625).

Rapport should not be misconstrued as involving only the initial "small talk" designed to put the counselee at ease. Rather, it is a dynamic emotional bridge that must be maintained throughout the counseling process. During the relationship, the participants continuously take stock of each other. They notice how the other presents her- or himself—what is said and how it is said. The nature of the communications, explicit or implicit, can cause the counselee, or even the counselor, to alternate from trust to tacit reserve or even to overt hostility. Exploring content that is threatening to the ego generally requires a more positive relationship bridge than is needed in more usual social encounters.

It is a matter of common experience that individuals find it more difficult to establish empathy with those unlike themselves (Katz, 1963, p. 6). Differences in racial or ethnic backgrounds, in socioeconomic class, and in language patterns—these and other factors singly or interactively create problems in establishing rapport in the counseling relationship. Often the differences or similarities are so imperceptible that the counselee cannot verbalize them. He or she can only feel them. For example, the counselee can only express good feelings toward the counselor by the statement, "He talks like us," which is equivalent to saying "He is one of us."

However, it is important to indicate that differences do make a difference when all other things are equal. In the United States, most minorities are so disadvantaged that any one of their kind who succeeds often is suspect by members of his own racial or ethnic group. On one hand, they view the achiever as a collaborator with the "enemy." How else could he have risen above his own people! On the other hand, they are consumed by destructive envy of him because he is better off than they who have not achieved. The ambivalence is aggravated when self-hatred pervades the minority group in question. For example, in order to understand the complex dynamics of the black-black counseling dyad, one must consider the client's ambivalence toward the counselor and the self-hatred of the interactants. Self-hatred causes each to reject the other, as he rejects himself. This phenomenon helps to explain why Caucasian counselors may be more effective counselors for some black clients than are black counselors themselves.

In spite of these observations, it is still possible to offer some general advice for establishing rapport with minorities, especially with those who have not had a continuing relationship with members of the dominant cultural group. First, the counselor should try to avoid extremes in behavior. For example, he should refrain from over- or underdressing;

that is, he should dress so as not to call undue attention to himself. American reservation Indians appear to be extremely suspicious of too much talking, too many questions, and too much "putting on the dog." Similar attitudes are pervasive among Appalachian whites, who historically have been suspicious of the "city slicker."

In general, the counselor should curtail his small talk in the beginning of the interview, especially if he does not know just what small talk is appropriate. Small talk may be perceived as an attempt by the counselor to delay the unpleasant. Therefore, it can be anxiety-producing. The counselor should start the interview with a direct but courteous, "How can I help you?" This will allow the client to chit-chat, if he is uncomfortable going immediately into his reason for coming to the counselor. Some Spanish-heritage clients may annoy the Anglo-Caucasian counselor with the penchant to pry into his personal life. In such a case, the counselor should not be alarmed and should reply to such a question as "Are you married?" and get on with the interview.

Structuring

On the whole, disadvantaged minority group members have had limited experiences with counselors and related therapeutic professionals. Their contacts have been mainly with people who tell them what they must or should do in order to receive wages, to get well, or to stay out of trouble. Relationships with professionals who place major responsibility upon the individual for solving his own problems are few. Therefore, the counselor working within such a context should structure or define his role to clients; that is, he should indicate what, how, and why he intends to do what he will do. It is also important to communicate to the client and sometimes to the client's loved ones what is expected of everyone involved in the relationship. Failure to structure early and adequately in counseling can result in unfortunate and unnecessary misunderstanding, simply because the counselor's interest and concern are unclear to the client, the client's parents, or significant others.

The counselor of deprived minorities needs to realize that he is working with persons who, because of their cultural and experiential backgrounds, are unable or unwilling to participate in introspective explorations. Therefore, techniques such as prolonged silences should be avoided, at least until positive rapport has been established, for their use tends to become awkward and to increase the distance between the counselor and his client (MacKinnon & Michels, 1971, p. 398).

The counselor may find it particularly difficult to conduct an interview in which personal issues must be explored. Appalachian whites, for example, may find to be very offensive personal queries which the counselor may perceive to be innocuous. Often parents of counselees are the first to let the counselor know this, especially if he or she happens not to be "from round here."

In general, more than usual attention should be paid to structuring when the subcultural group is typically suspicious of outsiders, for whatever reason, and when the socialization patterns in the group encourage a structured, well-ordered approach to life. For example, the well-defined roles and expectations for members of the orderly Chinese-American family probably explain why high school and college students from such families prefer concrete and well-structured situations in and out of the classroom (Sue & Sue, 1972). The ambiguity typically inherent in the counseling process is terribly disconcerting to them, to say the least.

Resistance

The counselee's opposition to the goals of counseling is usually referred to as resistance. It may manifest itself in a variety of ways, such as self-devaluation, intellectualization, and overt hostility. Although the counselor may recognize the various manifestations when he counsels a middle-class Caucasian counselee, he often fails to recognize the phenomenon in the minority-group client, probably because he is so overwhelmed by the perceived differences between his client and himself that he fails to follow his usual counseling procedures.

Although many Spanish-heritage clients are unable to converse fluently in English, others may reveal to the counselor's subsequent surprise that they are quite adept in that language. The client's alleged inability to speak English must be viewed, therefore, as resistance, either to the counselor himself, to the Anglo-Caucasian establishment, or to both (MacKinnon & Michels, 1971, p. 394).

It has been observed also that many young blacks, urban or rural, appear to be shy and withdrawn in the counseling dyad or group. The counselor, unfamiliar with the nuances of black culture, may be quick to assess the behavior as just another unfortunate effect of social and economic deprivation. However, the client's perception of his own conduct may be very different: he's just "cooling it." He knows how to rap beautifully about whatever but is unwilling to do so until he is convinced that his audience is a person of good will. On the other hand, such clients may be so talkative that they refuse to let the counselor get a word in edgeways. Although such deportment may be perceived as an indication of positive rapport and desire for assistance, it can also mean that the client is "playing along" with the counselor. It is somewhat similar to a sandlot basketball game in which the ball is being passed to all players but one, the isolate. In this case, the counselor is the outsider.

Other examples of resistance among minorities in the counseling relationship can be cited. A very obvious one is failure to show up for an appointment. American Indians, for example, are very reluctant to disagree or be uncooperative, especially with someone of higher status than they. Such reluctance may be observed also among many low-status Southern blacks, vis-à-vis whites, although perhaps for different reasons. Indians and blacks of all ages may agree to come in for an interview or conference, when, in fact, they have no intentions of following through. They promise to do so out of courtesy, respect, or fear.

Transference

Transference refers to an individual's reacting to a person in the present in a manner similar to the way he or she has reacted to another person in the past (Greenson, 1964, pp. 151–152). In other words, transference is a repetition of an old relationship. It may be conscious or unconscious, positive or negative, and it is considered a form of resistance to the goals of counseling (Harrison & Carek, 1966, p. 77). Common in most therapeutic involvements, transference is especially knotty in the majority-minority counseling dyad or group, because minority group members bring to the relationship intense emotions derived from experiences with and feelings toward the majority group.

In counseling, the client expects the counselor to succor and support or to punish and control (Brammer & Shostrom, 1968, p. 234). Minority-group counselees usually anticipate that the majority-group counselor will exhibit the latter behavior, either because of direct experiences with persons who remind them of the counselor or because of socialization that has taught them to react to members of the majority group or those who identify with that group with suspicion. For example, preschool Pueblo Indian children know better than to tell the "white man" about anything that is happening in the village (Zintz, 1969, p. 207). In barrios of the Southwest, the Mexican-American's fear of and hostility toward Anglo-Americans are evidenced by the fact that 4- and 5-year-old children run ahead of any official-looking vehicle that enters their neighborhoods and scream *la migra, la migra* ("the migration officials") (Moore, 1970, p. 91). Such behavior implies that these children learn before they enter school that Anglo-Caucasians are not to be trusted. It is easy to understand why many of them associate a counselor in a private office with the "policia" or some other official who does not have their best interest at heart.

Black children also learn at an early age, often at the feet of their parents, that white people are not to be trusted. As they mature in decaying ghettos of great cities, blacks also have other experiences that lead them habitually to approach Caucasians with resentful anxiety, distrust, hostility, and ambivalence. In a similar way, many Appalachian children learn that outsiders, whatever color they happen to be, are people who "mean no good." Thus, their school counselors, especially those perceived as outsiders, find that mountain children appear to be fearful, shy, and reluctant to talk (Weller, 1966, p. 49).

Countertransference

Countertransference occurs when counselors react to particular counselees as they have reacted toward other persons in their past. The counterpart of transference, it may lead to persistently inappropriate behavior toward the counselee and result in untold strains in the counseling relationship. Although counselors are quick to recognize transference as a reality, they find it difficult to consider the possibility that they may not accept, respect, or like many of their counselees (Harrison & Carek, 1966, p. 192). Their professional training has tended to inculcate in them the notion that they should be imbued with empathy, with congruence, and with a positive regard that is unconditional. Therefore, they fail to admit that they are also mothers and fathers, voters, property owners, taxpayers, Northerners and Southerners, and Republicans and Democrats—in a word, that they are human beings with a variety of attitudes, beliefs, and values, conscious and unconscious, that invariably affect the counseling relationships that they have established with minority-group people.

As products of a society that has been characterized as racist, counselors bring to the therapeutic relationship preconceived attitudes and ideas about racial and ethnic minorities. The preconceptions manifest themselves in numerous ways. Because majority-group members occupy the most powerful and prestigious positions in society, they are often perceived, rightly or wrongly, by minority-group people as being authoritarian and condescending. In counseling, this phenomenon may be described as "The Great White Father Syndrome." Majority-group counselors may communicate to minority-group clients that they are not only omnipotent but that they mean their clients nothing but good. They literally guarantee them that they will 'deliver," if the clients will put themselves in their hands. Simultaneously, they communicate, albeit unconsciously, the implication that if the clients do not depend on them, they will be doomed to catastrophe. The Great White Father Syndrome may be interpreted as countertransference, because it suggests that the counselor is anxious to demonstrate not only his or her power and authority but also to prove that he or she is not like all the other majority-group people the minority-group clients may have known.

Another general manifestation of countertransference is the counselor's tendency to be excessively sympathetic and indulgent with minority clients. For example, the counselor's definition of achievement for them may be in wide variance with his or her achievement yardstick for members of the majority group. Is achievement for minorities viewed as that level of attainment—educational, social, occupational, and economic—considered meritorious, laudable, acceptable, or desirable as measured by criteria, explicit or implicit, that are established or espoused by the dominant cultural group; or is a different set of achievement criteria considered appropriate for minorities, simply because they are minorities? If the latter is the case, the counselor is guilty of saying, thinking, or condescendingly implying that the minority-group client is pretty good—for a black, a Mexican-American, or an Indian.

Language

Language is a part of an individual's culture or subculture. Failure to understand another's language is failure to comprehend much of another's culture. In order to communicate effectively with minority-group clients, the counselor must be able to understand the verbal and nonverbal language of his counselees (for each aspect is dependent on the other). If the listener hears only the speaker's words, he or she may get as much distortion as if he or she had "listened" only to his body language. To understand the meaning of gestures, postures, and inflections, one must know a people, their institutions, values, and lifestyle.

The counselor encounters varying degrees of difficulty when communicating with racial and ethnic minorities. For example, on Indian reservations, variations in the facility to use English can be illustrated, on the one hand, by some of the Pueblos of New Mexico who speak no English in everyday life, and, on the other, by the Fort Berthold Reservation Indians of North Dakota who nearly all speak English. On the Choctaw reservation in Mississippi, about 4 percent of the families use excellent English; 57 percent, good; and 39 percent use poor English (U.S. Department of Labor, 1968, p. 130). Although this description is fairly typical of English facility among reservation Indians in general, young Indians, having learned English in school, use that language with greater facility than do their olders. Even so, Indians of whatever age communicate with great economy of language, and they are given to the use of concrete words, as opposed to abstract ones. Therefore, counselors find that Indian clients are limited in the ability to express personal feelings, which is considered necessary by most counselors.

In the Southwest, Spanish-heritage people customarily live in enclaves isolated from the English-speaking community. In many counties in Texas and New Mexico, the children enter the English-speaking world for the first time when they enroll in public schools. In classrooms children unable to speak English are often threatened with punishment if they speak in their native language. Badly needed to assist these children and their parents are bilingual counselors whose native language is Spanish, because many Anglo-Caucasian counselors who have studied Spanish in school find that they are still unable to communicate with alingual or biculturally illiterate children who speak neither English nor Spanish that is standard (Moore, 1970, pp. 77–78).

The counselor is less handicapped in communicating with Appalachian whites than he is with American Indians and Spanish-heritage clients. Even so, he usually finds therapeutic communication difficult, because mountain people tend to use simple Anglo-Saxon words. Their speech is characterized by a reduction in qualifiers, adjectives, and adverbs, especially those which qualify feelings (Weller, 1966, p. 144). Therefore, the counselor who expects his Appalachian clients to talk a great deal about how they feel is apt to be disappointed. Unique idioms and pronunciations also may constitute communication barriers, at least until the counselor's ears become attuned to the language patterns.

Among lower-class blacks, the counselor, black or white, often experiences difficulties in understanding not only slurred pronunciations, but also idioms and slang endemic to the community. Some counselors, not wishing to reveal that they cannot or do not understand the counselee's argot, continue the dialogue, hoping to catch up later on. Unfortunately, they often discover that the more they allow the client to talk without clarification, the more confused they become as to what he or she is saying. If the counselor fails to understand the client for whatever reason, the most honest thing to do is to ask him for an explanation or repetition of his statement.

The counselor probably experiences more difficulty understanding implicit language in the lower-class black community than he does comprehending the explicit (Wachtel, 1967). Individuals speak not just with their voices alone; they use their entire bodies either to make a complete statement or to punctuate one (Kris, 1941). For example, the "hip" shuffle of the young black male, his slouched sitting position with chin in hand, his erect stance with genitals cupped, the apparently unconscious wipe at the chin or mouth with his hand when there is nothing visible to wipe away—all of these nonverbal expressions are filled with significant meaning to one who can interpret them (Beier, 1966, p. 279). To arrive at the correct interpretation, the counselor must understand both the general and contextual meanings of these expressions. He needs to recognize that the more emotionally charged the verbal language, the less definite is its meaning and the more important are the accompanying nonverbal expressions (Vetter, 1969, p. 125).

Occasionally, the counselor may need to use an interpreter with Indian and Spanish-heritage clients. If an interpreter is needed when counseling or communicating with Hispanic people, it is important to use someone whom the individual can respect (Hidalgo, n.d., p. 13). For example, the Anglo-Caucasian counselor would be advised not to ask a third- or fourth-grade Spanish-speaking student to interpret for him when he consults with a Spanish-speaking parent. Because of the demand for respect so characteristic among the Spanish-speaking, the counselor should obtain someone whom the parent will respect as he or she respects the counselor.

2. Knowledge of the client's language and its nuances is important in counseling, because so many customary counseling techniques demand fluency in this area. Paraphrasing, reflection, and interpretation presuppose understanding the client's language. In order to reflect accurately what the client is experiencing and feeling, the counselor must be able to interpret nonverbal behavior. He must not allow skin color or accent to blind him to cues which would be otherwise obvious if he were counseling a majority-group client.

Psychosocial Barriers

Several psychosocial characteristics of racial and ethnic minorities constitute, singly or interactively, barriers to the achievement of therapeutic goals in the counseling relationship. These barriers are usually unconscious aspects of the personality and are derived primarily from the American culture which both socializes and oppresses its minorities simultaneously. Occasionally, current behavior patterns, discussed below, can be traced back to the old country.

Self-Disclosure. Self-disclosure, or the willingness to let another person know what you think, feel, or want, is basic to the counseling process. It is particularly crucial in the rapport-establishment phase of the relationship, because it is the most direct means by which an individual can make himself known to another person and is, therefore, prerequisite to achieving the goals of counseling. People of African descent are especially reluctant to disclose themselves to others, probably because of the hardships which they and their forebears have experienced in the United States. Many of them, especially the males, are devoid of confidence in human relations (Kardiner & Ovesey, 1962, p. 308).

Reluctance to disclose is a problem in the white-black dyad, because few blacks initially perceive Caucasians as being individuals of good will. The client discloses himself when he feels that he can trust the target person, not necessarily when he feels that he is being understood (Jourard,

1964, p. 4). In fact, the black client fears being understood, for it carries with it the idea of engulfment, of loss of autonomy, of being known, and that is the same as being destroyed in a society that he perceives as racist. Obviously, the fear of being understood has grave implications for individual and group counseling. It is conceivable that, in the case of the black client, the counselor who understands too much is to be feared or even hated.

Self-Hatred. An individual who is a member of an ostracized, excluded, or oppressed group tends not only to despise that group but also to hate him- or herself for being a member of the group. In the United States, blacks, more than any other minority, have unconsciously identified with the majority group—their perceived oppressors—and, consequently, have developed contempt for, and hatred of, themselves (Vontress, 1971). In view of the generally acknowledged positive correlation between self-rejection and the rejection of others, the counselor may expect repulsion, passive or overt, from the black client for this reason alone. The counselor's helping the black counselee to accept himself more positively should result in the client's progressive acceptance of the counselor.

Machismo. When counseling the Hispanic male, it is important to understand the meaning of machismo, which refers to one's manhood, the manly traits of honor and dignity, to the courage to fight, to keeping one's word, and to protecting one's name (Steiner, 1969, p. 386). It also refers to a man's running his home, controlling his women, and directing his children. Therefore, machismo, which provides respect from a male's peers, is not to be taken for granted. It also suggests a rather clear-cut separation of the sexes. The male, *ipso facto*, enjoys rights and privileges denied women, who are generally reluctant to demand equality. It is probably because of machismo that Spanish-heritage boys and girls are often more uncomfortable and uncommunicative in coed group counseling than is the case with non-Spanish-heritage boys. Another implication of machismo is that female counselors should not be too aggressive or forward in the counseling interview with Hispanic males, not even with preadolescents. The right amount of deference must be shown at all times. The topic of machismo is particularly sensitive in a context in which we are being sensitized to the inequity of a sexist society.

Personalism. Personalism constitutes a rather stubborn counseling barrier among Appalachian whites, Spanish-heritage people, and blacks. Although a precise definition is difficult, the word suggests that individuals are more interested in and motivated by considerations for people than they are for bureaucratic protocol. The mountaineer derives self-identification mainly from his relationships with others (Fetterman, 1971). Therefore, he or she puts a lot of stock in being neighborly. For the mountaineer, it is more important to pass the time of day with a friend encountered en route to an appointment than it is to arrive at the destination punctually.

Refusing to be enslaved by clocks, mountain people transact their business by feeling, not protocol (Weller, 1966, p. 159). People who adhere to appointments, promptness, and protocol are suspect. In counseling, personalism encumbers the counselor in getting his clients to make and keep appointments. They prefer to drop by to "pass a spell" and "visit" and may get around to discussing something that has been "bothering my mind," while they are there.

As suggested earlier, asking a counselor personal questions may be the Hispanic person's way of getting close to an individual who might otherwise remain impersonal. Although lower-class blacks are reluctant to ask a counselor direct personal questions, they are generally more comfortable relating to the counselor after they have obtained at least a modicum of information about the counselor as a human being; i.e., they are apt to "check out the dude" before "spilling my guts" to him.

Listening. Counseling requires, among other things, listening, an area in which many lower-class blacks and Appalachian whites have little experience, probably because of their early socialization in large families. Often their homes are filled with din and confusion, with everybody talking simultaneously, as Surface (1971, p. 32) pointed out. In such an environment, young people soon learn not to listen to what words mean, but to the emotions speakers convey (Weller, 1966, p. 49). This is why the observant counselor may discern a blank stare on the face of his client, even when he perceives himself to be providing the youngster with much needed insight. The empty facial expression indicates that the client has tuned out the counselor until he stops talking. The inability of black and mountain people to attend to a speaker may help to explain why their conversation seems to have little continuity of ideas. Inability to listen hampers more directly group counseling than it does dyadic relationships.

Modesty. Modesty in the presence of superiors is a relationship barrier in counseling Japanese-Americans. The phenomenon may be attributed to the total respect customarily paid the father, whose authority in the family is beyond question, and toward whom one is forbidden to express overt negative feelings (Kitano, 1969, pp. 64–67). Many young Japanese-Americans are so imbued with awe of authority that they hesitate to express their feelings on any subject when they are in the presence of higher-status individuals or when they are expected to articulate their views in groups. It is easy to understand how their hesitancy intrudes in the counseling relationship, dyadic or group.

Characteristic reserve in the Japanese-American personality makes it difficult to determine where cultural patterns end and psychologically debilitating symptomatology begins (Kitano, 1970). Counselors must have two perceptual yardsticks for measuring normal behavior; i.e., they must be able to determine what is deviant behavior in the Japanese-American subculture as well as what is aberrant in the culture at large.

Reserve among many Puerto Rican females and rural lower-class blacks in general corresponds closely to that of Japanese-Americans. The well-bred Puerto Rican girl often avoids eye-to-eye contact, especially with men, a fact which may cause the Anglo-Caucasian counselor to draw false conclusions about her character and personality. Her hesitancy to interact voluntarily in group counseling may be attributed to socialization in the Puerto Rican culture in which boys are expected to assert their manhood, while girls remain retiring. Traditionally, southern blacks were expected by southern whites to be nonassertive and passive. The residue of such expectations remains today, especially among lower-class blacks in the South, and probably helps to explain why black youngsters are often hesitant to interact in interracial counseling groups.

These, then, are but a few psychosocial barriers the counselor may experience in therapeutic interactions with racial and ethnic minorities. Others could be cited to illustrate the importance of the counselor's being cognizant of subcultural factors when relating to culturally different clients.

THE DIAGNOSIS

To accomplish the goals of counseling, the counselor must be able to relate to, and communicate with, his client; he must be able to determine the client's state of adjustment; he is expected to make therapeutic recommendations designed to assist the client; and he must be able to intervene personally to assist the individual. Although relating to minority-group people is problematic, as has been pointed out, making an accurate diagnosis of culturally different counselees is probably fraught with more difficulties. Even though the clients are racially and ethnically different, the counselor perforce relies on the same assessment tools and procedures used in counseling majority-group clients.

Diagnostic Techniques

Commonly used diagnostic techniques, whether standardized or unstandardized, are generally questionable for assessing minority-group clients. The ones most used today are standardized and objective; i.e., their procedure, apparatus, and scoring have been regularized to allow replicated administration; and every observer of performance arrives at the same report. Included in this category is a variety of commercially available instruments labelled proficiency, achievement, developmental, intelligence, and personality tests, and a limited number designated interest inventories.

There are several problems inherent in using these instruments with minorities. The first one can be described as situational. For disadvantaged minority-group individuals, lengthy structured situations demanding assiduity are physically and psychologically annoying. Unusual surroundings, formal procedures, and unfamiliar people so characteristic of large-group testing environments, individually or combined, aggravate their annoyance and often account for anxiety sufficient to depress scores of reluctant examinees (American Psychological Association, 1969). In the case of blacks, examiners with regional accents which put them on guard can influence performance. In general, Caucasians with Southern accents are associated with prejudice and discrimination; therefore, as test administrators they are apt to produce in blacks an anxiety that may affect test performance.

Steps can be taken to assure an environment most conducive to optimum performance of minority-group individuals on standardized tests. First, test administrators should prepare the examinees in advance for the test. Individual and group counseling is one vehicle which can be used, not only to allay apprehension about test-taking, but to motivate toward optimum performance as well. Second, in order to ensure the most favorable testing conditions, the size of the testing group should be kept small; i.e., 10 or 20 examinees to a room. Herding groups of 50, 100, or 200 students into a large arena is most undesirable. Third, test batteries requiring from 6 to 8 hours to administer should be given in segments extending over several days. Finally, examiners and proctors of the same racial and ethnic background as the examinees should be used whenever possible.

In general, language constitutes a handicap for minorities taking standardized tests, not necessarily because it serves as a people's vehicle for communication, but because of its role in the transmission of culture from one generation to another. As a major aspect of culture, it is also a barometer which reflects changes in cultural demands and expectations, however subtle (Cohen, 1956, pp. 78–125). Those who observe that minorities are verbally destitute, and somehow connect the destitution with depressed scores on standardized tests, oversimplify a complex problem. Language differences are simply indicative of more global and significant cultural differences.

The more assimilated a minority group, the fewer problems its members are apt to experience in taking standardized tests. Groups may loose their total cultural identity as many ethnics have done; they may do as Jewish and Japanese-Americans have done, accept selectively achievement-related aspects of the host culture, while simultaneously retaining many components of the old; they may become equicultural, moving comfortably back and forth across the line separating the old culture from the new; or they may remain essentially cultural isolates. The majority of American Indians, Americans of African descent, and Mexican-Americans can be classified as cultural isolates, because they are excluded physically and psychologically from the cultural mainstream of the American society. The language difficulties that they experience in taking standardized tests is but one of the manifestations of their exclusionary status.

In view of this problem, counselors should determine informally the degree to which the individual is assimilated in the American culture before administering him a standardized test. If he is a cultural isolate, insisting that he take a standardized test in the idiom of the host culture is questionable. The examiner should determine also the reading level of the examinee before subjecting him to a test that demands reading facility. If the readability level of the test is beyond the individual's reading ability, there is little to be gained by using the test.

Because of the cultural barriers encountered in using standardized tests with racial and ethnic minorities, it is often felt that substitute procedures should be employed. The obvious alternative is the impressionistic approach; i.e., the counselor looks for significant cues by any means available and integrates them into a total impression of the individual's ability, personality, aptitude, or other traits. The unstandardized procedures include observations, anecdotal records, and interviews —analytic techniques well known to counselors. Unfortunately, for minorities, these assessment approaches are probably more unreliable than the objective, standardized techniques, because of cultural stereotypes which impair the counselor's ability to diagnose individuals from subcultural groups of which he is not a member. Culture determines the specific ways in which individuals perceive and conceive of their environment and strongly influences the forms of conflict, behavior, and psychopathology that occur in members of the culture (Horney, 1937, pp. 13–29; Horney, 1966, pp. 176–177). This fact helps to explain why, for example, Caucasian counselors generally find it difficult to determine through an impressionistic interview where the usual Japanese-American modesty and reserve end and psychological malady begins (Kitano, 1970). Caucasian counselors are also generally inept in assessing psychological morbidity in blacks, mainly because for so long whites have accepted, expected, or demanded bizarre behavior of Negroes.

Recurring Problems

Although each minority-group counselee should be perceived and counselled as an individual, several common problems plague identifiable minorities in the United States. The severity of each problem depends on, among other things, geographic location and level of assimilation and deprivation. Three recurring problems are economic deprivation, educational deficiencies, and negative self-concept.

In general, the unemployment rate of minorities far exceeds that of the majority group. On countless reservations and in many ghettos and barrios, more able-bodied persons are unemployed than are employed. Economic deprivation, resulting from unemployment and low-paying jobs, in turn leads to a complex of psychosocial problems. For example, inadequate and high-density housing fast give rise not only to family dissension but to increased morbidity as well. Life becomes so difficult that short-run hedonism necessarily becomes one's goal.

Intertwined with economic disability are educational deficiencies so much in evidence in black, Mexican-American, and Indian communities. Although there is no consensus on the causation of educational bankruptcy among minorities, it seems clear that a complex of factors such as poor nutrition, inadequate housing, insufficient or improper familial stimuli and role models, poor teachers, and limited school resources interact to constitute a formidable barrier to equal education.

Members of subcultural groups enduring victim status in a country, over an extended period of history, soon come to view themselves negatively. Illustrative are blacks who were abducted to this country, stripped of their language, heritage, and religion, and assigned an inferior status from which few of their kind have been able to escape. Their lack of identity and consequent self-contempt help to explain their lack of academic achievement, interpersonal conflicts, intragroup hostility, and drug abuse, especially among young black males in urban areas.

Among American Indians, confusion over cultural identity also leads to interpersonal problems that are expressed in terms of jealousy and suspicion of others (Samora et al., 1965). Envy and distrust of one's peers are reflected in the school performance of many Indians who are reluctant to surpass the achievement of their classmates; in their hesitancy to assume leadership roles that might lead to insidious comparisons; and in hostility and conflict between adolescents and their elders. Widespread alcoholism among Indians, even teenagers, may also be attributed to loss of cultural identity and the accompanying institutional and ritualistic restraints which provided significant meaning and direction in life (Kiev, 1972, p. 113; White man brings. . ., 1972).

THERAPEUTIC RECOMMENDATIONS   2nd p. 53

Having made a diagnosis of the client's situation, the counselor needs to conceptualize what needs to be done, why it should be done, and by whom it should be done, to alleviate, enhance, or insure continuous development of the trait or condition diagnosed. He also should be able to anticipate the probable immediate, intermediate, and final consequences of each action recommended. In order to do this, the counselor should know the demands and expectations of the client's subculture in addition to those of the dominant cultural group.

In counseling disadvantaged minorities, the counselor must make recommendations that reflect explicitly or implicitly, directly or indirectly, an immediate or long-range attempt to help the client move from his racial or ethnic cultural influences to mainstream status or living style. For example, an Caucasian counselor new to the black ghetto may recommend that a child be removed from his home, which the counselor considers deplorable, without realizing that by local community standards the home is quite good. Another counselor insists that a Puerto Rican girl who has scored high on the Scholastic Aptitude Test apply for admission to a college where she can surely get a scholarship, without first consulting with her father who believes that a nice Puerto Rican girl should get married, have children, and obey her husband. Illustrative also is the counselor who directs a black student to a predominantly white college instead of a black institution, without realizing that the young man in an all-white environment is apt to become very lonely for the culturally familiar.

The examples are cited not to suggest that the counselor should refrain from making what could be termed intercultural recommendations. Rather, the intent is to show that most therapeutic recommendations made by counselors are, in effect, slanted toward the mainstream life style. As such, they are often antithetical to the demands and expectations of the client's particular subculture. Therefore, the counselor must help his clients make a series of intermediate adjustments prerequisite to becoming comfortable with the demands and expectations of the host culture. Often the problems are related to guilt feelings associated with having left behind people who still suffer as he has suffered. There is also fear of achievement which is pervasive among disadvantaged minorities. This phenomenon, upon closer inspection, is essentially fear of the envy of one's racial and ethnic fellows.

Intervention

In intercultural counseling, often the counselor is unable to intervene effectively on behalf of his client for several reasons. The minority-group client himself may be resistant to the goals of counseling. Intervention involves change, and that may trigger a personal social cataclysm with which he is unwilling to cope. For example, the mountain boy who is the first in his community to go away to college may worry that his friends staying behind will find him different upon his return. A black youngster from the ghetto may be reluctant to accept a scholarship to a predominantly Caucasian university, choosing instead to attend a smaller all-black college, because he fears losing his "blackness," which his friends consider important.

Also, intervention can be blocked directly by the client's significant others. Counselors working with children in Appalachia are chagrined sometimes to discover that their counseling is undone by superstitious parents. In extended Oriental and Hispanic families, it is important to recognize that family members rarely make individual decisions. In such situations, the counselor may need to provide family counseling in order to intervene on behalf of a single member, no matter how old he happens to be.

That the counselor typically works within an institutional setting suggests that there are forces outside the counselor's office which can hinder his intervention efforts. For example, the school counselor may find that he alone cannot help Spanish-heritage or black children adjust to a predominantly Caucasian school if the janitors, teachers, fellow students, and administrators are hostile to their presence. In government, although the personnel counselor places a minority-group employee in a position commensurate with his experience and skills, he may be unable to control the indifferent reception of other employees or the demeaning tasks assigned by the supervisor.

Intervention on behalf of minority-group clients frequently is made difficult and sometimes impossible because the community at large is indifferent to the needs and problems of the minority group in question. For example, in the Southwest, many Spanish-heritage children are doomed to failure in the public schools, because English is the sole language of instruction. Although the counselor may recognize that some of his Spanish-speaking clients who are failing are in fact extremely gifted, often he is unable scotch their academic demise because the Caucasian community, which controls the purse strings, just does not care when it comes to "those kids."

CONCLUSIONS

Numerous problems exist in counseling minority-group counselees. They derive primarily from intercultural barriers, which cause communication static and distortion in interactions involving individuals from culturally different backgrounds. The fact that the client comes from a distinct subculture impairs the counselor's ability to determine not only what difficulties the client may be experiencing but also leaves him at a loss to prevent or alleviate them.

Now that the impediments have been described, what should be done? Concerned counselors ask for special techniques to use with minorities. Others want to know whether it is better for minorities to be counselors to other minorities, since racial and ethnic barriers are so threatening and difficult to penetrate. Few counselors ever ask what they can do to change themselves; few want to know how they can become better human beings in order to relate more effectively with other human beings who, through the accident of birth, are racially and ethnically different. The failure of counselors to ask these questions indicates essentially why counseling minorities continues to be a problem in this country. Counselors are products of a culture which has been characterized as racist. In spite of having had a few graduate courses in counseling and psychology, they are shaped by that culture.

Counselors in service and in training need to be exposed to new experiences if they are to be effective when counseling minorities. Although a course in counseling racial and ethnic minorities may be another exciting and rewarding cognitive exposure, what is needed most are affective experiences designed to humanize counselors. Therapeutic group activities extending over long periods, practicums and internships in minority-group communities, living in subcultural environments, and individual therapy—these are just a few suggestions for helping counselors grow as human beings. However, these experiences presuppose that counselor educators and supervisors have achieved enough personal insight and knowledge of minorities to help others develop in the manner suggested.

Finally, research is badly needed. However, there are so many complex and imprecise dimensions in intercultural counseling that they elude traditional empirical scrutiny. Variables such as transference, countertransference, self-disclosure, machismo, and personalism are considerations that demand novel research strategies. The investigator himself must be comfortably polycultural in order to perceive clearly across racial and ethnic lines, a prerequisite to designing research which allows rejection or acceptance of the assertions made in this paper. A glaring research pitfall is the investigator's assuming that racial and ethnic identities are unidimensional. Future research also must not fail to control for the degree of assimilation in the case of black clients and counselors, or the extent of prejudice in the case of white clients with black counselors and white counselors with black clients.

REFERENCES

American Psychological Association, Task Force on Employment Testing of Minority Groups. Job testing and the disadvantaged. *American Psychologist*, 1969, *24*, 637–650.

Beier, E. G. *The silent language of psychotherapy*. Chicago: Aldine Publishing Co., 1966.

Brammer, L. M., & Shostrom, E. *Therapeutic psychology* (2nd ed.). Englewood Cliffs, New Jersey: Prentice-Hall, 1968.

Buchheimer, A., & Balogh, S. C. *The counseling relationship*. Chicago: Science Research Associates, 1961.

Cohen, M. *Pour une sociologie du langage*. Paris: Editions Albins Michel, 1956.

Fetterman, J. The people of Cumberland Gap. *National Geographic*, 1971, *140*, 591–621.

Greenson, R. R. *The technique and practice of psychoanalysis*. (Vol. 1). New York: International Universities Press, 1964.

Harrison, S. I., & Carek, D. J. *A guide to psychotherapy*. Boston: Little, Brown & Co., 1966.

Hidalgo, H.H. *The Puerto Rican*. Washington: National Rehabilitation Association (Ethnic Differences Series No. 4), n.d.

Hinsie, L. E., & Campbell, R. J. *Psychiatric dictionary* (3rd ed.). New York: Oxford University Press, 1960.

Horney, K. *The neurotic personality of our time*. New York: W. W. Norton & Co., 1937.

Horney, K. *New ways in psychoanalysis*. New York: W. W. Norton & Co., 1966.

Jourard, S. M. *The transparent self*. Princeton, New Jersey: D. Van Nostrand Co., 1964.

Kardiner, A., & Ovesey, L. *The mark of oppression: Explorations in the personality of the American Negro*. Magnolia, Massachusetts: Peter Smith, 1962.

Katz, R. L. *Empathy*. New York: Free Press of Glencoe, 1963.

Kiev, A. *Transcultural psychiatry*. New York: Macmillan Co., Free Press, 1972.

Kitano, H. H. L. *Japanese Americans*. Englewood Cliffs, New Jersey: Prentice-Hall, 1969.

Kitano, H. H. L. Mental illness in four cultures. *Journal of Social Psychology*, 1970, *80*, 121–134.

Kris, E. Laughter as an expressive process. *International Journal of Psycho-Analysis*, 1941, *21*, 314–341.

MacKinnon, R. A., & Michels, R. *The psychiatric interview in clinical practice*. Philadelphia: W. B. Saunders Co., 1971.

Moore, J. W. *Mexican Americans*. Englewood Cliffs, New Jersey: Prentice-Hall, 1970.

Samora, J., et al. Rural youth with special problems: Low income, Negro, Indian, Spanish-American. In L. G. Burchinal (Ed.), *Rural youth in crisis*. Washington, D.C.: Superintendent of Documents, 1965.

Steiner, S. *La raza*. New York: Harper & Row, 1969.

Sue, D. W., & Sue, S. Counseling Chinese-Americans. *Personnel and Guidance Journal*, 1972, *50*, 637–644.

Surface, B. *The hollow*. New York: Coward-McCann & Geoghegan, 1971.

United States Department of Labor. *Role of manpower programs in assisting the American Indians.* Washington, D.C.: United States Employment Service, circa 1968.

Vetter, H. J. *Language behavior and communication.* Itasca, Illinois: F. E. Peacock, 1969.

Vontress, C. E. The black male personality. *The Black Scholar,* 1971, *2,* 10–16.

Wachtel, P. L. An approach to the study of body language in psychotherapy. *Psychotherapy,* 1967, *4,* 97–100.

Weller, J. E. *Yesterday's people: Life in contemporary Appalachia.* Lexington, Kentucky: University of Kentucky Press, 1966.

White man brings booze: New woes to frustrated western Indian. *Po-ye-da* (Friend), 1972, *1,* 11–12.

Zintz, M. V. *Education across cultures* (2nd ed.). Dubuque, Iowa: Kendall/Hunt Publishing Co., 1969.

4 Value Differences among American Indians: Concerns for the Concerned Counselor

JOSEPH E. TRIMBLE

WHY SHOULD A CLIENT FROM ONE CULTURE TRUST A COUNSELOR FROM ANOTHER?

Until recently, the American Indian, struggling to maintain indigenous values and culture without sacrificing access to power, was forced to urbanize, modernize, and progress on terms established by non-Indian society. The following chapter highlights some of the difficulties that the Indian has encountered in making that adjustment and suggests how non-Indian counselors might truly assist rather than inhibit an Indian client.

A typical complaint frequently registered by non-Indian counselors centers around the apparent nonverbal, almost passive posture assumed by American Indian clients. Most counselors despair of being able to break this barrier. Despite recognition of a general behavioral pattern in their Indian clients, non-Indian counselors persist in trying to crack that omnipresent shell even in the face of probable failure.

Research has indicated that the problem lies not with the Indian client but rather with the non-Indian counselor. In most instances the counselor believes that he or she has a thorough understanding of Indian culture and values. Other research strongly suggests that this apparent understanding is at best superficial and often is more indicative of the American Indian stereotype of a century or more ago rather than of the contemporary native American Indian. Most of that understanding has been gained by the counselor through readings of traditional literature on the American Indian. Little has been gained through experiencing the cultural and physical environment in which an Indian has been reared.

Indians are very quick to point out that their values and cultural ways are quite dissimilar as a group from those of any other culture. And, in general terms, they will list those values that set them apart from non-Indians. A close examination of these general values finds that they are not radically different values but are simply different in terms of the emphasis placed upon various aspects of a value system shared by other cultures.

65

To substantiate this notion, Trimble conducted a value study on 245 students who were attending a high school in southeastern Oklahoma. The school is integrated, with approximately 40 percent of the students being of American Indian background. It is a unique setting in that the school is partially funded by the federal government, and the majority of the Indian students are boarders. The entire student body was administered an unstructured, projective instrument designed to isolate value systems in intercultural settings. Results supported the hypothesis that Indian values differ qualitatively from those of non-Indians, and do correspond with those generally believed to be indicative of the American Indian in general.

A counselor must concern him- or herself with two salient attributes that are specific to the issue of values in a counseling setting involving American Indians. In general, Indians tend to value trust and understanding more than almost any other attribute. They are even more sensitive to distrust than to trust, particularly when the counselor is non-Indian. Understanding is closely tied in with trust and, in general, Indians will relate better to persons who attempt to understand them from their own perspective rather than from non-Indian orientations or from some schedule that fits within a counseling theory. Traditional counseling methods such as nondirective therapy, psychoanalysis, group therapy, etc. are not conducive to a trusting relationship with Indian clients. In fact, some studies indicate that more harm than good has resulted for the Indian when traditional approaches were used. Indians place a great deal of emphasis on familial relationships. They highly value kinship relations and will more than likely look to their kin for assistance when they are troubled. In many instances, non-Indian counselors are looked upon as meddlesome professionals. Yet the training and expertise of non-Indian counselors can be extremely valuable provided that they take the time to familiarize themselves with the psychological aspects of Indian culture, particularly those that are concerned with the value system.

Counselors function under a dual handicap of being biased by their non-Indian professional values as counselors and their non-Indian social values. Both hindrances act as a barrier between themselves and their Indian clients. The differentiations within the Indian community among tribes and nations are an essential aspect of the total person seeking counseling and must be attended to by sensitive counselors. Trimble highlights the pressing need to articulate value differences as well as similarities and to deal with this special population in a way that will allow its members to trust non-Indian counselors.

The pressure of population growth, migratory movements of varying groups, added improvements and advances in communication networks, and increased interest in the welfare of certain residual groups, have resulted in more and more persons who reflect diverse cultural backgrounds coming into direct contact with one another. People are becoming more conscious of the salient differences between individuals and between groups. The recognition of differences has become not just simply one of sorting out and isolating physical attributes but also one of uncovering differences in psychosocial intergroup characteristics. Many groups are begining to place an emphasis on such attributes and are attempting to develop and project a sense of pride in both the physical and psychosocial aspects. Increased social contact and group-centralism seem to be two forces that are destined to dissolve or resolve the question of nationalism. Certainly these forces will raise issues with those who believe in the existence of national characteristics.

American Indians constitute one such group that is intensely involved in both increased social contact and group-centralism. Years ago social contact between Indian and non-Indian groups usually was either one of choice on the part of the non-Indian, contingent on that group's or person's acceptance by the Indian or one imposed on the Indian by outside dominant forces such as the federal government. In each case, Indians typically viewed the encroachments as being disruptive and an attempt to break up their stable social system that was developed in a state of self-imposed isolation. The elements of colonialism caused Indian groups to be even more conscious of differences and to become more cautious about internalizing the different systems that were being thrown their way.

Contemporary Indians seem to be much more conscious and cautious than were their ancestors. They are being affected by the pressures of an ever-growing population and by developing technologies. Isolationism is no longer considered to be a safeguard against intergroup contact. The government's employment relocation and educational and career development programs, coupled with the implicit but not necessarily accepted assumption that life and opportunity are better in urban areas, have caused many to leave the typically rural Indian communities. Because of these and other processes it should be no surprise that approximately 50 percent of the United States American Indian population resides in urban areas.

The increasing social contact of Indians with non-Indians has resulted predictably in more conflict, both between Indians and non-Indians and within the Indian community itself. It is more difficult to deal with conflict within the Indian community because of the sovereign status of the community, reservation, or pueblo. Unfortunately, the conflicts could not and cannot be shut out with the closing of a gate. The forces that create them must be confronted, dealt with in one form or another, and in many instances accepted and internalized for better or worse. Although it may not have to be this way, more often than not it is.

A partial consequence of intergroup contact is an immediate recognition of differences in beliefs and values and a pattern of concomitant behavior between the contact groups. Social psychologists would predict that an awareness of value differentials is one source that could lead to eventual intergroup conflict, with a resulting tendency for the groups to emphasize more strongly their basic value systems. Aside from this, the contact places persons at differing levels of evaluation, particularly when one or the other group is in a dominant position. One may attempt to evaluate the foreign element in ethnocentric terms and perceive the exotic as a reflection of one's own behavior; such perceptions, however, result in confusion and error. Let an example speak to this point. A Lower Elwha Indian woman in Oregon sent a big lunch to school along with her grandson. He came home that day and asked her not to fix that kind of lunch for him again. It seems that the non-Indian teacher had made him eat the entire sack of food, assuming it had been prepared totally for him. What the teacher didn't understand was that, contrary to the white man's values, he had brought the lunch to share with other children.

Obviously, the vignette calls for a sensitivity on the part of both parties, plus their willingness to look at the obvious aspects of the behavior. Neither knew or was aware of each other's different frame of value reference and the consequence was indeed a bit overbearing for the child! The confusion and misunderstanding could have been avoided. But value conflicts are quite common between contemporary Indians and non-Indians, which can lead and have led to tragic consequences in some instances.

The process of understanding values has typically emphasized the psychological level of analysis, although anthropologists have done a great deal to bring out value differences between cultures. Scheibe (1970, p. 42) has defined values as, "... what is wanted, what is best, what is preferable, what ought to be done. They suggest the operation of wishes, desires, goals, passions, valences or morals." More concisely, English and English (1958) indicated that values "... define for an individual or for a social unit what ends or means to an end are desirable." In either interpretation, there is a reference to the process that defines a very generalized set of goal-oriented expectations that are based on a specific anchor inherent within the person's immediate frame of reference. An attempted distinction between such concepts as attitudes, beliefs, ideas and values would prove to be simply a futile exercise in intellectual word games. Suffice it to state that most social scientists would concur with the definitions by Scheibe or English and English.

Admitting that Indian groups are different from non-Indian groups, one asks what values can be listed to distinguish one group from another. Unfortunately, a complete definitive catalogue is not immediately available despite the attempts of certain social scientists to develop one. Their efforts, or the efforts of anyone who would take on the task, would be hampered indeed by the diversity of Indian groups themselves. To begin with, one would have to differentiate between Indians residing in different sectors of the country on reservations, in rural nonreservation communities, in small towns, and in large metropolitan areas. If one manages to make this differentiation, then one must face the task of differentiating and discriminating among tribal differences. The process of deduction is seemingly endless. The federal government alone recognizes 478 tribes. There are 52 identifiable groups or tribes that are Indian but are not recognized as such. Each tribe considers itself distinctly different from the other even if it may in fact be in name only.

There is more to this. By now most persons are familiar with the notion that the term "American Indian" is really a misnomer, a case of mistaken location and subsequent identity on the part of one Christopher Columbus. Nevertheless, the term has stuck for some 480 years. Arising out of this though is the question of who or what is an American Indian. For many non-Indians it is an image of a person portrayed in books, in cinema, or on television. To them an Indian is a person with black hair and eyes and brown skin and distinguished facially by the presence of high cheek bones. For still others it is this plus the added attributions of clothing and hair styles that were characteristic of Indian life 100 or so years ago (cf. Trimble, 1974a). The physical description is in part true.

Unlike other ethnic, national, or minority groups in this country, the American Indian has a legal definition. Basically, the federal government's agent of Indian affairs, the Bureau of Indian Affairs, defines a person as an American Indian if his or her blood quantum is one-fourth or more; any less than that and the person is not legally Indian. This alone has enormous implications for self-identity and the identification of Indians by non-Indians. Some tribes have set a lower blood quantum such as one-eighth or one-sixteenth in order that more persons could take advantage of tribal benefits. One tribe in Oklahoma, after receiving a land claim adjustment, maintained that if a person could prove lineage he or she was entitled to a share regardless of blood quantum. Some who cared little and in no way identified with the tribe obviously benefited financially.

The United States Bureau of the Census has not complied with the hard and fast criteria of the Bureau of Indian Affairs. It uses a form of self-enumeration, but will also check with neighbors for verification. Its criteria are more a form of social-cultural affiliation than of a legal and sanguinolent one.

For many Indians and non-Indians, a person is not Indian unless he or she is a pure blood—a full-blood or four-fourths. Any person of a mixed marriage was typically an outcast in both communities; "half breed" (an offensive and pejorative term in some areas) usually implied nonacceptance. In the Sioux language such a person was *iyeska* (one who talked many languages or mixed blood). Originally it was a descriptive term, then for years it was a pejorative one, and lately it has been losing its punch and is often used in a humorous vein.

The real issue centers on the conflict of identification for both Indian and non-Indian groups. For many, it is difficult to accept someone as Indian who also happens to possess light hair, blue eyes, and fair skin. More often than not such persons are not accepted, despite the extent to which they may have been reared in a traditional Indian manner. What this amounts to is that if one says he or she is of Indian background, then he or she is. But there are those who would argue even with this.

In view of these extensive tribal and individual variations, small wonder that a catalogue of their values has not been attempted. It seems that the next best approach is to list those values that Indians recognize as differing most from those of the dominant culture. Bryde (1972) considered this and developed a list which reveals what he believes to be the basic value differences between the two cultural groups. The list was compiled from the general responses he had received from his informants. The list plus a brief annotation includes:

1. Present-oriented versus future-oriented—The Indian lives in the present. He or she does not become concerned about what tomorrow will bring, but enjoys *now*. The non-Indian lives for tomorrow, constantly looking to and planning for the future.
2. Lack of time consciousness versus time consciousness—In many tribal languages there is no word for time that is equivalent to the English word. There is always time to get things accomplished even if not accomplished today. The non-Indian's life is governed almost entirely by time. Those who are prompt are respected and those who are not are usually rejected and reprimanded.
3. Generosity and sharing versus personal acquisitiveness and material achievement—The Indian gets in order to give. The one who gives the most is the most respected. By contrast, the non-Indian is judged by what he has, so that material achievement means acquiring many possessions and that carries with it the hope of social mobility.
4. Respect for age versus emphasis on youth—The Indian respects a person who has knowledge of the people and the world around them. The older Indians who have lived a long time are respected for their wisdom and knowledge. The non-Indian society places a greater importance on youth. We see this emphasis on television, in politics, etc.
5. Cooperation versus competition—The Indian learns to get along with others. He or she values working together and fitting him- or herself

to others. In the Indian group there is conformity not competition. The non-Indian believes that competition is essential. Progress results from competition and lack of progress may be synonymous with lack of competition. Every aspect of daily living in the non-Indian culture is quite competitive.

6. Harmony with nature versus conquest over nature—Nature, in the Indian view of the world, is one thing and a person is only a part of that one thing. One accepts the world and does not try to change it. The non-Indian attempts to control the physical world, to assert mastery over it. The more nature is controlled, the better.

Zintz (1963, p. 175) drew a finer distinction between the two cultures in his comparison of Anglo-Caucasian and Pueblo values. His list identifies the basic value differences as including the following:

PUEBLO	ANGLO
Harmony with nature	Mastery over nature
Present-time orientation	Future-time orientation
Explanation of natural phenomena	Scientific explanation for everything
Follow the old ways	Climb the ladder of success
Cooperation	Competition
Anonymity	Individuality
Submissiveness	Aggression
Work for present needs	Work to get ahead
Sharing wealth	Saving for the future
Time is always with us	Clock-watching
Humility	Win first prize if at all possible
Win once, but let others win also	Win all the time

Aberle (1951, pp. 95–96), in his psychosocial analysis of an individual Hopi, discussed those values that make up what the Hopi construe as the ideal person. In a word, it is the word *hopi* itself which usually is translated as "peaceful." To be *hopi* one must adhere to the values of: (a) strength, including self-control, wisdom, and intelligence; (b) poise, tranquility or "good" thinking; (c) obedience to the law, which includes cooperation, unselfishness, responsibility, and kindness; (d) peace or the absence of aggressive behavior; (e) protectiveness or preserving all life forms; and (f) health. A person who follows the opposite values of the *hopi* is typically referred to as a *kahopi*, "not *hopi*." That person is usually thought of as a witch or a "two-hearted" person.

A comparison of the Bryde and Zintz lists reveals a common dimension of agreement. More importantly, there apparently exists an area of general value orientation for which many groups have developed a specific perspective. This suggests the possibility of the existence of some universal

patterns of behavior for which persons must find solutions. Kluckhohn
and Strodtbeck (1961), and Kluckhohn (1953) suggested this possibility
and narrowed down the seemingly inexhaustible array of general possibilities to three universal value perspectives: man-nature orientations
(mastery over nature, subjugation to nature, and harmony with nature);
time orientation (temporal past, present and temporal future); and rela-
tional orientation (status and power positions along lineal orientations,
group consensus, and individualism). The possibility of universal reactions
to value orientations was supported by Osgood (1966). He showed that a
number of words are evaluated positively across many cultures and possess
much the same intrinsic meaning. Since words are closely linked to ways
of thinking and behaving, Kluckhohn's position may not be as outlandish
as some might make it out to be.

Tefft (1967), by using a slightly modified version of her scale on Shoshone and Arapaho youth, tested the Kluckhohn value perspectives. She
found that both groups hold values similar to Caucasian students, with
the Arapaho students showing more despair and disillusionment with
their social environment. That is, the Arapaho students revealed more
internal disagreement over preferred values in contrast to the Shoshone
and Caucasian. Tefft cautiously attributed this finding to increased culture
contact situations with the dominant culture, with that group being regarded as the reference group.

The notion of the reference group setting standards for role behavior
is common to social psychologists. Anthropologists have used it to study
value shifts resulting from acculturation. Berreman (1964), using this
idea, found that Aleuts are involved in what he calls "evaluation group
alienation." They perceive that Caucasians dislike them. As a consequence,
when they are in the presence of Caucasians and in an effort to compromise,
they assume roles which differ markedly from their typical behavior. The
roles often serve to reinforce the perceived expectations that Caucasians
have of them, sometimes reinforcing general Indian stereotypes. Chance
(1965), in support of this, found that the St. James Cree act more "Indian"
when they are in town than when they are in their own village.

Often it is difficult to separate out the differences between role expectations and value orientations, as one is invariably reflected in the other.
Much of the research on value shifts is directed at the basic world view
or "ethos" of a culture and what others consider as influential processes
are built into the analysis. The values of a culture are then viewed as part
of the process of social change. In this approach, acculturative forces
would not be viewed as the cause of value shifts but only as one of the
many aspects of change itself. Honigmann (1949) has applied such a view
in his study of the Kaska. His findings suggest that the Kaska "ethos" of

strong emotional constraint, inhibition of emotional expression in inter-personal relations, and apathetic withdrawal from or mistrust of others is related to their low density of population, isolation, and general style of life, one characterized by hunting and trapping. This may or may not be indicative of what some would call traditional Kaska values. Alter-natively, they may be values that have developed because of fear of social contact and acculturation. In either case, they could be viewed as simply functional values arising out of the Kaska's remote ecosystem.

Certain values and traditional personality characteristics have been shown to persist in spite of the variations in social contact and accultur-ation. The return of conservative patterns, unconscious persistency, and generosity have been identified among Cherokees and certain Plains Indians (Meekel, 1936; Devereux, 1951; and Gulick, 1960). Schusky (1970, p. 115) noted that differences persisted between Caucasians and Lower Brule Dakotas. He stated that "one readily observes personality differences between Indians and whites . . . on first acquaintance the young seem excessively quiet. Although this shyness lessens with greater familarity, children are quite reserved before adults, waiting to be 'spoken to before speaking'. Whites frequently comment on the good behavior of Indian children in this respect." Freyre (1956) also noted that the practice of and value placed on mercy killing still persists among certain Eskimo groups (who are legally defined as American Indians), despite Caucasians' insistence that such practice is murder and Eskimos who commit euth-anasia should be punished accordingly.

Despite the apparent persistence in the Indian cultures of certain indigenous, traditional values, there are individual Indians who experience a great deal of conflict in attempting to internalize alien values. The mere presence of a contact group is known to create some value conflicts. In reference to the Teton Dakota, Macgregor (1970, p. 99) related that "in this environment the basic personality has become almost schizophrenic. Individuals were torn between desires to gain status and role outside the reservation and to enjoy warm, stable and positive interrelations by remaining at home. Through failure to realize either goal, many of the younger generation slipped into a life of apathetic resignation and passivity. . . ."

The same disruption in values apparently can occur when an Indian leaves the reservation for a short period of time. Vogt (1951) found that many Indian veterans who had returned to the reservation from a term in the Armed Forces had modified their value orientations. Some veterans had adopted a concern for future time that went beyond that which the Navajo traditionally values, and had taken a position that a person con-trols nature rather than one where a person is subject to the control of nature. Vogt further indicated that those Navajo males who tended to accept Caucasian values were characterized by personal conflicts and feelings of insecurity.

Similar value conflicts emerge for the Indian who leaves the reservation and takes up residence in urban communities. There is typically a strong tendency for urban Indians to retain their "Indianness," while struggling with the almost daily contact with the dominant culture. In so doing an urban Indian typology has emerged that places an emphasis on internalizing values indicative of Indians in general. Invariably these values are elaborations with modifications of typical tribal values and are more characterized by pan-Indian ideologies. The stretching of the tribal values to accommodate one's conflict with Caucasian values has produced what White (1970) has called "the lower class 'culture of excitement.'" In his studies of lower-class Sioux in Rapid City, South Dakota, he found that Indian values may represent the official ideal for the person but the behavior may suggest different intracultural dimensions contingent on the situation. One cannot then infer the value from the role or the role from the value, because the intrinsic value of any behavior is situational. This may well be an explanation for the discrepancies in Tefft's findings on Arapaho-Shoshone values, as well as those of Berreman and Chance.

Value conflicts may not be attributed strictly to intergroup relations but may arise from the measurement or assessment of values themselves. Of course, these issues are not just applicable to the measurement of values, especially at a intercultural level but are equally applicable to the assessment of psychosocial characteristics.

There has been a limited number of scales and inventories developed to assess values directly. For intercultural research there is even a lesser number. In most instances those instruments that do exist attempt to assess the presence or absence of a value or they measure it in some way. Blum (1950) developed the Blacky Pictures Test as an indirect measure for psychoanalytically interpreted values; Allport, Vernon, and Lindzey (1951) developed a scale to assess six specific rather general constellations of values; Peck (1967) developed a sentence completion test that served to differentiate between value systems of Mexican and American youth; Kluckhohn (1953, 1961) developed the Value Orientation Inventory to assess values among the Southwestern Pueblos and tribes. She believes, however, that it is applicable to all groups. Rokeach (1973) likewise holds the same thesis, but has expanded his Rokeach Value Survey to include two sets of 18 descriptive and evaluative values.

To assess single values, certain investigators have developed specific instruments such as achievement orientation, internal-external control, powerlessness, religiosity, etc. Few investigations have provided for meaningful research at the sociocultural level of analysis.

Studies of need-achievement have been conducted on a number of Indian groups. It will be remembered that generally Indian groups describe themselves as emphasizing individual achievement orientation (see Bryde, 1972: Zintz, 1963). Through an analysis of folktales, McClelland and Friedman (1952) found high imagery towards achievement and innovation. Parker (1962), utilizing McClelland's theory, found that Ojibwa are much more oriented toward individual achievement than are the Eskimos. Lantis (1953) found similar orientations among Eskimos which Parker's findings tended to support.

There needs to be more emphasis placed on improving and developing instruments to assess value orientations, particularly in view of the increased level of sociocultural interaction. The Value Orientation Inventory of Kluckhohn (1953) is a worthy contribution, but the instrument is much too lengthy and has been criticized for its possible lack of validity and reliability. Rokeach (1973) has developed a clever testing device, but it is too early to tell whether the universality of his value inventory will hold up under the severe test of intercultural research. Peck (1967) and Peck and Michalis (1968) have attempted to develop a culturally relevant sentence completion instrument, which appears to show strong promise.

To determine the feasibility of using a sentence-completion type instrument to assess value differences between Indians and non-Indians in 1971, I conducted an exploratory study among high school students in southeastern Oklahoma. This setting was chosen primarily because of the high level of interaction between the two groups and because of the unique setting of the high school. The 86 Indians, most of them of mixed blood, were supported by the Bureau of Indian Affairs. Some of them were boarded at the school; others lived with Indian or non-Indian families in the community; and still others were natives of the local area. All of the non-Indian students lived in and around the community in which the school was located.

The Indian subjects represented a wide variety of tribal groupings. However, most of them were members of one of the so-called Five Civilized Tribes of Oklahoma (Cherokee, Choctaw, Chickasaw, Creek, and Seminole), a collective group greatly integrated through intertribal and intergroup marriages.

The specific instrument consisted of 40 sentence-completion items. The significant feature of the instrument is that it is designed to elicit information from children and adolescents in five different areas of behavior: task achievement, interpersonal relations, authority, aggression, and anxiety. The instrument makes no reference to values in an intrapsychic sense; that is, it refers to the behavior that is assumed in some instances to be goal-oriented.

The instrument was administered on a randomly chosen school day to the entire student body present. Then the sentence stems were analyzed by two judges according to the criteria set up by Peck (1967). Because the basic intent of the instrument was to determine its sensitivity in differentiating between rural, nonreservation Indians and non-Indians, a two-group, stepwise, linear, discriminant-function analysis was used to treat the data (Overall and Klett, 1972). Of the 40 responses to the instrument, 31 were adequate to discriminate significantly between the two groups (F [31, 185] = 1.5, p < .05). According to the mean responses of the 217 subjects on the 40 stems, 50 of 84 Indians were classified as rural, nonreservation Indians while 103 of 137 non-Indians were classified accordingly (X^2 = 30.26, p < .001). These results suggest that a number of significant statements can be made about the groups and the test. The reader must recognize that the test used in the study was still in the pilot stages. But an analysis of the norms, reliability, and validity suggests that it is relatively stable. For example, there was little variation from the norms in the mean response patterns of the non-Indians (obviously there was for the pan-Indian sample). Again, a factor analysis of the 40 stems produced the same number of dimensions indicated in the manual with an almost complete loading of the same stems. But let us focus on group differences.

To give a general impression of the differences in response patterns of the two groups, certain stems have been selected that served to differentiate significantly one group from the other. What follows after each is the mean generalized response according to the coding manual for each group. A good indication of the difference in orientation, coping, and, in general, the value systems can be gleaned from just these responses alone.

> STEM: If I lose most of the time at playing a certain game, I _____.
> NON-INDIAN RESPONSE: "would try another game" or "start something else"—a general substitute or compensation for the activity would be pursued. INDIAN RESPONSE: "would feel bad" or "would get a little upset"—a general negative depressive or anxious affect would result.
>
> STEM: When I get mad, I _____. NON-INDIAN RESPONSE: "get mad at myself" or "feel terrible"—a general negative depressive or anxious affect. INDIAN RESPONSE: "sulk" or "am grouchy"—a general repressed hostile or aggressive affect.
>
> STEM: When there is something difficult to do, I _____. NON-INDIAN RESPONSE: "go find someone to help me" or "ask the

teacher"—a general request for aid or advice. INDIAN RESPONSE: "do it depending on who tells me to" or "don't do it unless I want to"—a general compliance conditional on the circumstances.

STEM: I really get angry when _____. NON-INDIAN RESPONSE: "I see someone mistreated" or "someone is cruel to a dog"—a general mistreatment of people or animals occurs. INDIAN RESPONSE: "I do something bad" or "I do something unsatisfactorily"—a general reaction to one's own behavior or shortcomings that have caused the anger.

The significant finding in this exploratory study is not the responses given, but rather the nature of the Indian subjects who gave the responses. The Indians were not representative of one tribe, nor were they "reservation-types." Most of them had had close contacts with non-Indians and consequently had had to deal with non-Indian values at one level or another. Through all of this interaction, a different value system has been retained somewhat intact in spite of the influence of the dominant culture; but, at the same time, the value system has undergone a change from tribal-specific values to a more generalized set of rural pan-Indian values.

Even in a relatively integrated environment two salient sets of response patterns can be differentiated, each indicative of a cultural dimension. Whether they are values is moot. The key point is that many of the Indian subjects didn't "look Indian"—did not possess the stereotypical Indian physical characteristics—but culturally most of them were Indian. To the unskilled observer some of those students would not have been identified as Indian. If this misidentification were to occur in a counseling setting (and it has), the results could be tragic.

The understanding of salient and specific value differences is the key to successful counseling and psychiatric interviewing. Such understanding is even more critical when the members of the customary counseling dyad have come from different cultures, where each is looking at the other's behavior from a different frame of reference. This would predictably occur whether the counseling took place in one or the other's cultural setting.

The core of the problem between a non-Indian counselor and an Indian student is one of communication and mutual understanding. Each is aware that the other is different and each is alert to the complications that these differences typically produce. While both may be given the responsibility of working through the client's difficulties, most responsibility would, of course, rest with the counselor. A counselor not only works from a set of value references indicative of his or her own culture but also works from those value references bound to a selected theory of counseling.

In many ways counselors who work with persons from other cultures act very much like social anthropologists. They intrude—that is, they invade the domain of the client's head ideally for the sole purpose of giving the person what the counselors perceive as much-needed assistance, whether the person has asked for it or not. The counselor knows that the client is different not only because he or she acts out the stereotype of expected behavior but also because of the fact that the client does belong to another culture. The counselor, by becoming so engrossed in the cultural differences that may lie hidden in the client's every sentence or gesture, might completely ignore the problem. Now this can occur to even experienced intercultural counselors who may not be aware of their unintended fascination and preoccupation (cf. Trimble, 1974b).

There is yet another subtlety involved in the counseling process. Indians may be reluctant to discuss their problems, for they know, perhaps from previous experience, that the counselor just does not nor could not ever understand how they perceive themselves and the world around them. If this should occur, then Indian clients may, in general, resort to responding to the direction that the counselor wishes the relationship to take but on the counselor's terms; at that point it would be under the counselor's naive terms. There may be complete compliance or acquiescence; that is, the Indian may go along with the theory or approach that the counselor wishes him or her to follow and may show very little, if any, resistance. Naturally this is contingent upon whether or not the counselor could manage to sustain a manageable relationship. If that relationship is not there, the client is lost and becomes another "therapy drop-out."

An Indian client may react negatively to a counselor's advice for two reasons. First, the counselor's solutions to the problem may be rejected by the client because of his or her personal set of values or, second, when the effect of the recommended behavior for the client would not be helpful. In either case, the client would become alienated from the counselor, and this alienation could cause the eventual dissolution of the relationship. This, in fact, has occurred more often than one would care to admit. To avoid this difficulty, counselors must sensitize themselves to the Indian's frame of reference.

All too often non-Indian counselors believe that they are sensitive to the cultural variations among American Indians, particularly to their value systems. However, there is not a simple list of Indian values. Neither Indians nor all members of a tribe or clan are alike. As should be evident by now, the variations in values and beliefs are extremely diverse.

Understanding may come with the counselor's implicit realization that Indians do possess different value systems, and that the clients must be given ample opportunity to emerge within the context of the counseling relationship under their own conditions and from their own conceptual frame of reference.

To avoid the obvious discrepancies that emerge out of errant interpretations, counselors should accept the limitations of their personal values and of their techniques. At the same time they should encourage their clients to compare values with those of other Indians. Other Indians could be invited into the setting and encouraged to do the same. Opler (1957) referred to this as the "cultural punch," a kind of support system which he has used with different ethnic minorities in group therapy. Through the dialogue the counselor might even encounter substitutes in language patterns as has been suggested by Krapf (1955). The client may lapse into colloquial speech patterns or even his or her tribal language to express certain emotions and recreate certain experiences. The essential nature of close contact on the part of the counselor is crucial at this point.

This technique of inviting other Indians into the therapy sessions obviously calls for a modification of the customary two-person relationship, the specific aim being to intensify the counselor's understanding of the Indian's frame of reference. The Indian is not accustomed to self-analysis nor is there a familiarity with the process of discussing with a non-Indian one's emotional conflicts. Sharing difficulties with others or allowing others to assume the counselor's role may allow the counselor to play a self-effacing role. Prompted by their need to understand, the counselors will be confronted with their own set of values, personal and applied. Progress can then be achieved in stabilizing the relationship, and the subsequent process of understanding and mutual growth can proceed with fewer difficulties.

REFERENCES

Aberle, D. F. The psychosocial analysis of a Hopi life-history. *Comparative Psychology Monographs*, 1951, *21* (1): 80–138.
Allport, G. W., Vernon, P. E., & Lindzey, G. *A study of values: A scale for measuring the dominant interest in personality* (Rev. ed.). Boston: Houghton Mifflin Co., 1951.
Berreman, G. D. Alienation, mobility, and acculturation: The Aleut reference group. *American Anthropologist*, 1964, *66*, 231–250.
Blum, G. S. *The Blacky pictures: Manual of instructions*. New York: Psychological Corporation, 1950.
Bryde, J. F. *Indian students and guidance*. Boston: Houghton Mifflin Co., 1972.
Chance, N. Acculturation, self-identification, and adjustment. *American Anthropologist*, 1965, *67*, 372–393.

Devereux, G. *Reality and dream.* New York: International Universities Press, 1951.

English, H. B., & English, A. C., *A comprehensive dictionary of psychological and psycho-analytical terms: A guide to usage.* New York: David McKay Co., 1958.

Freyre, G. *The masters and the slaves.* New York: Alfred A. Knopf, 1956.

Gulick, J. *Cherokees at the crossroads.* Chapel Hill, North Carolina: Institute for Research in Social Sciences, 1960.

Honigmann, J. J. *Culture and ethos of Kaska society.* Yale Publications in Anthropology, No. 40. New Haven, Connecticut: Yale University Press, 1949.

Kluckhohn, F. R. Dominant and variant value orientations. In C. Kluckhohn & H. A. Murray (Eds.), *Personality in nature, society, and culture.* New York: Alfred A. Knopf, 1953.

Kluckhohn, F. R., & Strodtbeck, F. L. *Variations in value orientations.* New York: Harper & Row, 1961.

Krapf, E. E. The choice of language in polyglot analysis. *Psychoanalytic Quarterly,* 1955, *24,* 343–357.

Lantis, M. Nunivac Eskimo personality as revealed in the mythology. *Anthropological Papers of the University of Alaska,* 2, 1953.

McClelland, D. C., & Friedman, G. A. A. A cross-cultural study of the relationship between child rearing practices and achievement motivation appearing in folk tales. In G. E. Swanson, T. M. Newcomb, & E. L. Hartley (Eds.), *Readings in social psychology.* New York: Holt, Rinehart & Winston, 1952.

Macgregor, G. Changing society: The Teton Dakotas. In E. Nurge (Ed.), *The modern Sioux: Social systems and reservation culture.* Lincoln: University of Nebraska Press, 1970.

Meekel, H. S. *The economy of a modern Teton Dakota community.* New Haven, Connecticut: Yale University Press, 1936.

Opler, M. K. Group psychotherapy: Individual and cultural dynamics in a group process. *American Journal of Psychiatry,* 1957, *114,* 433–438.

Osgood, E. C. Language universals and psycholinguistics. In J. H. Greenberg (Ed.), *Universals of language* (2nd ed.). Cambridge, Massachusetts: M.I.T. Press, 1966.

Overall, J. E., & Klett, C. J. *Applied multivariate analysis.* New York: McGraw-Hill Book Co., 1972.

Parker, S. Motives in Eskimo and Ojibwa mythology. *Ethnology,* 1962, *1,* 517–523.

Peck, F. R. A comparison of the value systems of Mexican and American youth. *Revista Interamericana de Psicologia,* 1967, *1* (1), 41–50.

Peck, F. R., & Michalis, E. *ITEC instrument manual: Sentence completion instruments—child version* (Coping Styles and Achievement: A Cross-National Study of School Children, Working Paper). Unpublished manuscript, University of Texas at Austin, 1968.

Rokeach, M. *The nature of human values.* New York: Macmillan Co., The Free Press, 1973.

Scheibe, K. E. *Beliefs and values.* New York: Holt, Rinehart & Winston, 1970.

Schusky, E. L. Culture change and continuity in the Lower Brule community. In E. Nurge (Ed.), *The modern Sioux: Social systems and reservation culture.* Lincoln: University of Nebraska Press, 1970.

Tefft, S. K. Anomy, values and culture change among teen-age Indians: An exploration. *Sociology of Education,* 1967 (Spring), 145–157.

Trimble, J. E. *Say goodbye to the Hollywood Indian: Results of a nationwide survey of the self-image of the American Indian.* Paper presented at the 82nd annual convention of the American Psychological Association, New Orleans, Louisiana, September 1974. (a)

Trimble, J. E. *The intrusion of Western psychological thought on Native American ethos.* Paper presented at the Second International Conference of the International Association for Cross-Cultural Psychology, Kingston, Ontario, Canada, August 1974. (b)

Vogt, E. Z. Navajo veterans: A study of changing values. *Papers of the Peabody Museum of Archeology and Ethnology,* 1951, *41* (No. 1).

White, R. A. The lower-class "culture of excitement" among the contemporary Sioux. In E. Nurge (Ed.), *The modern Sioux: Social systems and reservation culture.* Lincoln: University of Nebraska Press, 1970.

Zintz, M. V. *Education across cultures.* Dubuque, Iowa: William C. Brown & Co., 1963.

5 Psychotherapy and the Foreign Student

A. A. ALEXANDER, FIKRÉ WORKNEH, MARJORIE
H. KLEIN, AND MILTON H. MILLER

SHOULD A COUNSELOR FROM ONE CULTURE CHANGE THE VALUES OF A CLIENT FROM ANOTHER CULTURE?

Alexander, Workneh, Klein, and Miller bring the perspectives of psychiatry to the problems of intercultural counseling. Their distinctive contribution to this book has been drawn from longitudinal data on the adjustment of Chinese and other foreign students attending the University of Wisconsin. They generalize from empirical data to a particular clinical context. When a counselor from one culture intervenes to help a client from another, he or she must face a profound ethical question as to his or her right to change that client's own values and ways of looking at problems. This chapter deals directly with that question and provides specific suggestions for the intercultural counselor.

The chapter moves from the general issue of what it is like to be a foreign student to specific questions or problems. What is it like to be a foreign student who seeks professional help? By the time the student has presented himself as a patient he will probably need more than a psychological Band-Aid. He will have waited until the last minute and will have exhausted other resources. He will usually be all alone by that time and may well feel that he has caused himself and others much embarrassment, if not humiliation.

What it is like to be the clinician who sees the foreign student? How does the therapist respond to a patients' passive reserve, sensitivity to interactional cues, language difficulties, dependency demands, and manipulation? What do you do with a therapist's frustration, mistaking the communication pattern for the person, distinguishing the culture from the pathology, and his fear of that which he does not understand?

How are foreign student patients similar and how are they different from native-born patients? There are differences in self-concept, autonomy, the meaning of family membership, minority identifications, sources of stress, and others.

What are the modes and styles of psychotherapeutic intervention which may be beneficial to foreign student patients, and what approaches may be inapplicable? The alternative of applying psychological gimmicks to foreign patients to capitalize on their expectations will be compared with other authoritarian or confronting interactions. The suitability of encounter techniques is also considered.

This chapter provides valuable evidence for the need to accommodate a client's values without violating one's own ethical responsibilities, and is thus of use to professionals who do not work with foreign nationals as well as to those who do. Differences which are more apparent at the international level operate with a more subtle, but nonetheless compelling, force in all counseling relationships. All counseling can be viewed as intercultural to the extent that the counselor's values might differ from those of his or her clients. The importance of each client's total and unique background is perhaps most apparent in working with international students, an experience which can quickly erode the stereotypes and generalizations of mono-cultural counselors.

This paper is concerned with the experience of the foreign student who seeks professional help or who is brought to the attention of mental health professionals during his or her stay in the United States. Our general statements about treating the foreign student in psychotherapy stem from our clinical contacts with foreign student outpatients or with psychiatric inpatients in the University of Wisconsin Hospital setting and from the wider perspective of ongoing research into the adaptational processes of foreign students on campus (Klein, Alexander, Tseng, Miller, Yeh, Chu, & Workneh, 1971). Indeed, our research findings and contacts with our "nonpatient subjects" have provided an invaluable frame of reference for the clinical work. One way of bridging the cultural barriers in therapy is to know the background, hopes, concerns, and the day-to-day campus life of the nonpatient foreign student.

RESEARCH ON ADAPTATION

Briefly summarized, our research has shown that the vast majority of non-Western, or Third World, students—nonpatients and patients alike—feel vulnerable and at risk during much of their time in the United States. In addition to suffering culture shock when dealing with external matters such as differences in food, climate, language, mannerisms, and communication, these students also suffer from status change and status loss. Most foreign students have been academically successful at home and are often professionally well established. Suddenly they face intense academic pressures and adjustments and a painful social vulnerability as well. Having lost cultural and personal structure when they separated from the home country and feeling fearful or pessimistic about the possibility of making contact with Americans, very few are successful in coming close to American peers. Instead, they create a conational "subculture," which recapitulates the home setting and provides necessary support but which also erects barriers to deep intercultural contact (Klein, Alexander, Tseng, Miller, Yeh, & Chu, 1971).

In making the transition from favored professional or favored student at home to the student role in the United States, foreign students themselves give highest priority to academic adjustment and consider interpersonal happiness more as a luxury (Chu, Yeh, Klein, Alexander, & Miller, 1971). A questionnaire survey was made of 250 foreign students as they registered at the Foreign Student Reception Center at the University of Wisconsin campus at the beginning of their stay (Klein, Miller, & Alexander, 1974). Asked about their goals while in the United States and the problems they anticipated, nearly 90 percent of those students responding stated that their most important goal was obtaining professional training, with 80 percent seeking a specific degree. The desire for personal involvement with Americans or curiosity about the culture was secondary. Only 15 to 25 percent ranked interpersonal goals high, and only 5 percent expressed strong concerns with learning about American culture and government. Only in the professional context were interpersonal contacts given emphasis. Forty-six percent of the respondents stated that "finding out how their professional colleagues worked" was a very important goal.

Specific problems anticipated also reflected these practical concerns and the dominant professional academic goals. Finances, course arrangements, academic performance, and living arrangements were expected to be greater problems than were homesickness or making and establishing social contacts.

The secondary status assigned to social contact with Americans was more clearly illustrated in follow-up (spring term, $n = 59$) questionnaire data for Far Eastern students from the larger survey, and in the results of over 40 interviews (often lasting more than 2 hours) carried out with respondents from Taiwan, Hong Kong, and Ethiopia. The recurring finding was one of isolation from the American culture and the maintenance of a rather exclusive or closed relationship with a supportive conational subculture. Only half of the Asian subsample expressed any initial interest at all in contact with Americans. Fewer (33 percent for the Far East, 26 percent for Southeast Asia) expected these contacts to be intimate. In their responses to questions concerning interpersonal problems anticipated with and expectations of Americans, they revealed what might be called the stereotypical view that Americans would be superficially friendly but would not be open to the kind of intimate,

interdependent friendship based on mutual consideration and trust that
was valued at home.

Turning to the questionnaire responses for the 59 students who were
willing to be followed up after 6 months at the university, we found that,
despite the presence of Americans in the students' housing and work
settings, only one-third of the respondents reported a substantial level of
friendship with Americans. Instead, there was a widespread disillusionment with the quality of interpersonal relationships. Only half of the
respondents reported making as many friends over the year as they would
have wished; 14 percent reported making no friends. Consistent with the
initial expectations, Americans were described as being difficult to know,
with some showing little interest in contact with foreign students.

The importance of the conational subculture as a barrier to contact with
the host culture was clarified in additional studies of Formosans and
Koreans on the Wisconsin campus. The Formosan study was a questionnaire survey of members of a self-defined subculture, a student social
organization. The sample contained 44 respondents—30 males and 14
females (wives of male students). Most had been in the United States for 1
year or more, with 11 percent having been here for over 4 years. When
asked about the presence of Americans, conationals, and other foreign
students in housing, most respondents indicated that they lived with or
near Americans. However, responses to other questions regarding the
frequency of various social activities with Americans and with conationals
indicated a clear preference for the conational groups (see Table 1).
Comparing their casual contacts (talking about studies or daily events)
with their more personal contacts (talking personally, going out or eating
together), we found no difference in the rate of casual contacts with
Americans versus conationals but found a substantial difference in the
rate of personal contacts. As Table 1 indicates, personal contacts with
Americans were rare. For example, 87 percent reported that they either
never or rarely ate with Americans, 7 percent reported that they ate
with them occasionally, and only 3 percent reported a frequent sharing
of meals with Americans. Looking at the whole range of activities, we
found that for the modal respondent, the only activities carried out weekly
with Americans were superficial talks about classes or daily events, with
all other discussions—from those covering politics to home and family
or personal activities—occurring either less than once a month or never.
All discussions were carried out with conationals on either a weekly or
several-times-monthly basis for most respondents.

Another study of Korean students by Bae (1971) revealed the role of
value orientation in social adjustment. A range of social activities

TABLE 1: FREQUENCY OF SOCIAL CONTACT WITH AMERICANS AND
CONATIONALS, AS REPORTED BY FORMOSAN RESPONDENTS ($n = 44$)

ITEM	RARELY OR NEVER	OCCASIONALLY	FREQUENTLY	NO RESPONSE
Personal Contact				
Personal Talk				
Americans	64	5	20	11
Conationals	29	29	32	9
Go Out Together				
Americans	83	13	0	3
Conationals	57	34	4	5
Eat Together				
Americans	87	7	3	3
Conationals	27	41	27	5
Casual Contact				
Talk about Studies				
Americans	7	33	65	3
Conationals	23	23	50	4
Talk about Daily Events				
Americans	11	27	55	7
Conationals	5	29	61	5

NOTE: Figures represent percentages of the total. Rarely or never, less than once a month or never; occasionally, several times a month; frequently, several times per week or daily.

similar to that listed in Table 1 was included in the questionnaire and was grouped for scoring purposes into casual, friendly, and intimate. Although there was no relationship between the respondent's traditional Korean values and the frequency of either casual or friendly relations with Americans, there was a strong association for intimate contacts involving the sharing of important personal experiences. Only those Korean students who were low in traditional Korean values reported substantial levels of intimate involvement with Americans. Patterns of contact with Koreans were the reverse. Again, there was no difference among the respondents when their attitudes were grouped according to traditional values for the frequency of casual or friendly activities, but the high-value group reported more intimate activities with Korean friends. We found a contrast between the high and low value groups: highly traditional students report more intimate activities with Koreans than with Americans; low-tradition students report more activities with Americans than with Koreans. This same pattern of findings was reported for other kinds of contacts, such as relationships with professors and the frequency of organized extra-curricular activities with American and Korean groups.

If it is true, as the above studies suggest, that wide differences in values serve as barriers to intercultural friendships, it is then important to consider under what conditions individuals are able to overcome these barriers. To know that an individual who disassociates himself from home country values is more easily able to move into the American culture is not sufficient to understand exactly how the barrier is crossed. Previous work with Japanese respondents (Bennett, Passin, & McKnight, 1958) reported that the alienated Japanese student, despite expressing an interest in identifying with Americans, was clearly unable to sustain satisfying relationships and became bitter and disillusioned with both home and American groups. The results of the follow-up study of 59 Asian students previously described suggest some positive correlates of intercultural contact (see Table 2). Here we see that initial motivation for friendship was not predictive of the number of American friends reported, whereas what might be labelled as self-confidence factors were predictive. The more American friends a respondent reported as having in the spring, the more likely he was to have anticipated in the fall, and experienced by the following spring, few problems in getting along with Americans and in understanding or speaking English. Among the "outcome variables" reported in the lower portion of Table 2, we see that the frequency of American friends was associated with the respondent's general sense of well-being and confidence, including feelings of having made satisfying friendships over the year, of not being lonely, and of having done well academically.

One way to summarize the implications of these research findings for psychotherapeutic contact with foreign students is to say that:

1. warm, intimate international contacts are the exception rather than the rule for foreign students on a large American campus.
2. those who bridge the barrier may be special—may be less strongly identified with home country values and may be relatively high in self confidence and in communication skills.
3. those who remain estranged from Americans and who continue to be oriented toward a home country subculture are both more traditional and probably more inhibited and shy socially.

Who Seeks Help

In general, our research and clinical experiences with foreign student patients suffering from medical or emotional problems have indicated that:

1. foreign students are a high risk group, under considerable stress.
2. this stress is more likely to be experienced in the form of physical complaints than psychological complaints.

TABLE 2: Factors Related to Number of Close American Friends as Reported by Asian Students ($n = 59$)

VARIABLES	CORRELATION WITH AMERICAN FRIENDS r	NUMBER OF REPORTED p VALUE*
Predisposing Variables (Measured on Arrival)		
Motive		
Strength of Goal to Get Involved with Americans	.01	NS†
Degree of Intimacy Desired with Americans	.19	NS†
Confidence		
Anticipated No Problems in Getting Along with Americans	.28	.05
Anticipated Few Problems in Understanding or Speaking English	.23	.05
Process Variables (Measured in Spring)		
Lived with or Near Americans	.44	.01
Actually Reported no Difficulty Speaking English	.24	.05
Actually Reported no Difficulty Understanding English	.30	.05
Actually Reported no Difficulty Having Behavior Understood	.16	NS†
Found Americans Friendly	.25	.05
Had Few Problems Making Friends with Americans	.24	.05
Outcome Variables (Measured in Spring)		
Overall Level of Self-Confidence High	.23	.10
Satisfied with Ability to Make Friends Here	.31	.05
Not Lonely	.25	.10
Satisfied with Degree Progress	.33	.05
Satisfied with Courses	.31	.05
Satisfied with Studying	.32	.05
Satisfied with Overall Academic Performance	.23	.10
Satisfied with Help Received for Problems	.27	.05

*One-tailed p values given for relationship predicted in advance; two-tailed p values for other variables, including outcome variables.
†Not significant.

3. the foreign student is more likely to seek medical than psychological help, with the latter sought only after all other resources have been exhausted.
4. there is considerable commonality to foreign student psychosomatic and emotional problems.

These generalizations are supported by a number of small studies that were carried out at the University of Wisconsin. In one survey of all students, both foreign and American, using the Student Health Service during 1 week in December, we found no difference in the overall rate of utilization between the groups but did find a significant difference in the types of illnesses reported. Non-Western foreign students complained more often of gastrointestinal problems or of generalized, undifferentiated pain. Treating physicians were more likely to rate foreign student problems as having a primary emotional component, although there were no differences in assessments of seriousness of illness. A survey of foreign students' health records revealed case after case of students coming to the health service with a mixture of physical complaints and psychological and situational stress.

Other studies of the utilization of psychological, psychiatric, and counseling services on this campus indicated, however, that foreign students are not likely to take their stress-related problems to these sources of help. In one sample group of 491 foreign students followed over a 5-year period, we found only 35 who used either psychiatric, psychological, or counseling services, and only 3 who became psychiatric inpatients. This rate of 7.6 percent over 5 years or 1.5 percent on a year-to-year basis can be compared with overall utilization rates of 2.6 percent for the psychiatric outpatient, 2 percent for counseling services, and with the estimate that one out of five students seeks some sort of help for mental health problems over his or her stay at the university. Finally, there is no evidence to suggest that the rate of psychotic breakdown, or suicide, is greater for foreign students. A review of all inpatient records for foreign students suggests, however, a heavy concentration of acute paranoid and severe depressive episodes. This is consistent with other studies and suggests that there are typical patterns when foreign students do succumb to stress (Zunin & Rubin, 1967; Yeh, 1972).

With these findings as background, we, as clinicians, are able to assume that when the international student is referred (by self or other) for help with emotional problems, then this patient is in greater need of help than his American counterpart. There are a variety of reasons why this may be true. Students from Eastern and African cultures especially do not tend to gravitate toward professional help with the same alacrity as do Americans. The home culture has rarely offered such resources so they have no familiarity with them. The home value system often is such that the need itself for professional help, even overseas, would constitute a loss of status in the student's own and his or her fellow nationals' eyes. Treatment typically is delayed even further because many non-Western cultures have elaborate networks for dealing with psychological stress through family, peers, and social structures that are approximated locally —all of which the foreign student patient will have tried unsuccessfully.

Finally, the patient and his fellow nationals are very reluctant to attract the attention of what they see as the "authorities" for fear of damaging their personal student status and the national image of their own country.

While these factors serve as barriers to the entrance of the foreign patient to the North American mental health system, they may also serve as coping or therapeutic measures. For example, the impulse of fellow nationals to cluster around, support, and protect one of their number who seems to be in trouble is often sufficient support for a successful, albeit limited, survival in the alien culture. It is only when the members of a cultural subgroup become overly protective of a seriously depressed, paranoid, or schizophrenic friend that their support becomes a liability. The individual then becomes worse and attempts (but rarely completes) suicide, disappears, or becomes so troublesome and embarrassing to the home group that they abandon and disassociate themselves from him, thereby compounding his troubles. This is most often the situation we find when a foreign student is brought to our psychiatric inpatient service. Even in less extreme cases, however, we have found our foreign outpatients have already exhausted their familiar resources and are in need of more than a psychological Band-Aid. The only exception to this general rule is when the foreign student becomes involved with an overly excitable administrator, advisor, or professor. The authority's intolerance for cultural or characterological differences is often translated into a perception of psychopathology in the student: dependence may be interpreted as psychological weakness; passive-aggressiveness as alienation; autonomy as irresponsibility; shyness as depression; or privacy as paranoia. Treatment in such cases takes on a family therapy flavor in which the goals are to open up communication channels rather than to modify the behavior of the designated patient.

COMMUNICATION BARRIERS IN THERAPY

All who have worked with foreign students are acutely aware that the stakes are higher in therapeutic contacts with international students, because, if unsuccessful, the almost inevitable result is the enforced return of that student—disgraced, wounded, and often professionally dead-ended—to his or her home country. The therapist's awareness of this and what it is like to be subject to it is essential to a successful therapeutic beginning.

The therapist must also be especially aware of his own feelings when attempting to relate to foreign patients. First impressions and gut reactions may be dreadfully misleading in intercultural encounters. The assumption that there is a common ground of shared experience or the notion that this level of similarity is the only path to understanding is misleading, as Stewart stresses in chapter 6. We must take the time and care to empathize with differences, to learn the latent messages in intercultural communications, and to bring our intellectual as well as our emotional awareness to bear upon these encounters. Too often have we found with our own psychiatric trainees who are attempting therapy with foreign students that the intercultural difficulties the visitor experiences in establishing intimate relationships in the host culture, and which have added to his psychological distress, are easily recapitulated in the therapeutic encounter. The students from the Far East, in our experience, tend to enter therapy looking scared, reserved, and passive. This is not unusual in any beginning therapy; what is different is that it often does not change over time. North American therapists may interpret passivity in a North American patient as resistance, but when they encounter passivity in an Asian patient, they may simply feel frustrated, blocked, and eager to find ways to terminate. For a variety of reasons, an Asian will maintain his reserve long after the American patient will have "let it all hang out." American therapists in such relationships then tend to doubt their skill, the patient's motivation, or the possibility of overcoming "cultural differences." The result, though, is to end the relationship, which for the foreign patient may be just one more encounter in a long list of non-gratifying contacts with the "foreigners."

What the therapist needs to keep in mind is not that the patient is uncommunicative or uncooperative, but that the therapist must take time to learn the different cues and signs by which the patient is communicating. He must also learn to recognize when he is presuming anything and then try not to presume. For example, as with all patients, the presenting symptom may be merely a symbol or cover for unspoken difficulties; what may be different is that the patient may be using a different code book than the one the therapist knows. Therapists working with foreign patients must become sensitized to the importance of and patience required for social ritual in the ancient cultures from which many of the patients have come. Relatively speaking, Western societies value "getting to the point," "telling it like it is," being "open and genuine." Patients from Eastern cultures have spent too many years developing their own formalized ways of "getting to know" one another, where they "stand," and what the limits of a relationship are, to be able to discard them because their therapist may be urging it as healthy. (The extreme case would be the attempt to employ encounter techniques with foreign patients.) The therapist must himself guard against interpreting patient ritual or reserve as guardedness. Passivity may well be the patient's accepted and appropriate way to relate to authority; to do otherwise, in his system, would constitute not only impropriety but even an aggressiveness or a hostility which he simply does not feel. And the patient most often expects an authoritarian, supportive, directive role of his therapist and may see the absence of these qualities as the therapist's lack of concern. Much of American psychotherapy has within it, both in technique and values, the importance of stripping away the "style" of a patient, of confronting, of challenging, of laying open the patient's dynamics—all of which may constitute a disgrace for the foreign patient (and for some Americans). Being urged to do this by the person they sought out to help them save face is often more confusing to the patient than he or she can tolerate.

If the therapist cannot tolerate his own frustration at not knowing what is happening with his patient, he, too, will give up, convinced that the patient is too alien or inscrutable to be reached or is too reluctant to try behaviors that the therapist knows to be therapeutic (such as confrontation or catharsis). When the therapist and patient reject cultural differences between them, they often reject each other as people. Yet our experience with international students has taught us that, above all, the needs, the feelings, the vulnerabilities that we experience as people are the same the world over. Cues are different, values are different, styles are different, communication patterns are different, but the people are the same (Miller, Yeh, Alexander, Klein, Tseng, Workneh, & Chu, 1971). A rejecting mother, with no surrogates, will likely have the same pathological effect anywhere. Schizophrenia is as easily recognizable in Benares, Addis Ababa, and Taipei as it is in Chicago, even though there are still many questions about different etiologies in different cultures (Torrey, 1973). Psychological trauma is handled universally by mechanisms such as withdrawal, depression, regression, denial, and the like; however, what is traumatic and what defines withdrawal varies widely around the world. (Could one talk meaningfully of "primal scene" to a patient who grew up in a family living nine to a room?) The need for self esteem is also universal, though the ways it is played out may vary greatly. The Asian student in the United States, for example, has within his or her identity much more of the homeland, student status, family, minority status, and future responsibilities and obligations than does the average American student. Such a student has less concern about autonomy and independence and much less stake in rebellion. Yet, when his or her identity is threatened, this student is no less distressed than is an American student. Therapists must not mistake the values or the style for the person. And they must not assume the Western way to mental health is the only way. In psychoanalytic terms, one would say that a therapist dealing with foreign patients is in danger of developing a countertransference to the cultural differences. Therapists, like all of us when our authority or expertise is threatened, may respond with anger—or dogma. Therapists, when faced with what by Western standards may be seen as excessive dependency may be frightened, or may feel manipulated. These and similar factors may bring the therapist to the point where his or her answer and stance are "I must teach this patient to handle his problems in the way I know works best—the Western way."

SITUATIONAL FACTORS VERSUS PERSONAL PROBLEMS

The foregoing has consisted largely of what not to do. To move on to specific modes of intervention with foreign patients, we might start with the importance of considering situational aspects in the treatment. Whereas some therapies emphasize keeping the real world outside the door of the office, it is especially important to focus on it with foreign patients. For most foreign students, this is often the first time in their lives that the day-to-day world has not automatically carried them along. They find academic structure and expectations to be vastly different from the home country where the university system, families, professors, and their government often combined to keep them moving along. As well as being much more academically adrift and unsure of how to proceed, the foreign student patient may also be having specific problems with language (in lectures or readings), with subject matter for which he is ill-prepared, with pleasing academic authority figures, and with discomfort with the American educational system itself. Financial and other practical aspects of the patient's situation must also be fully explored. The loss of anchorage inherent in moving from one culture to another only heightens anxiety, self-consciousness, paranoia, vulnerability, and concern with status. This has been documented, as have the reactions of depression and withdrawal. The therapist should not hesitate to recommend or intervene where appropriate in these practical issues, since they are likely to have a significant effect on the psychological status of the patient. The therapist's efforts in these regards will also serve to reassure the patient on what may be his worst fear—that he is not worth saving. We have yet to find a patient who resents such participation on the therapist's part, since that is often the very expectation he came with.

CONATIONAL SUPPORT

Another very important therapeutic step may be the active involvement of the patient with the conational network. Whereas the absence of contact with conationals may be pathognomonic, reinstatement of contact can be enormously therapeutic if orchestrated properly. The therapist is often in a uniquely critical position to be the agent for such rapprochement, since to the patient he or she may appear to be an ally who can ask and arrange for such a contact when the patient no longer feels justified to do so. The therapist is also seen by the friends of the patient as an authority who both certifies the patient's worth and is taking responsibility for him, thereby relieving the conational group of some of their doubts and fears. On smaller campuses where there may not be any or many conationals, the arranging even of an introduction to a professor of the same background, or a local businessman, or a friend of a friend, can be beneficial.

ENCOUNTERS WITH STRANGERS

In contrast, we have found that group therapies, or inpatient milieu approaches, often have little or no therapeutic impact on foreign students. When placed in the midst of numbers of Americans, the foreign patient tends either to comply with what he or she imagines will please or to withdraw. Group functions or exercises are seen as lacking in dignity and intimacy. The personal pride of the foreign patient runs against the psychological stripping which communal therapies require. The foreign patient's difficulty in discerning the structure implicit in the host culture's modes of interaction may be further compounded in the typical therapeutic setting. When our patient groups have dealt specifically with one another's behaviors, our foreign student patients have tended to feel insulted, demeaned, and attacked. In many of the cultures from which they came, to volunteer one's own response to what someone else is doing (outside of the defined social order) is beyond the bounds of good taste. The therapist must never underestimate the sense and importance of dignity to the foreign student patient. To have others pry into your affairs, to be urged to be open and informal, is not only threatening but demeaning as well.

Specific behavior therapy approaches, if properly presented, can be of value in the treatment of foreign student patients. Yet a behavioral program instituted without considerable orientation and explanation will probably end in failure. In the first place, it would be difficult to enlist the understanding or cooperation necessary to do the proper behavioral analysis required to develop the program, for the patient would have difficulty in seeing the relevance of the questions necessary for the analysis and might simply give whatever answers he or she believes the therapist wishes to hear. But more important, by the time the foreign patient has reached therapy he may have gone beyond specific target problems and is primarily seeking (but not asking for) warm, human, interpersonal contact. If that is first achieved, behavioral approaches may be tried and may fit in quite well with the task-oriented approach of many foreign students. But the relationship aspects of the therapeutic intervention must always trump the behavioral ones.

MEDICATION

The use of psychotropic medicines is similarly complicated. We have found a general pattern in which medications are prescribed more frequently for the foreign student patients than for their American counterparts, and these prescribed medications are less often taken by the foreign students. It is, of course, easier to prescribe a drug than to try to bridge cultural, language, and interpersonal difficulties. This message is not lost to the patient, who will often abjure the drug along with the professional contact itself. There is the added difficulty that unless the therapist has taken the time and endured the stress of really coming to understand this difficult patient, the medication tried may not be appropriate—a conclusion that the patient may reach long before the therapist does. This is especially a problem where there may be side effects of the medication. These must be anticipated and discussed with foreign patients, especially if such side effects may upset the patient's ability to study.

On the other hand, if a sense of trust and understanding is first developed, foreign patients will be quite eager and responsible in regard to medication. Such approaches are familiar; i. e., a knowledgeable authority dispensing the specific remedy for their trouble—and are less demanding than interpersonal contact. The patient is not being asked to explore his own interior with a Westerner's map; he is not being asked to bare his soul in what to him is an unseemly manner; and he will be eager to please someone he trusts. In sum, medication therapies are effective if they are not perceived by the patient as being a dismissal but rather as the authoritative answer to his problems in the context of a secure relationship.

TO STAY OR RETURN

One of the most agonizing issues a therapist may have to confront with a foreign student patient is the question of whether or not the patient should return home before completing studies. It sometimes becomes clear that a return to family, familiar environs, and cultural structure, and the sanctuary that they represent, is the only therapeutic option. Invariably, however, the patient's consideration of that option raises appropriate fears of being considered a failure, of abrogating a promise to be a special person (in his mind or that of his family), and the possibility of being disqualified from progress within the home country's professional or governmental system. In spite of these concerns, some patients unconsciously or privately may have concluded that this is their only option, but they cannot bring themselves publicly to say so. The patient may then be waiting for the therapist to put it into words.

In any case, the therapist should discuss these matters openly from both the practical and psychological points of view. Speaking the unspeakable most often has a reassuring effect, and once again the weight of the therapist's authority can counterbalance to some degree both the patient's sense of responsibility in the matter and the validity of the decision. And, as with most fears, anticipation and honest consideration can contribute to mastery. Some smoothing of the return can often be effected by the therapist. Acute symptoms should be treated. Separation from local boyfriends or girlfriends must be worked through. The cooperation and understanding of professors and deans can be obtained, so that letters or certificates for academic work already completed can be transmitted to relevant governmental or private agencies. Communication with the student's family before the return can be encouraged, and countrymen who have had either successful or unsuccessful foreign sojourns themselves can be enlisted. But most essential of all are a full, open, practical, and honest consideration of the meaning of the return to the patient and the inherent legitimizing of the decisions and the feelings about it.

SUMMARY

In making and establishing therapeutic contact with a foreign student patient, the therapist:

1. must keep in mind that it has not been easy for the patient to have come for help;
2. must remember that on initial contact what to the therapist might be construed as openness and honesty may be to the patient an invasion of his or her privacy;
3. must *not* assume that he or she intuitively or automatically understands the meaning, source, or significance of symptoms, feelings, or styles;
4. must be aware of his or her own responses to a person from another culture, so that he can work at bridging cultural gaps and difficulties and not contribute to them;
5. must never underestimate the foreign patient's sense of both national and personal pride and the threat to it that is represented by the situation in which the patient now finds himself;
6. must take care that he or she does not rely on cant or bluster when communication becomes difficult, or when he or she does not understand or agree with the value system of the patient;
7. must, above all, forego the temptation to define therapeutic movement in American terms or attempt to "Americanize" the foreign patient;
8. must never lose sight of the foreign patient as an individual—unique, distinct, and nobody's stereotype.

Client-patient roles differ from culture to culture and clients must be educated in what to expect and what to do. But more important, helper roles differ too, and we must learn to be more flexible in how we are willing to play them. Just as we may vary treatment techniques to fit specific problems, we must vary the way we mobilize and shape the non-specific factors of the helping relationship to fit the cultural style of the client. The therapist must accommodate the foreign student patient to his own culture—the one he carries with him. While there are a few individuals who seek to expand their identity through intercultural experiences, they rarely seek out therapists to help them do so. More likely the issue for the foreign patient will be to reestablish a concept of himself with which he can once again be comfortable. We must recognize that therapists carry real and considerable power with these patients, and this power must be used against the patient's problem rather than against the client's sense of self.

REFERENCES

Bae, C. K. *The effects of traditional Korean values on social adjustment and brain drain of the Korean students in the USA.* Unpublished doctoral dissertation, University of Wisconsin, 1971.

Bennett, J. W., Passin, H., & McKnight, R. K. *In search of identity: The Japanese overseas scholar in America and Japan.* Minneapolis: University of Minnesota Press, 1958.

Chu, H.-M., Yeh, E.-K., Klein, M. H., Alexander, A. A., & Miller, M. H. A study of Chinese students' adjustment in the U.S.A. *Acta Psychologica Taiwanica*, March 1971, No. 13, 206–218.

Klein, M. H., Alexander, A. A., Tseng, K.-H., Miller, M. H., Yeh, E.-K., & Chu, H.-M., Far Eastern students in a big university: Subcultures within a subculture. *Bulletin of the Atomic Scientists*, January 1971, *27*.

Klein, M. H., Alexander, A. A., Tseng, K.-H., Miller, M. H., Yeh, E.-K., Chu, H.-M., & Workneh, F. The foreign student adaptation project: Social experiences of Asian students in the U.S. *Exchange*, 1971, *6*, 77–90.

Klein, M. H., Miller, M. H., & Alexander, A. A. When young people go out in the world. In W. P. Lebra (Ed.), *Youth, socialization, and mental health* (Vol. 3 of Mental Health Research in Asia and the Pacific). Honolulu: University Press of Hawaii, 1974.

Miller, M. H., Yeh, E.-K., Alexander, A. A., Klein, M. H., Tseng, K.-H., Workneh, F., & Chu, H.-M. The cross-cultural student: Lessons in human nature. *Bulletin of the Menninger Clinic*, March 1971, *35*, 128–131.

Torrey, E. F. Is schizophrenia universal? An open question. *Schizophrenia Bulletin*, 1973, *7*, 53–59.

Yeh, E.-K. Paranoid manifestations among Chinese students studying abroad: Some preliminary findings. In W. P. Lebra (Ed.), *Transcultural research in mental health* (Vol. 2 of Mental Health Research in Asia and the Pacific). Honolulu: University Press of Hawaii, 1972.

Zunin, L. M., & Rubin, R. T. Paranoid psychotic reactions in foreign students from non-Western countries. *Journal of the American College Health Association*, February 1967, *15*, 220–226.

6   Cultural Sensitivities in Counseling

EDWARD C. STEWART

HOW CAN A COUNSELOR FROM A DIFFERENT CULTURE DEVELOP EMPATHY?

The counseling of persons from other cultures can ignite cultural sensitivities on the part of the participants, particularly when their cultural predispositions are challenged as a result of the intercultural interaction. The cultural predisposition of participants may be analyzed according to their similarities and/or differences with one another. American cultural values have emphasized the importance of finding similarities in intercultural exchanges, in which an interface of sympathy for other cultures is created. A different kind of interface accents dissimilarities and leads to an analysis of interaction in terms of bridging value differences. This alternative is an interface of empathy. It is unfortunate that the notions of empathy and sympathy have been frequently confused and the important differences in meaning have been diffused.

Stewart describes a model that accommodates cultural differences, to the extent that they are similar and/or different, through analogy to a hologram. The holographic analysis of counseling draws attention to the principle of similarity as the basis for establishing an interaction between the counselor and the client. Like a pattern in a hologram, each cultural event contains the cues by which a client may be understood if those cues are properly illuminated by the appropriate insights. The holograph analogy provides a model that tolerates cultural differences between clients and counselors without either partner having to assimilate the other. Stewart pursued the implications of this analogy in its application to intercultural counseling.

Stewart's paper is the most theoretical treatment of intercultural counseling in this volume. He provides a means of conceptualizing the practical problems involved in communicating with clients from other cultures. The client must be viewed within his own natural environment and as a totality. Counseling has more typically required the client to accommodate the counselor's culture as a prerequisite to receiving help.

In distinguishing between the ideas of empathy and sympathy, Stewart makes a valuable contribution to the way in which counselors can improve their skills, not just to work with clients from other cultures but also to sharpen their insights into the essence of counseling processes. His discussion of the hologram analogy provides a structure to sort out similarities and differences from the client's cultural point of view as being conducive either to sympathy or empathy. Although Stewart emphasizes the counseling of persons from foreign countries in his examples, his model provides the means of looking at counseling in a wide range of intercultural relationships.

Counselors of college students often adopt the view that the counseling situation should be expanded into an event embedded in the wider context of the total life of the student. The need for this humanizing perspective arises spontaneously when one is counseling with foreign students. The problems foreign students convey to the counselor frequently bring to the surface values and patterns of thinking underlying education and cultures that undermine implicit assumptions in counseling. These asumptions usually are considered to be universal and, though seldom examined for their cultural limits, should be so examined when one is counseling foreign students.

Our concern is to expand the context of counseling to gain a slice of time for the client to become a person, to give him perceptions and memory that go beyond temporary rewards, and to see that his past experiences still loom prominently in the present. The counselor must perceive the client as a human continuity of experience in time and space and must set aside a perception of the foreign student as being made up of incoherent and unconnected events in counseling and outside. If the counselor is able to enlarge the counseling situation to encompass wider activities, to include time leading to the past, to memory, and to anticipate the future, then the counselee will perceive him- or herself as a total person (Hampshire, 1973), one who may abide by unexpected cultural assumptions, values, and patterns of thought.

At the same time as the cultural perspective in counseling provides a focus, it also introduces a knot of complexity. Counseling may be defined as an event of intercultural interaction, which resembles other events in which persons of different cultural backgrounds participate. Intercultural communication then becomes the key to the problems of counseling, and simplifies the role of the counselor, who applies knowledge and experience from the field of intercultural communication.

The counselor sacrifices some of the objectivity usually associated with behaviorism, but the loss is more apparent than real. Current trends from objective psychology in decision-making, problem-solving, criteria of evaluation, and in modification of behavior propose three ideas. First, actions are probably judged by their consequences; therefore, students should practice adjusting to norms that provide benefits from attending school, and fulfill the purposes for which they came. Along with this stress on practicality (utility), there is secondly the implicit assumption that both rewards and punishments can be combined in a calculus that yields choices. Priorities are established according to an unspecified criterion. Finally, the time frame for making choices is brief. Choices refer to relatively immediate objectives, since these tend to be practical and concrete in comparison to more long-range goals, even those which have implications in the present. The implication of these three factors is that the individual is given limited choices that diminish the dignity and sensibilities which so many students, both American and foreign, expect.

In counseling, the person should be perceived as going beyond the limits of temporary behavioral contingencies and making choices according to values, patterns of thinking, and other predispositions which shape him as a cultural being. For this purpose objective measures of psychology fall short. Decision-theory has failed to explain how the decision maker combines subjective estimates of his own situation and makes a rational choice from among conflicting and contradictory factors. The experimental evidence, after 15 years of investigation, is inconclusive (Tversky, 1967). Reviews of decision-making in social contexts have fared no better. The theory of utility provides no way to compare the preferences of one actor with those of another (McIntosh, 1969).

In his review of how people combine individual preferences into social choices, Lieberman (1969) ended on an inconclusive note, very similar to the positions of Tversky and McIntosh, that drew attention to an area that has not been studied. He stated (p. 110) that "One set of processes that undoubtedly have great influence on the social choice problem, but have been virtually unstudied, are the processes involving the effect of past commitments and decisions, and anticipations of the effect of future social choice situations and commitments on the present problem."

Reviews of the subject essentially concur that everyday behavior cannot be handled by decision-making theory. When these theories are adequate, the conditions and issues are highly artificial and accentuate a narrow perception of the foreign student. We perceive a stranger from another culture and see only a small part, the larger, more important body of unshared experiences being buried in his own unique culture. We judge and counsel him on only the small part we see and how it looks to us, rather than on how it looks to him. The reverse view is likewise limited. For our purposes it is necessary to describe actions and choices in a context of the person's total environment and identity.

BASIS OF INTERACTION: SIMILARITIES AND DIFFERENCES

The interaction between counselor and client may be seen as a deliberate intervention in the activities of the client, conducted and constructed to yield insight, understanding, and benefits for the client's satisfaction and improved effectiveness. The participants must create an interface which will sustain the counseling relationship and which will benefit the client. It is widely accepted that the interface that is needed should be genuine, warm, and should generate empathy. The last concept is critical for intercultural communication, since empathy suggests establishing a bond, a link, based on a state of similarity between the two participants. Intercultural counseling, by definition, does not permit a totally accurate interaction, since empathy, defined as understanding others on the basis of shared qualities, cannot occur. Before abandoning the possibility of intercultural counseling, we should look into the similarities needed to sustain empathy.

Perhaps it is fair to say that counselors derive most of their beliefs, practices, and methods from a body of values in American society, from a residue of clinical insights, and from conventional wisdom in education. Counselors would appear to be less affected by systematic research findings in psychology and anthropology. For these reasons I will first discuss the importance of similarity in American life, then of its status in the culture, and conclude with research findings.

Similarity has been an important influence in American life since the colonial days, when travelers already remarked on the remarkable uniformity of the American language (Boorstin, 1958). In social relations similarity is expressed as conformity, and by the 1830s Tocqueville had perceived the "tyranny of the majority" in the United States, and believed that public inquiry had already intruded more deeply into the private affairs of Americans than in those of the French. Nearly every observer of the United States has commented on the conformity and standardization of American life. Most of these observations have been made on the basis of European cultures and can be summarized by the observation of Richard Müller-Freienfels, who stated in 1929 (in Williams, 1970, p. 484) that "distance, uniqueness, and originality are European values, which are foreign to the American. His values are the very reverse of these: adherence to type, agreement, similarity."

Robin Williams (1970) associates conformity in American life with several themes, chief among these being the economic order and the heterogeneity of American culture. Equality and the stress on activity probably also contribute to the predisposition for conformity in American culture. Despite the agreement of observers about conformity, their opinions should not end the matter. It would be desirable to obtain more objective comparisons with other societies, for to some degree all men must conform with standards in society if any kind of social existence is to take place. It would be very important to determine not only the degree of conformity, but also the nature of it, whether there is full compliance, and whether a *J*-curve can be found in which a few comply fully while others deviate. Although Americans are perceived as conformists by Europeans, are they also seen as conformists by non-European societies?

Although research may modify the significance of similarity, the principle continues to influence values in American society. Its importance perhaps is great enough for it to qualify as an assumption in American thought, in American social life, and in communication. Thus, the more similar two persons are, the better they should be able to communicate; whereas differences impede communication. In some other cultures, however, differences may be assumed to be necessary for communication to take place, and the degree of success is not measured by agreement and conformity as it tends to be in American life.

Research of diffusion of innovation provides a critical "incident" for demonstrating the strength of similarities in American culture. For nearly a generation Americans have gone throughout the world and developed programs to stimulate economic-social development. Their efforts have invariably involved working and living with people of a different cultural background. Innovators have developed two ideas that have widely influenced innovation. These are homophily and heterophily, referring respectively to similarity and differences. The concept of homophily/similarity apparently originated with Tarde (1903), who stated that social relations are closer among people who are similar in occupation and education. The term now is used primarily in the literature on innovation, and homophily or similarity is declared to underscore the adoption of innovations (Rogers & Shoemaker, 1971). A crucial comment from this source states that: "when source and receiver share common meanings, attitudes and beliefs, and a mutual language, communication between them is likely to be effective" (p. 210).

This quotation underscores the importance of homophily. It is a position which is now undergoing modification as heterophily is discovered to underlie diffusion of innovation (Rogers & Shoemaker, 1971). Dodd (1973) reached a similar conclusion in his study of the spread of Christianity in Ghana, in which he focused on nontechnological innovations. He concluded (p. 8) that heterophily prevails in the adoption stages of innovation, while homophily characterizes a sociometric bias of opinion leaders. It would seem that diffusion of innovation, by definition, involves heterophily, since innovation requires that change be diffused among dissimilar people.

Leaving the level of social theories, we turn to examine the bias toward similarity as a predisposition of the perceiving and thinking individual. Similarity and difference may be two separate ways of describing the same situation. A dark gray may be described according to its similarity to black, or its difference from white. Laboratory experiments with sound have shown that sounds judged to be the same and sounds judged to be different are not equivalent obverse aspects of a unitary judgmental process, such as two sides of the same coin. Subjects take longer to decide that two tones are the same than that two tones are different (Bindra, Williams, & Wise 1965). At the perceptual and judgmental level there exists a difference between perceiving and judging same and different, with difference apparently the easier and preferred response. The experimental results disclose a dual judgment, which is available to all subjects.

Building on this basic psychological process, cultural learning may well establish a perceptual set to find similarities versus meeting differences. If the laboratory findings can be extended to the levels of social perception, we can make a hypothesis that in some societies, American for instance, cultural learning encourages the perception of similarities, while in others, the French perhaps, the predisposition established is to perceive differences. These are general observations which need to be confirmed or rejected.

At a more complex level of thinking, it perhaps can be said that Americans prefer similarities in their logical rules. Induction and conjunction are clearly American preferences, and both of these aspects of thinking rely more on similarity than on deduction and disjunction. In the course of his research, Cole and colleagues concluded that the Kpelle of Liberia were better at disjunctive reasoning, while Americans were better at conjunctive. This result was later modified, if not neutralized, by Cole's following research. If sustained, such findings would offer a clear example in the area of cognitive concepts in which American culture predisposes toward similarity (Cole, Gay, Glick, & Sharp, 1971, pp. 197–203). It is not necessary to show that there is a cultural difference in proficiency between different styles of thinking, with one being better than the other, to demonstrate a cultural predisposition or preference. It can be demonstrated that Americans in their daily behavior consistently search for similarities and sameness and avoid difference. This tendency is reflected throughout their mental health service systems.

There is a final area of research that is relevant to the predisposition toward similarity, this being in the field of interpersonal attraction.

Researchers who have examined the psychological bases for social interaction generally conclude that attraction is positively influenced by personality similarities (Byrne and Griffitt, 1973). The research has usually been conducted with American subjects, but a recent study systematically extends the finding to other cultures and concludes that there is a ubiquitous relationship between attitude similarity and attraction (Byrne, 1973).

The argument for similarity frequently associates similarities of social environment and of learning with transcultural properties of behavior, which view in turn launches the proposition by Byrne (1973, p. 205) that "our supposition is that the response to attitudes is based on common learning experiences which stress the desirability of being logical and correct in perceiving the world as others do."

This statement implies the presence of universal qualities of logic and of perception and suggests that there is a "correct" view. The inquiry can be advanced one more step to stress universal similarities in basic processes. In learning, for example, food serves a similar function as a reinforcer. Specific details differ. The effectiveness of chocolate or whale fat varies from society to society (Byrne, 1973, p. 201).

It is clear that at some level of abstraction a general psychological theory shall contain behavioral laws independent of cultural backgrounds and hence be based on similarities. There are universals of human behavior, such as in basic processes in psychology and physiology. Attraction theory has revealed some universal qualities in interpersonal interactions.

Personal attraction theory is usually based on experimental studies in which the alternative responses of subjects are limited. These conditions for collecting responses on the basis of similarity are necessary, since it has been shown that strong situational variables will otherwise obscure the role of individual differences (Mischel, 1973, p. 276). In unscrambling the effects of similarity and difference, one must stress the difficulty of attributing behavior to the personalized situation or the global qualities of personality (Mischel, 1973). This is a demanding research task, but a beginning has been made. Mettee and Riskind (1973) have shown that under circumstances of competition the defeated prefer to lose to those who are different, not similar. There are other examples in a useful analysis of similarities and differences from the perspective of attraction theory, but the ways in which human beings are like other human beings and are also different remain a challenge for research. The level of similarity/difference is often combined with the third level of how every human in some respects is like no other human. Theory tends to search for similarities, to discover differences, and then to focus on individuality. Fromkin (1973, p. 1) examined "the prevailing theories and research of interpersonal similarity, their limitations, and the ways that the notions of uniqueness limit, clarify and expands [*sic*] upon the range of behavior encompassed by them."

Fromkin's analysis suggests that the experimental basis of most of the research in attraction theory has been too limited in scope. Several important variables, such as the degrees of similarity, number of attitudes compared, and the characteristics of the comparative criteria, have been neglected. When these variables are examined in the research, the conclusions reached are more realistic and the claims made for similarity must be revised. Fromkin (1973, p. 51) concluded that "when a person engages in social comparisons of a *large* number and high proportion of *similar* attributes with a large number of similar comparison others, he will tend to assign himself a position with high degrees of similarity." These are the conditions under which a person experiences a loss of uniqueness, a sense that he or she is not different from others. According to Fromkin (1973, p. 51), the favorable self-evaluation found under conditions of moderate similarity is replaced by unfavorable self-evaluations.

The work on the psychology of uniqueness is significant for a revision of the attraction theory. The principle of difference is approached from the vantage of individual difference, uniqueness, which is used to limit the applications of similarity. The two limiting conditions of similarity/difference, universal and unique, provide a theoretical basis for intercultural communication, which starts with an assumed cultural difference between communicators.

We have stressed the work on uniqueness, because it provides the most relevant research for counseling that establishes the significance of differences. It also raises the problem of self-identity of a client in counseling and his relationship to the counselor. In the next section we shall turn to the preferred interface of empathy and examine its appropriateness for intercultural communication. We will have occasion to refer to similarity/dissimilarity and uniqueness, which provide the basis for introducing the self-concept into the discussion of intercultural communication in counseling.

THE INTERFACE BETWEEN COUNSELOR AND CLIENT

Empathy has scaled the pinnacle of success and attained an unchallenged nominal status in American society, a status unmarked by a cloud of either negative connotation or negative functional meaning. Its history in American psychology goes back to 1909 when Titchener translated the writing of Theodore Lipps (1903), specifically his translation of the concept of *Einfühlung* as "empathy." The original German refers to an esthetic experience, and its meaning lies close to motor mimicry (Allport, 1968). It is only later that the concept acquired the meaning of the generalized ability to understand others.

Empathy can be understood as transformed in meaning by the influence of values in American society, particularly those of the stress on similarity and the self-perception of many Americans. Its original meaning is now changed, and its current definition is confused with a second potential interface between persons—sympathy. This concept has a much longer and troubled history. Preceding the time of Adam Smith, it eventually declined, fell into disrepute, and now is confined primarily to pleas for compassion and to studies of children (Allport, 1968).

The rich history of empathy has yielded some subtle analyses that have frequently been conducted in German, a language that stimulates a richness of emotional analysis that is difficult to translate into English. The peak of analysis may have been reached with Scheler (Allport, 1968), who distinguished eight different levels ranging from motor mimicry, *Einfühlung*, to a mystical union of all with the One. A quick glance at the eight levels yields an interesting, although perhaps superficial, rhythm between differences and similarity. Thus all the even-numbered levels of Scheler suggest states of similarity, which can be summarized as 2, simultaneous feelings; 4, identification between persons; 6, affiliative fellow feelings, though the feelings themselves are separated; and 8, referring to the unity of all. These similarities of the even levels appeal to Americans and contrast with the odd stages, which refer to differences, or at least they lack the common bond of the even levels. Thus, level 1, *Einfühlung*, refers to motor mimicry and is correctly translated as empathy, but the concept does not necessarily suggest a similar feeling. The similarity is in terms of the act, not of the persons. It even has been used to describe the impulse to tilt the head to look at a picture hanging on a wall at an angle. Level 3 refers to the emotional contagion which sweeps from person to person in a crowd. (It is the emotion which brings people together, not the persons themselves as in identity, level 6.) The next two levels reflect increasing degrees of intellectual detachment that are altruistic but lack the common emotional bond of level 6, characterized by affiliative fellow feelings. Level 5 represents persons who know how others feel, but the understanding of the other is conscious and detached and distinguishes the self from others. The self understands how others feel but does not necessarily endorse their actions. At the final level of empathy, 7, the self senses the state of mind of the other and prizes and respects it.

Scheler's levels easily incorporate the ideas both of sympathy and empathy. Even levels 2 to 8 show a clear progression from a temporary fusion of self with others to the complete unity of Scheler's mystical level 8, often identified with religious feelings. Empathy, the odd levels of 1, 3, 5, and 7, suggests a separation between self and others. It is a more complex progression than sympathy: uniqueness and difference would appear to have infinite roots.

The analysis of Scheler's levels is tentative and must be considered suggestive at best. Nevertheless it draws attention to at least two interfaces that occur in intercultural communication. Empathy, based on differences, has been described in terms similar to the conclusions derived above. In the words of Lauren G. Wispé (1968):

> Empathy may be defined as the self-conscious effort to share and accurately comprehend the presumed consciousness of another person including his thoughts, feelings, perceptions, and muscular tensions, as well as their causes. Empathy may more briefly be defined as the self-conscious awareness of the consciousness of others. Empathy as used in psychology requires the empathizer to maintain an awareness of the imaginative nature of the transposition of one self into another. . . . Empathy, unlike sympathy, denotes an active referent. In empathy one attends to the feelings of another; in sympathy one attends to the suffering of another, but the feelings are one's own. In empathy I try to feel your pain. In sympathy I know you are in pain, and I sympathize with you, but I feel my sympathy and my pain, not your anguish and your pain. Empathy as an act, and "empathic understanding" as a therapeutic process, are not necessarily coterminous. [p. 441]

Wispé derived the etymological structure of both sympathy and empathy and found that the connotations of negative affect predominate; hence, the negative affective tone of the comments following the discussion of the etymology. The quotation has been selected to stress the psychological meaning of sympathy and empathy; it is agonistic and does not accurately reflect the range, thematic intent, and intricacies of Wispé's article. However, the quotation does present the essential but theoretical point about the two interfaces. To relieve the abstractions and to bring the discussion closer to the issues encountered by counselors and clients, I will describe examples of sympathy and empathy.

The incidents occurred in a workshop built around psychodrama and involved a police officer who was called to the house of a private citizen to investigate the citizen's threat to kill the president of the draft board. The officer was informed that the citizen had just been notified that his son, a draftee, had been killed in Vietnam. When the officer approached the citizen, he encountered a man possessed by grief and hate, who freely threatened the life of the president of the draft board. The officer responded by taking great pains to identify his own feelings as a young man and to refer to others of his acquaintance who were in Vietnam. This is *sympathy*.

In the same psychodrama, a second police officer entered the house of the citizen, spotted a picture on the wall, began to talk about it, and engaged the man in conversation about the objects that both perceived. Out of this conversation developed information about the family and the son who had been reported killed, without the police officer ever establishing a basis of personal similarity with the man of the house or with the dead son. The officer did respond to the emotions of the citizen but did not use his own emotional identity to guide his responses. This is *empathy*.

The two interfaces may be approached from another direction, and described in relation to defense mechanisms. Sympathy, encircling personal responses and emotions, falls into the domain of introjection. The outward movement of empathy, in which the person engages the emotions of the other, clearly brings the interface close to the mechanism of projection. The distinctions between the two sets of concepts seem to match, so that we can refer to sympathetic introjection and empathic projection. The important question for counseling and communication posed by the matching concepts is whether sympathy goes along with projection and empathy with introjection. The choice in American society seems to have been made both for introjection and sympathy.

Perhaps it is rash to propose sympathy as the interface Americans prefer when it is empathy that has attained a nominal status. But by whatever name, Americans create a sense of understanding and of intimacy with others when they refer to a common experience in the past, as Mead (1964) has pointed out. They search for a place visited in common. They search their lives for people they have known and examine shared experiences. They identify similar roles in sympathy. For persons who develop interfaces of empathy, however, there is a shared domain but there is no intent or desire to share identities in either time or space or to integrate roles. The sympathetic or empathic interface exhibited by a person can be seen as an extension of the self-concept, which probably governs the kind of interface that the person habitually employs in social exchanges. In American society, the confusion between sympathy and empathy can also be associated with the dominant concept of the self which has prevailed in the society.

The dominant pattern of the American self-perception lacks clearly recognized structures of values and beliefs (McClelland, Sturr, Knapp, & Wendt, 1958). There are motivating needs and required responses, but the self is known by actions and a general belongingness with other persons. The inner core of the self is private (Rogers, 1964), inaccessible, and exists in a subjective world isolated from the "selves" of all other persons. Others are not usually given the same subjective existence so that the "self" is different from other selves in a sweeping subjective sense that cannot be matched by differences between any two "others." The American self is unique, it is the quantum of the culture (Stewart, 1971a), but there is no reason for its existence other than in itself. Simone de Beauvoir commented that Americans consider their existences as accidents (1964). Meaning and values are derived from an almost impersonal affiliation in social groups. The only bond for persons whose real selves are inarticulate and inaccessible—since there is no reason or "cause" for them—is a common purpose or goal in action, in groupings that accommodate persons on the basis of needs which are seen as universal.

The reluctance of Americans to perceive themselves as members of a category (a class) has been often noted and is reflected in the lack of ideology in political parties, relative disengagement from philosophies, and constant stress on performance. Pragmatism replaces abstractions, theories and even a priori values as criteria for choice and decisions. The high value placed on concepts of decision, choice, and preference in American society suggests that the favored terms employed to describe personality ideals have the effect of severing the individual from the group.

It is doubtful if the self exists as an empirical phenomenon completely separate from attitudes, values, or other psychological constructs. At the same time there is no question that the subjective feeling of having a self is an empirical phenomenon, although it is one that is often taken for granted (Epstein, 1973, p. 405). These aspects of self-perception have led to the view that the self is a theory held by the individual about himself, even though he may not necessarily be aware of the significant features in his own self theory (Epstein, 1973). The individual also holds theories about the nature of the world, the nature of the self, and the interaction between the two. These are subjects that have been treated as aspects of the culture of the individual (Stewart, 1971b) and that open up the area of cultural differences in personal theories about the self.

The undifferentiated notions of American identity, dependent on social norms for direction, help explain the confusion of empathy and sympathy while still maintaining the label empathy as a historical relic. The tendency among Americans is to insist on their own individual feelings, choices, and preferences and to use their evocation to establish a bond, i.e., a similarity basis, with another person. Thus the distinctions between the two interfaces seem appropriate. Sympathy has been the ideal of conventional wisdom in American society, while empathy is the necessary interface in intensive interactions of intercultural communication.

MODEL FOR COUNSELING SESSION: THE HOLOGRAM

The counseling process symbolizes a condensation of the individual's total life experiences, emphasizing some of them more than others. The counseling situation is a "simulacrum" of the client's life space. This way of describing it is timeworn and difficult to analyze, but we have had occasion to turn to technology and use the hologram principle as a model for the counseling situation. "In a hologram the information in a scene is recorded on a photographic plate in the form of a complex interference, or diffraction, pattern that appears meaningless. When the pattern is illuminated by coherent light, however, the original image is reconstructed. What makes the hologram unique as a storage device is that every element in the original image is distributed over the entire photographic plate" (Pribram, 1969, p. 73). The hologram represents an image that is not intelligible; the original can be obtained only through a reconstruction, and this process parallels the process of reconstructing the interaction between a counselor and the client in the intercultural situation.

There are several characteristics of a hologram which are important for the model of counseling. First, the usual hologram resembles intricate patterns of contour lines on a map. The observer cannot identify the objects it represents from the incomplete holographic image, since there is no photographic similarity between the two. Thus, the principle of similarity, which often functions in both perception and thinking, does not operate to represent the object in the hologram. By analogy there is no reason to find in the counseling situation superficial resemblances to the other life experiences of the client. Second, every aspect of the hologram reproduces the entire image and, inversely, the image spreads out over the entire surface of the hologram. I am again drawing an analogy with counseling and suggesting that any aspect of a counseling session can be enlarged, elaborated, and decoded to yield the basic patterns of life experiences. (We incur the risk of overdetermination and hence stand to lose objectivity in the behavioristic sense.)

The correspondence between a counseling situation and other life experiences of the individual is not one of similarity or of representativeness. Counseling is a deliberate intervention, analogous to a pattern of interference encoded in the hologram, which serves to bring out that which is meaningful in counseling and to link it to other life experiences of the individual. Interference—a term which seems too strong for counseling—is used in holography. When the interaction in counseling involves cultural differences, cultural concepts can be used to illuminate the process of interaction and its relationship to the life experiences of the student.

The hologram provides an accurate analogy for the "deliberate interaction of counseling." The recorded light patterns of the hologram represent the meaningless reflected light from an object recorded with a reference beam of light from the same source. The image, the hologram, records the interference pattern from the two beams (Leith & Upatnieks, 1965). It does not represent distinctive features of the object. To make sense of the meaningless hologram and to identify the object contained, one needs to flash a coherent light, which in optics is defined as a narrow wave (ideally monochromatic) as provided by laser lights. In counseling we lack the precision of narrow-band laser lights, but we have the developing field of cultural differences in values and thinking that can be used as a coherent light cast on the interactions and problems of the foreign client.

There is one final point of analogy which is important—the relationship of the hologram to time. The hologram represents light waves stopped in an instant of time. Two light waves are frozen and recorded in their interference patterns. In counseling, time is brief and meaning is concentrated and reconstructed in cultural terms. Identifying the counseling session with the model of a hologram permits us to isolate a brief slice of time and yet accept the client as a person existing in the broader landscape of his cultural existence. The analogy suggests a holographic analysis of what happens in the counseling situation reconstructed in relation to other life experiences which clarify the meaning of counseling. The model draws attention to the crucial issue of how the student can be assisted to live and function more effectively out there through the mediation of events in counseling. How does counseling generalize to affect the actions and satisfactions out there? An answer to this question requires the drawing of a link between counseling and the life experience of the cultural client.

The holographic model for intercultural counseling provides a perspective on the relationship between a segment of behavior and other aspects of behavior. It also suggests a criterion for success which is reached when counseling attains holographic meaning. The criterion of success, it must be stressed, is inseparable from the model itself, which introduces criteria for choices in counseling that contrast with other principles of explanation. First, the principle of similarity assumes that each individual is in search of immediate behavioral reinforcements. It is difficult for the counselor to generalize from the counseling situation to the life experiences of the client. There is no link other than that found in similarities. Inasfar as the counseling situation is not the same as other life events, then the two are mutually exclusive and similarities are misleading.

A second principle of explanation is derived from information theory. The central idea is that any item of information about a topic used in communication is meaningfully related to other items from the same domain of total information about that topic. Information selected for communication implies items not selected. Thus a student coming to the counselor has ruled out going to friends or others for assistance at this time when he states that he has made the decision to come. The two kinds of resource persons, selected and not selected, are inextricably linked. An acceptance of the counselor implies a rejection of the friend. The problem with this view in counseling is that all items of information may be related, but some of the alternatives are less meaningful to the student. Any decision assumes the ability to make alternative choices in the abstract. The information on which any given choice is made refers to events or situations that may not be meaningful to the student. This pattern of thinking uses utility as the criterion of choice. It does not allow for the decision-maker with a past, present, and future. The decision between information selected and not selected is not made exclusive of experience, perception, or values of the student. The atomism of simplistic decisions is artificial. It should be noted that the counseling event is connected to other life experiences of the individual in terms of the potential choices which he or she may make. The client's own experiences or history does not necessarily provide the connecting link.

Turning to the holographic explanation, we consider a fusion of abstract ideas and concrete emotions that occur in a field of past, present, and future relationships. Holography illuminates both counseling and outside events in an esthetic relationship rather than a logical or statistical one. The psychology of both counselor and client is approached in terms of layers and embeddedness. In addition, this principle of the hologram allows us to look at the individual's cognitive processes, the relationship between the individual and culture, and the connection between cultural influences and the total environment.

The counselor adopts a fixed illumination to perceive the counseling of foreign students as an intercultural experience. This view of counseling does not apply to all counseling situations, since foreign students may have problems that do not require a cultural intrepretation. Because counselors should not overreact to cultural differences, the model presented is not intended to cover all counseling situations with foreign students, only those in which the coherent light of culture does provide resolving insight to the student and the counselor.

Leaving theory behind, we find that this model of counseling leads to several practical consequences. First, it focuses attention on counseling as an event in the life experiences of the client and compels the counselor to discard the stereotype of foreigners prevalent in American society. The stereotype might otherwise lead Americans to respond in the same way to a Japanese as to an Arab. The counselor should be aware of his own foreignness in the eyes of the client. Cultural perception influences perception of physical features to the extent that all those who are foreign seem to resemble one another.

Secondly, the approach places the various methods and beliefs with respect to counseling in a different perspective. The traditional definition of counseling is discarded and we are able to see where role-playing, esthetics, and simulations could be used together with dialogue between the counselor and the client. The hologram model has been used in part to demonstrate the contributions of these other methods, which sometimes seem merely to enliven counseling techniques, but appear in their therapeutic effect more central and significant than the traditional dialogue or psychometric approach. These approaches, as well as any other innovative technique in counseling, should be carefully evaluated, since both methods and the content of counseling convey cultural assumptions.

In leaving the hologram model, I shall proceed to describe two main effects of using this model in counseling situations. I will first turn to the resistance or interference in the interface between client and counselor and then shall turn to culture.

The emphasis in counseling on the analogy of the hologram and the reference to esthetics leads to a conception of counseling as drama. It is important to stress that the drama is internal; it occurs in the perception, feelings, and emotions of the participants. The relationship between the counselor and the client is transitory and cannot become a permanent aspect of the resolution of the counseling problem. The purpose of the drama is to use counseling to bring about a change in the client. The change and the drama in counseling are internal to the persons involved. For this reason, it will be necessary later on to develop a view of cognitive structures.

NATURAL EMPATHY

The theoretical and the practical clarification of empathy still leaves one question standing, that of how one person, the counselor, can have an understanding of consciousness of another person, the client. Some have claimed for empathy an intuitive primordial existence (Stein, 1964). The idea is not new: Vico (in Bergin & Fisch, 1969) stressed something like it, and many persons today subscribe to "gut feelings," which refers to the acceptance of the outcome of a blind process, similar to empathy, obfuscating objective understanding. A natural explanation of empathy in intercultural counseling is essential, since the counselor cannot use sympathy for an interface and hence cannot freely employ his own emotions to understand the client. To grasp natural empathy, one should understand what happens in the perception of an event.

The layman usually assumes that what one perceives is stored in the brain in the form of a fair replica of what really happened. Inaccuracies intrude and the original perception fades, but the trace retains the features of the original. The brain, in this view, is assumed to be an automatic storing box from which memory may later on be retrieved. Any explanation of how the individual knows or learns from his experience assumes that all stored traces derive, in all of their essential features, from original perceptions. If the original perception has not been stored in all of its essentials, then the automatic storing box has lost traces, and the individual has forgotten. On the other hand, if the individual can act on "understandings," which cannot be associated with stored traces and, in turn, with original perceptions, then the psychologist is confronted with the problem of discovering the source of the understanding. The problem resides with the assumed identity between perceived reality and stored traces—the knowledge, information, and feelings acquired by the individual. The gap between "nonperceived" reality and stored traces is bridged by "empathy," "gut feeling," and extrasensory perception, which, in the latter, reveals in some undisclosed way understandings that cannot be traced to original perceptions.

The model of the brain accepted by many psychologists until recently resembles that conceived by conventional wisdom. Within the subdiscipline of behaviorism, the brain was treated as a master muscle or as a gland. Behaviorists focused on stimuli, the input, and on responses, the output. They paid scant attention to what intervened in between when they described or explained behavior. Mind did not exist. Within the last 10 years, however, this view of the brain has changed drastically; the pressures of internal disagreements in psychology, the development of computers, information theories, and the contributions of linguistics (Segal & Lachman, 1972) have contributed to that change. The intervening stage, called mind, has been reinstated, inasmuch as the previous concept of the brain made no provision to store and transform deep structures of language, organization of information, consolidations in memory, or various other aspects of perception. For these reasons it became necessary to insert mind between stimuli and response and also to suggest a causal system.

The model that is gaining in favor describes the mind as being much more active than was previously believed. Because the brain senses and scans the outside world, Gyr (1972) has described the process of perception as taking place from inside out as well as outside in. A given stimulus that impinges upon the sensory organs is abstracted or modified before it is transmitted to the brain, where the incoming impulses are again modified as they are encoded and stored (Weimer, 1973). A replication of reality, the *eidola* theory of perception held by the Greeks (Boring, 1950), never arrives at the brain, which can only know the ends of its nerve, so to speak. The act of storing in the brain, or memory, establishes a new order of events with its own principles governing that which is stored. This world of mental representation, or subjective space, does not correspond directly to the physical world of objects. One of the startling implications of this idea is that the only thing which an individual can know directly is a mental representation which corresponds to an abstraction rather than to a concrete manifestation in the physical world of objects (Pylyshyn, 1972; Weimer, 1973). Whereas the influences on mental representations from the outside are severely limited by time, those from the inside regulate subjective space in a timeless order.

The world of mental representation, however, is not a static condition, since what is stored does not remain impervious to other cerebral events which take place and which further modify the stored perceptions according to principles largely unknown. At some future time the original perception may be retrieved and brought to conscious awareness, but this process itself distorts what is recognized as being past experience. Memory is dynamic and changing. As in a hologram, something remembered is distributed over wide parts of the mind. Remembering is an active process of reconstruction, one that is holographic in nature, as Pribram (1969) has suggested. Conscious memory seems to match this process of holographic memory. In keeping with the holographic principle, any of many fragments of the experience can serve to reconstitute the entire experience. The same experience probably can never be recovered, however, since the act itself of retrieving and bringing to conscious awareness an original perception distorts what is recognized as a past experience.

This view of the brain and mind involves one additional factor, which again is related to the holographic principle, or, perhaps more accurately, the gestalt principle. It is the consciousness (Sperry, 1969) that assumes a role in the causal sequence of a complete explanation of the cerebral process (Sperry, 1970, p. 588). This view of consciousness, attained from the field of psychobiology, resembles conclusions reached from information-processing models (Shallice, 1972). The data on consciousness have only begun to appear and the issue is far from settled. Whatever the eventual resolution, it is clear that in this complex process there is plenty of room for the past experience of the individual to provide "input" into a raw perception so that, when it is served up, the retrieved outcome perceived as the original event may well reveal features which are novel to the original perception, and we have an instance of understanding which differs markedly from original observations. When the understanding refers to others, we have an example of empathy, and it does not seem to require an intuitive primordial process to explain it. The sources of information and knowledge are quite sufficient to provide the mysterious source of insight so frequently associated with empathy. Our task ahead is to show that the influences from the past and from the immediate present are shaped up at least in part by culture, and that intercultural sensitivity in counseling implies knowing and observing the appropriate cultural forms.

The essential point in the analysis of empathy given in these pages consists of the source of the understanding, which is the experiences and the memory of the person himself. Thus, the understanding is not derived from external sources of stimulation but comes instead from memories and traces of language, images, emotions and from unformulated perceptions in the present. They may be fleeting sensations and experiences which lend their flow to the empathic understanding. It is a knowledge obtained from the inside, constructed by imagination and memory, and it depends on participation to take root. It is a way of knowing, discovered by Giambattista Vico (in Bergin and Fisch, 1969), that assigns to memory, to imagination, and to the immediate apperception of human interaction and communication a modality of knowing radically different from thought formed as induction or deduction (Berlin, 1969).

Empathy leads to understanding of another individual. In an intercultural situation, empathy should generate regressions toward cultural assumptions, values, and patterns of thinking. This kind of understanding through empathy is cultivated by inducing the mind to contribute its past experience for encoding tracings, revealing the assumptions and the categorizations used in encoding and decoding perceptions.

Empathic understanding should be assisted by quick, fleeting perceptions which register stimulation coming in as another's body language and tone of voice, and as smells, touches, etc., which are encoded as symbols and as information close to the perceptual domain. These quick, often peripheral, perceptions come close to revealing the deep structure of thought and of values. The patterns of thought, the use of analogies, the train of thought—all contribute to a latent level of communication which is the basis of empathy. These assumptions and values should be understood in the ways in which they function to guide behavior and not necessarily according to the operational definitions they receive when employed to collect research data. Operational definitions often have little in common with the way in which the "concept" is stored and in which it functions to guide behavior. Apparently there is a natural conflict between firm research parameters and operational categories or stereotypes as applied in psychology, this being evidenced by encoding strategies and personal constructs (Mischel, 1973, pp. 267–268).

If we define empathy as response to the latent level of communication, and then if we accept it as the desired interface in counseling, there follows an important consequence for the use of intercultural communication in counseling. In behavior modification or in sensitivity training, the client examines his or her personal constructs, style of life, and feelings and incurs the risk of surrendering his or her privacy. When counseling is conducted as an intercultural communication, however, the counselor attempts to ascertain and to work with cultural values. The client examines qualities in himself which he shares with an ethnic reference group. He is provided with a safety factor if he personally believes that he has encountered unpleasant or undesirable qualities or aspects of his behavior that he is unprepared to accept as being self-descriptive. He can assign them to qualities of the cultural group to which he belongs without necessarily ascribing to them. The counselor also has a clear task. He should consider the behavior of the client within a cultural context. He is not required to make a choice or even impose a change on the client. Both participants work with cultural factors and are partly spared from making moral or ethical judgments. At least the freedom for choice would seem to be clearer.

CULTURAL REFERENCES IN EMPATHIC UNDERSTANDING

The use of the holograph as the model for the counseling situation implies that the interaction between the counselor and the client is not directly meaningful. It is necessary to establish a cultural reference as a backdrop for the description and the analysis of counseling interculturally. An analysis of culture provides the analogy in counseling to the reference beam in the hologram. The hologram is understandable, is coded in a meaningful manner only in reference to the beam of light with known characteristics. Thus the objectives, motives, action, and, in general, the dimensions of the problem of the client should be perceived as particular manifestations of cultural predispositions. Attention given to cultural dimensions acts as reference lights to the counseling situation and provides a personal understanding of the client. Interpreting the counseling event means transforming an abstract (etic) into a specific (emic) analysis.

A successful counseling session implies that the client has attained meaning at three different levels: abstract, from reference to culture; general, from the interaction with the counselor; and personal, from the internalized personal constructs and strategies of encoding that provide the particularized meaning of the counseling (Lounsbury, 1955). Thus the etic analysis is followed by an emic one, which eventually yields to a personal analysis, but developed in cultural terms, with all three levels fused as in a hologram.

The analysis of culture yields abstractions of code, patterns of thinking, emotions, values, motivation, roles and events—but these concepts are not readily tied to the personal constructs of clients. The success of counseling depends on how the results are encoded or represented in the perceptions of the client. The problem is how to express results of counseling with the imagery, verbal representations, and acts that will guide and govern desired actions. This is a problem which has not received very much empirical attention. To put the problem squarely as a question: If the counselor and the client establish that it is desirable for the client to pursue a course of action, how is the result to be represented to the client? As procedures and schedules? As purposes and utilities? As visual images? Kinesthetics, as associations with the time and place of action? How is the action represented—encoded in the client's thoughts, emotions, and values?

There is a need to examine the methods used to impart information, knowledge, and attitudes so that encoded knowledge should accurately guide and govern behavior. The analysis of culture yields abstract concepts which do not readily engage the personal constructs of Americans. The concepts of culture and cultural differences are, for this reason, frequently conveyed in the context of human relations training. The patterns of interaction provide experiences that can be used to define the nature of cultural differences. The combination of culture and human relations training is not always successful, since human relations training tends to assume a goal of sympathy, i.e., similarity, whereas in the area of intercultural situations, empathy should be the preferred interface.

There are other methods such as simulations and exercises, that can be employed successfully to convey cultural predispositions. Implications must be drawn from analyses of similarities and of differences. Those differences that are important for communication and those that are not must be identified. Although there are many intuitive studies and analyses, at this time neither theory nor field experience yields conclusive answers. Similarity and the self-concept were advanced as being important for Americans, but the counselor must exercise personal choices until research illuminates the field of cultural differences and reveals the differences and similarities that are most important for a given client and the counselor.

Identification of meaningful cultural differences in counseling implies that the differences affect the client or the counseling situation. Working with the differences requires that they be perceived as relevant by the client, that they be grasped intellectually and accepted emotionally.

Finally the client should derive benefit from counseling that will lead him to guide his own actions according to the insights obtained in counseling. One measure of success can be attained by drawing concrete examples to the attention of the client. These examples can be related to a single principle which the client, in turn, can use as a guide to behavior under different situations.

SUMMARY

There are increased pressures in intercultural counseling to consider the client as a person and to perceive him as the sum total of his or her experiences. The counseling context should be expanded to include an awareness by the counselor of both the client's past and future; it should be treated as an intercultural event embedded in the total life and cultural experiences of the client.

The literature on counseling usually assumes that the interface between the client and the counselor should generate empathy, which reposes on similarities between the two concerned individuals. Because intercultural counseling assumes cultural differences, empathy might not be an effective interface.

The apparent necessity of similarity to undergird the process of empathy in counseling may be associated with conformity in American life, this conformity having been observed by Europeans and persons from other cultures. Recent research in the diffusion of innovations, in perception, and in patterns of thinking has begun to distinguish between similarities and differences in psychological and social processes. It is in the field of attraction theory—how people make social comparisons—that recent research has begun to disclose the complex relations between similarity, uniqueness, and the self-concept. An individual needs to be different and unique, as well as similar to others. The unique attribute is associated with differences and with empathy, similarity with sympathy.

The empathy interface was described. Practical examples were offered of empathy and sympathy. Intercultural counseling can be analyzed as possessing the qualities of a hologram. Each counseling event can reconstruct and symbolize the life pattern of the client. Nevertheless, these overlapping counseling and life events do not necessarily resemble one another. It is necessary to analyze counseling with a cultural perspective to reconstruct the meaning of the counseling event for the client as applied to his experience.

The holographic analysis of counseling draws attention to the limits of the principle of similarity as the basis for establishing an interaction between the counselor and the client and to the need for empathy based on differences. The holographic model can provide a way of conceptualizing intercultural counseling according to intercultural relationships. An analysis of culture provides the analogy in counseling to the reference beam in the hologram.

The two interfaces, sympathy and empathy, are considered to be extensions of the self-concept and, to explore the hold of similarity in American culture, a view of the American self-concept is presented. The emphasis on conformity has been seen as an American characteristic by Europeans and by persons from other cultures. Apparently this emphasis has contributed to the shift in the meaning of empathy.

Some have argued that empathy has an intuitive primordial existence, but this view has been derived from problematical analyses of the processes of perception and recall. Empathic understanding requires a sensitivity to experience, personal constructs, and cultural predispositions for an encoded trace to be retrieved. Empathy involves a response to these factors which constitute latent levels of meaning. In the intercultural counseling situation, the interface of empathy relieves both counselor and client from making moral judgments and from evaluating the other's point of view.

There are no firm guides to enable one to formulate concepts of differences or similarities that are important in intercultural counseling. Cultural variations of the self-concept and of similarity are two likely factors that influence intercultural communication. Insights attained through the process of empathy may be conceptualized within a cultural frame.

REFERENCES

Allport, G. W. The historical background of modern social psychology. In G. Lindzey & E. Aronson (Eds.), *The handbook of social psychology* (Vol. 1). Reading, Massachusetts: Addison-Wesley Publishing Co., 1968.

Beauvoir, S. de. Adieu to America. In M. McGiffert (Ed.), *The character of Americans*. Homewood, Illinois: Dorsey Press, 1964.

Bergin, T. G., & Fisch, M. H. *The new science of Giambattista Vico* (Rev. translation of 3rd ed.). Ithaca: Cornell University Press, 1969.

Berlin, I. A note on Vico's concept of knowledge. *The New York Review of Books*, April 24, 1969, pp. 23–26.

Bindra, D., Williams, J. A., & Wise, J. S. Judgments of sameness and difference: Experiments on decision time. *Science*, 1965, *150*, 1625–1627.

Boorstin, D. J. *The Americans*, Vol. 1, *The colonial experience*. New York: Random House, Vintage Books, 1958.

Boring, E. G. *A history of experimental psychology*. New York: Appleton-Century-Crofts, 1950.

Byrne, D. The ubiquitous relationship: Attitude similarity and attraction. *Human Relations*, 1973, *24*, 201–207.

Byrne, D., & Griffitt, W. Interpersonal attraction. In P. H. Mussen & M. R. Rosenzweig (Eds.), *Annual Review of Psychology*, 1973, *24*, 317–336.

Cole, M., Gay, J., Glick, J. A., & Sharp, D. W. *Cultural context of learning and thinking: An exploration in experimental anthropology*. New York: Basic Books, 1971.

Dodd, C. H. *Homophily and heterophily in diffusion of innovations: A cross-cultural analysis in an African setting*. Paper presented at the Speech Communication Association convention, New York, November 1973.

Epstein, S. The self-concept revisited: Or a theory of a theory. *American Psychologist*, 1973, *28*, 404–416.

Fromkin, H. L. *The psychology of uniqueness: Avoidance of similarity and seeking of differentness* (Paper No. 438). West Lafayette, Indiana: Institute for Research in the Behavioral, Economic and Management Sciences, Krannert Graduate School of Industrial Administration, Purdue University, 1973.

Gyr, J. W. Is a theory of direct visual perception adequate? *Psychological Bulletin*, 1972, *77*, 246–261.

Hampshire, S. Morality and pessimism. *New York Review of Books*, January 25, 1973, pp. 26–33.

Leith, E. N., & Upatnieks, J. Photography by laser. *Scientific American*, 1965, *212*, 24–35.

Lieberman, B. Combining individual preferences into a social choice. In I. R. Buchler & H. G. Nuttini (Eds.), *Game theory in the behavioral sciences*. Pittsburgh: University of Pittsburgh Press, 1969.

Lipps, T. Einfühlung, innere Nachahmung und Organempfindungen. *Archiv für die Gesamte Psychologie*, 1903, 20, 185–204.

Lounsbury, F. G. The varieties of meaning. *Georgetown University Monograph Series on Languages and Linguistics*, 1955, *8*, 158–164.

McClelland, D. C., Sturr, J. F., Knapp, R. H., & Wendt, H. W. Obligation to self and society in the United States and Germany. *Journal of Abnormal and Social Psychology*, 1958, *56*, 245–255.

McIntosh, D. *The foundations of society*. Chicago: University of Chicago Press, 1969.

Mead, M. We are all third generation. In M. McGiffert (Ed.), *The character of Americans*. Homewood, Illinois: Dorsey Press, 1964.

Metee, D. R., & Riskind, J. *When ability dissimilarity is a blessing: Liking for others who defeat us decisively*. Paper presented at the American Psychological Association convention, Montreal, September 1973.

Mischel, W. Reconceptualization of personality. *Psychological Review*, 1973, *80*, 252–283.

Pribram, K. H. The neurophysiology of remembering. *Scientific American*, 1969, *220*, 73–86.

Pylyshyn, Z. Competence and psychological reality. *American Psychologist*, 1972, *27*, 546–552.

Rogers, C. Toward a modern approach to values. *Journal of Abnormal and Social Psychology*, 1964, *68* (2), 160–167.

Rogers, E., & Shoemaker, F. F. *Communication and innovation*. New York: Macmillan Co., Free Press, 1971.

Segal, E. M., & Lachman, R. Complex behavior or higher mental process: Is there a paradigm shift? *American Psychologist*, 1972, *27*, 46–55.

Shallice, T. Dual function of consciousness. *Psychological Review*, 1972, *79*, 383–393.

Sperry, R. W. A modified concept of consciousness. *Psychological Review*, 1969, *76*, 532–536.

Sperry, R. W. An objective approach to subjective experience: Further explanation of a hypothesis. *Psychological Review*, 1970, *77*, 585–590.

Stein, E. *On the problem of empathy*. The Hague: Martinus Nijhoff, 1964.

Stewart, E. C. *The self: Quantum of American culture*. Paper presented at the American Psychological Association convention, Washington, D.C., 1971. (a)

Stewart, E. C. *American cultural patterns: A cross-cultural perspective.* Pittsburgh: Regional
    Council for International Understanding, 1971. (b)
Tarde, G. *The laws of imitation.* Gloucester, Massachusetts: Peter Smith, 1903.
Titchener, E. B. *Experimental psychology of the thought processes.* New York: Macmillan
    Co., 1909.
Tocqueville, A. de. *Democracy in America.* New York: Random House, 1945.
Tversky, A. Additivity, utility and subjective probability. *Journal of Mathematical Psycholo-
    gy,* 1967, *4,* 175–202.
Weimer, W. B. Psycholinguistics and Plato's paradoxes of the *Meno. American Psychologist,*
    1973, *28,* 15–33.
Williams, R. M., Jr. *American society* (3rd ed.) New York: Random House, Alfred A.
    Knopf, 1970.
Wispé, L. G. Sympathy and empathy. *International Encyclopedia of the Social Sciences*
    (Vol. 15). New York: Macmillan Co., Free Press, 1968.

7 The Use of Social Learning Theory in Preventing Intercultural Adjustment Problems

KENNETH H. DAVID

CAN INTERCULTURAL COUNSELORS ASSIST CLIENTS TO ADJUST TO OTHER CULTURES?

Problems of intercultural adjustment may be viewed as a consequence of the punishment encountered in the host culture. Punishment may occur as a result of the removal of a reinforcer or the presentation of an aversive stimulus. In attempting to prevent intercultural problems, the sojourner should learn the stimulus cues of the host culture that are instrumental in attaining reinforcers and in avoiding punishers. To prevent the removal of reinforcers when traveling to another culture, the sojourner should attempt to transfer those reinforcers that approximately fit the host culture and to develop new reinforcers that are congruent with the social structure of the host culture.

To avoid aversive stimuli in the host culture, the sojourner should learn how to avoid or neutralize aversive stimuli. For some situations the sojourner may be able to change host culture events that are initially aversive to ones that are reinforcing. The sojourner may learn to avoid many of the punishing events in the host culture by modeling his behavior after those persons from his own culture who have adjusted well to the host culture. The simulation of host culture conditions may help to identify many of the punishers that a sojourner will encounter. The use of desensitization by counterconditioning procedures may be particularly effective in decreasing the potency of aversive stimuli in the host culture.

David's article breaks down the problems of intercultural adjustment into their components, with some parts having a reinforcing and some a punishing effect. He looks at clients from other cultures, identifying significant aspects both of the host and the back-home cultures. Like Stewart's chapter, this chapter provides another conceptual framework for looking at counseling communications in an international context. It also provides practical suggestions and recommendations that a counselor can use when working with clients in multicultural environments.

Not only does it describe a way of looking at intercultural adjustment, it identifies specific ways that a counselor can apply the models of social learning theory to facilitate the client's intercultural adjustment.

This chapter attempts to explain how social learning theory can be used by intercultural counselors to assist in the prevention and alleviation of intercultural problems of adjustment (see also David, 1973). A major supposition of the approach to be described, which is based in part on the principles espoused by Bandura (1969), is that problems of intercultural adjustment are a consequence of punishing events. A punishing event, as defined within the context of this chapter, refers to (a) the removal of a reinforcing event or (b) the presentation of an aversive event.

A person who intends to live temporarily in another culture (referred to as a sojourner in this paper) can prepare himself, prior to his sojourn, for a more effective adjustment. Further, according to David and King (1973), similar preparations should be appropriate to assist the immigrant to adjust to his adopted country. Such preparation should consist of arranging systematically to prevent certain punishing events from occurring in the host culture. Also, after the sojourner's arrival in the host culture, potentially punishing experiences should be modified or removed, which should result in a concomitant increase in his adjustment. A similar approach should be used to prevent or eliminate punishing events upon the sojourner's return home (the occurrence of serious problems of adjustment at this time are sometimes termed the "reentry crisis"). The counselor should provide the sojourner with much of the information and direction that are crucial for the prevention of punishing events. A requirement for the intercultural counselor, regardless of his theoretical approach, should be some degree of familiarity with the differences and similarities between the sojourner's home and host cultures. In the terminology of the social learning approach, the counselor should be knowledgeable about the commonly occurring reinforcing and punishing events that sojourners tend to experience when in the host culture.

The intercultural counselor should attempt to match the existing set of reinforcing and punishing events of the individual sojourner to the situational context of the host culture. The sojourner may need assistance in adjusting to the host culture because of his or her difficulty in preventing many punishing events from occurring. These events may result from insufficient information about the situational context within which he or she will be living and/or from the new culture's presenting punishing events that the sojourner rarely or never encountered before. For instance, would an American sojourner know, prior to his trip, that children in Korea are apt to greet him by yelling "Hello"? Further, would he know whether such a greeting is friendly or hostile? Peace Corps volunteers in Korea have reported this ostensibly friendly greeting to be quite irritating (an aversive event), especially as it continues for months, without always being able to identify the source of that irritation. Or would the sojourner know that many situations will intrude upon his "privacy" (for example, it is uncommon for men and women to have separate toilet facilities) and whether or not these events will act as punishers? Consequently, we might expect the typical sojourner to be unaware of, and unprepared for, many of the events that he will find reinforcing and punishing in the host culture. On the other hand, the intercultural counselor could be in a better position to relate the experiences of previous sojourners to a theoretical framework and to employ methods of predeparture orientation in a systematic manner, thereby assisting the sojourner in being more effective and in having an enjoyable sojourn.

Verbal and nonverbal cues in the host culture are the means by which a sojourner learns how to avoid punishment and how to receive reinforcement. Such cues, although not discussed in this paper, must be learned if one is to adjust satisfactorily to another culture (see Brein & David, 1971, for a review of intercultural adjustment from the perspective of intercultural communication). Consistent with the social learning approach, learning the cues that indicate approval and disapproval in the host culture would seem to be essential for the sojourner's effective adjustment (for example, raising one's eyebrows in Tonga indicates agreement—a necessary cue to learn).

Reinforcing Events

The removal of reinforcing events is a basic contributing factor to the adjustment difficulties of sojourners. After living in the host culture for a few weeks, the sojourner may feel "homesick" and long for and day-dream about the ordinary and everyday reinforcing events that were taken for granted at home (American sojourners, for example, may long for ice cream, hot showers, and the *New York Times*). The most serious problems of intercultural adjustment usually seem to occur during the sojourner's first year of living in the host culture (see Brein & David, 1971, for a review of the sojourner's adjustment problems). The removal of reinforcing events may account for such defensive behaviors as increased sleeping, decreased social contact with the host culture, and self-deprecation resulting in depression.

It is likely that it is not the loss of the entire home culture that is upsetting to a sojourner but rather the removal of a select few reinforcing events. These "potent reinforcers" would be the primary source of satisfaction for a particular individual. If a counselor could identify a handful of these potent reinforcers for a particular sojourner, he or she might then be able to assist the client in making a satisfactory and effective intercultural adjustment.

The identification of potent reinforcers may be a difficult task because a reinforcer may be taken for granted; full awareness of the satisfaction received from a reinforcing event may occur only after the event has been removed. For instance, many Peace Corps volunteers in Korea learned, after the removal of everyday ordinary events taken for granted in the United States, that these events had been sources of satisfaction to them. Among the missed activities were eating American food, discussing intellectual topics, watching television, watching American motion pictures, and playing baseball. More complex sources of satisfaction would be working at a meaningful job, feeling that something worthwhile is being accomplished, having common beliefs about privacy and private property, a social agreement about the amount and type of physical and social contact that is acceptable, and the capability of expression by means of language without tripping over the culture. Once the potent reinforcers for an individual sojourner have been identified, procedures may then be taken to prevent their removal.

Transfer of Reinforcing Events

How to prevent the removal of a reinforcer essentially becomes a question of how to transfer a reinforcing event from the home to the host culture. Because reinforcers are situational in nature—"events" rather than entities—the problem is one of how to transfer the essential elements of the reinforcing event to a new cultural setting. For example, a fairly simplistic example could be when "tennis playing" may be a potent reinforcer to a person, but only when played with friends and during the evening. If such a person should sojourn to another culture, he or she may derive no satisfaction from playing tennis with strangers in the heat of the day (only one of the three essential elements would have been transferred and it may no longer be a reinforcing event). However, if the person were able to play tennis with friends in the heat of the day, he or she may derive some satisfaction (two of the three essential elements would have been transferred). Or, again, if he or she could play tennis during the evening with strangers, there may also be a partial source of satisfaction (again, two of the three essential elements would have been transferred).

A more difficult example would occur when a more abstract reinforcer is separated into its essential elements. For instance, a "meaningful job" may actually refer to helping ill children under the direction of an approving supervisor. Without both of these elements being present, the worker would derive practically no satisfaction from the job.

It seems reasonable to expect that a systematic approach to the transfer of reinforcers would be quite helpful if intercultural problems are to be prevented. The preliminary planning and preparation of any sojourner is the same, in many respects, to what is being proposed in counseling. The traveler attempts to make his trip more enjoyable and to avoid hardships by making reservations in advance, by carrying traveler's checks, and by taking sufficient money. Viewing them as positive reinforcements, the sojourner should arrange for the continuance of potent reinforcing events in the host culture, especially during his or her first few months in a foreign culture. For instance, the person who enjoys playing tennis should take along his tennis equipment; and the person who is an avid reader of science fiction should ensure an ample supply of reading materials. These simple aspects of back-home routine might serve as an integrating function in the unfamiliar host environment.

To plan and prepare for the transfer of reinforcing events, one must first identify these events. Once they have been identified, the sojourner should determine the likelihood of being able to transfer these reinforcers to the host culture. The tennis player intending to live in an area with neither tennis courts nor tennis players would probably be denied this source of satisfaction, except for what might be gained vicariously through reading, discussing, thinking, and writing. And the reader of science fiction should determine in advance whether science fiction materials will be accessible and whether the opportunity to read them will be available. Living in a rural area may preclude the easy accessibility to reading materials, and social and occupational obligations may allow little time for reading. It is because these routinized details of our everyday life are taken for granted that we are likely to overlook their importance in making us feel "at home."

To determine the likelihood that a reinforcing event can be transferred to the host culture, the individual should consult previous sojourners, who may be valuable sources of information. For example, if other sojourners who had enjoyed playing tennis at home did not play tennis in the host culture, it would seem that conditions in the new culture would seem to mitigate against the transfer of this reinforcer. Conversely, if many former sojourners have played tennis in the host culture, the probability of transferring this reinforcer would seem to be increased.

Although it is desirable to plan for the adaptation of potent reinforcers to the host culture, the fact remains that the typical sojourner appears to do relatively little systematic planning for transferring them. (In fact, during Peace Corps training projects, trainees have stated that prior learning about the host culture would detract them from the enjoyable experience of learning something new!) Consequently, the typical sojourner is apt to find himself in the host culture with his potent reinforcing events removed, because he failed to make adequate preparations for their transfer. However, the identification of a potent reinforcing event is an easier task after the sojourner has arrived in the host culture. It is then that the sojourner can describe many of the events which have been removed and which no longer can be enjoyed. When this happens, steps may then be taken to transfer the missing reinforcing events. The tennis player, for example, may have his tennis racquet sent from home. The sojourner who enjoyed reading the *New York Times* may subscribe to it. The science fiction reader may have a friend send along several books on science fiction. Unfortunately, after potent reinforcing events have been removed, the sojourner may fail to begin transferring potent reinforcing events (for example, a depressed person may refuse to do anything that would actively improve his adjustment). Consequently, the sojourner should try to arrange for the transfer of reinforcers before he or she leaves home and make any necessary modifications after arrival in the host culture.

The state of Hawaii provides an excellent example of how various immigrant groups have transferred reinforcing events from their culture and, in the process, have influenced and modified the host culture. For instance, many available activities in Hawaii provide reinforcements primarily for the Japanese immigrant population and, to a lesser degree, for the Japanese-Americans of the second, third, and fourth generations. Such reinforcements include a Japanese-language television station which is devoted almost exclusively to Japanese programs, several Japanese-language radio stations, several motion-picture theatres that show only Japanese films, Japanese-style restaurants, and a Japanese-language newspaper. Some of the other immigrant groups that have changed Hawaii by transferring their reinforcing events to the host culture include the Chinese, Filipinos, Portuguese, Koreans, and Samoans.

Developing New Reinforcing Events

For the sojourner who is unable to transfer any of his potent reinforcing events to the host culture, it would be crucial that he develop a set of new reinforcing events which would be compatible with the host culture. Rather than waiting until arrival in the host culture before developing these new reinforcers, he or she should begin their initial development while still at home.

There are several guidelines for choosing new reinforcing events. First, an understanding of the host culture will help to provide some information about what types of events may be available as reinforcers. Second, those events that are to be developed into reinforcers should be compatible with the host culture and should not be events that will result in the hosts' labeling the sojourner as eccentric, stupid, or worse. Some American sojourners have found that the use of drugs (a potent reinforcing event for many persons) in other countries has resulted in severe punishment such as imprisonment without "due process" that would not have occurred in the United States. Third, the sojourner should consider events that have previously appealed to him, even though these events have never been potent reinforcers. In fact, some sojourners seem to go to another culture with the intent of developing a potent reinforcing event from one that in the past had been little more than a fleeting thought. The sojourner who has prior knowledge about the host culture may be able to develop reinforcing events that coincide with some of these long-term and budding desires. For instance, the American who has occasionally thought that she would like to learn Korean dancing might develop this activity into a potent reinforcer before sojourning to Korea. Associated activities, such as practicing, reading, observing, discussing, and thinking about Korean dancing, could all contribute to the development of a potent reinforcer. Or the person who has thought occasionally about learning a system of self-defense might learn the Korean method of self-defense, Tae Kwon Do, into a potent reinforcer before moving to Korea. Upon the sojourner's arrival in Korea, an important source of satisfaction for maintaining the sojourner's adjustment would already have been established.

Sojourners often seem to allow the development of new reinforcements to be dictated by seemingly uncontrollable circumstances in the host culture; that is, what develops as new reinforcing events appears to be determined primarily by the situational context of the host culture (in conjunction with the prior learning of the sojourner) in which the sojourner is living.

Upon returning home, the sojourner may experience what is sometimes termed a "reentry crisis." From a reinforcement approach, the reentry crisis may be viewed as resulting from the loss of the reinforcing events developed by the sojourner in the host culture. For instance, the woman who receives satisfaction from Korean dancing may find that the essential elements of this event cannot be transferred to her home country. In other cases, the newly developed reinforcements may actually be punished when the sojourner returns to his home culture. For example, a male Peace Corps volunteer in Korea may derive satisfaction from the physical contact between male friends, which would be approved of in Korea, but the same behavior might be labeled as perverse in his own country. The sojourner may also receive a great deal of attention in the host culture and, in a sense, become a celebrity. The Peace Corps volunteer may enjoy a role in another culture that provides social influence and responsibilities far beyond what he or she could expect in the United States. Not surprisingly, such sojourners sometimes seem to undergo a reentry crisis that results from the removal of these potent reinforcers that were developed in the host culture.

The remedy for the reentry crisis is similar to that for the culture-shock experience. Upon returning home, the sojourner should attempt to transfer potent reinforcing events, to reestablish some of the reinforcing events used prior to the sojourn, or else develop a set of new reinforcing events. The sojourner who returns home may then become aware of the amount of satisfaction he received from potent reinforcing events in the host country. He may then become homesick for the host culture, question the values of his home culture, and wonder why he ever returned home. In fact, a sizable number of Peace Corps volunteers and other sojourners have returned to their host cultures on a more or less permanent basis.

AVERSIVE EVENTS

An aversive event, as the term is used in this paper, refers to a noxious stimulus that is experienced as pain or discomfort. Some aversive events, such a those that produce physical injuries, have a strong sensory component in which the role of learning is minimal; others are primarily dependent on past learning experiences, as when an individual suffers an experience that causes him or her to fear crowds. Aversive events may result in fear responses in anticipation of the painful event itself. It seems likely that the sojourner may develop in the host culture a generalized level of anticipatory fear, because of the seemingly unpredictable nature of the aversive events that may be encountered. Also, because the sojourner will inevitably make numerous intercultural mistakes and will in all probability have many painful experiences, and because he lacks control over the antecedent conditions of the aversive events, he may suffer—or be prone to suffer—a severe culture shock experience.

The identification of aversive events is the initial step for preventing their occurrence in the host culture. A simple procedure would be to develop a frequency list of aversive events that previous sojourners have experienced. (Lonner, in chapter 9, refers to the Michigan International Student Problem Inventory, which is a checklist, derived from interviews with foreign students in the United States, of potential problems.) For example, a list could be developed for Americans who have sojourned to Korea; another list, for Koreans who have sojourned to the United States. Such a list would help to identify, by the sojourner's home culture, those events most likely to be experienced as aversive in the host culture. Further refinement of the list would consist of looking at such variables as sex—

types and frequency of aversive events between the sexes; age—elderly versus youths; economic positions; and so on. Similar information has been provided by questionnaires aimed at Peace Corps volunteers living in various countries; one such is the Overseas Volunteer Questionnaire developed by Jones (Jones & Popper, 1972).

The sojourner frequently has difficulty in identifying aversive events prior to his trip, not only because he is usually unaware of what events he will encounter in the host culture, but also because he is not very accurate in predicting whether an event will be reinforcing, punishing, or neutral. One method to improve the identification of aversive events would be to simulate in a systematic manner some of the more commonly found aversive events of the host culture. All of the essential elements of the potential aversive event should be included in the simulation, so that the person would respond as if he were actually in the host culture. A somewhat similar procedure consists of having the person visualize the most frequently occurring aversive events in the host culture and then reporting on the degree of aversiveness of such events. Measures of physiological responses during the simulation or imagery may provide additional information about the intensity of the aversive event.

Another approach consists of the development of a questionnaire to measure aversive events (Wolpe & Lang, 1964) in an intercultural setting. Cautela (1972) reported that he has been developing an Aversive Survey Schedule, which would be similar to the Reinforcement Survey Schedule developed by Cautela and Kastenbaum (1967). When presented before the sojourn, an intercultural questionnaire can help to identify those events that are presently aversive to a sojourner and can indicate which events would be aversive in the host culture. If presented after the sojourner arrived in the host culture, more accurate responses would probably be given to the questionnaire items. However, regardless of when the survey is to be presented, it is necessary that all of the essential elements in the description on the event be included. This could prove to be a rather difficult task in view of the complexities involved in validating tests across cultures. David and Uhes (1972) have noted some of the other difficulties in developing a comprehensive survey to determine reinforcing or aversive events.

Avoiding Aversive Events

Many of the aversive events that may be encountered by a sojourner can and should be avoided. As I mentioned previously, information from prior sojourners about the more commonly occurring aversive events can help to identify which events may be noxious and thereby indicate which events should be avoided. In fact, as any seasoned traveler knows, pretrip preparations can prevent many later hardships. The intensive predeparture training that has been required of Peace Corps trainees has taught many volunteers how to avoid some of the aversive events in the host culture. Nevertheless, aside from the intercultural training programs of the Peace Corps, there is much that a sojourner can do by himself to avoid aversive events. Guide books written for the tourist can provide information about the more common (albeit potent) aversive events likely to be encountered in the host culture, and they usually discuss how approval and disapproval are expressed by the hosts. (For instance, in Korea, the passing of objects to another person with one's left hand is sometimes considered to be an insult—indeed, an aversive event for the Korean recipient.)

Some aversive events in the host culture are actually tangible objects, in which case the sojourner should ensure that the object is removed. For instance, American sojourners to Korea may encounter the aversive event of sleeping on a thin Korean mattress—an event easily avoided by taking along a thin foam mattress. It would be advisable to consider, however, how the hosts would respond to one's bringing along one's own mattress. If such an act might be offensive to the hosts, the sojourner should develop other means of reducing this source of discomfort.

Other aversive events encountered by some American sojourners to Korea have been intestinal illnesses, having to sit cross-legged on the floor when eating, riding the trains, being requested to give English language lessons, walking down crowded streets, and being asked personal questions such as "Why aren't you married?" The likelihood of remaining healthy is increased by avoiding nonboiled water and uncooked food. Such avoidance behaviors, although seemingly simple, may be quite difficult to perform, because at times the social situation may call for the sojourner to drink nonboiled liquids and to eat uncooked food. More subtle methods of avoiding the potentially aversive events can be employed at these times, without offending one's host, if the refusal is conducted in a culturally acceptable manner. For example, for an American simply to refuse to eat uncooked vegetables by saying "No, thank you" would probably be considered rude by the hosts. However, to refuse uncooked food because of "My doctor's orders" would most likely be acceptable. More complex aversive events would include poor communication with Koreans, being "laughed at," and observing various aspects of a "poverty culture." Commonly reported aversive events related to a Peace Corps volunteer's job have been language difficulties, meaningless work, ambiguous job responsibilities, and uncooperative government agencies.

To maintain his effective adjustment to the host culture, the sojourner should minimize the number of aversive events that he creates for his hosts. The sojourner will inevitably, although unintentionally, produce some aversive events for his hosts because of cultural differences in the meaning of cues. However, the sojourner who prepares for a culture should learn how to avoid at least some of the more common aversive events that persons from his home country create in the host culture. In Korea, to prevent offending his hosts, the sojourner should avoid such acts as passing objects to others with one's left hand, using one hand when passing objects to one's elder or superior, failing to bow (especially to one's elders), smoking in sight of one's elders, smoking in public if a woman, wearing shoulder-length hair if a man, wearing a beard if a young man, displaying affection between the sexes in public, wearing sport clothes when working in an office, and responding "No" or "I don't know" to questions. Failure to avoid such acts and many others as well may result in a number of derogatory labels being attached to the sojourner. And, as Mischel noted, negative labels tend to be formed early and to be relatively long-lasting (Mischel, 1968).

Neutralizing Aversive Events

Many times it is possible to neutralize the aversiveness of events that cannot be avoided in the host culture. Such neutralization can occur either prior to the sojourner's departure or after his arrival in the host culture. Prior neutralization would be preferable, however, especially for the more extreme aversive events.

It may not be possible to neutralize some aversive events, although partial neutralization may still be attained. With partial neutralization, the event would decrease in the degree of its aversiveness. Examples of aversive events that some Peace Corps volunteers in Korea have neutralized are eating kimchee and other Korean foods, sleeping on a thin Korean mattress, sleeping on wooden pillows, being bumped into on the street, slurping soup, and shopping in the marketplace. Various other situations have also been neutralized, including such complicated problem areas as one's role in a Korean family, one's role at work, and the conditions under which one should be candid, be on time for an appointment, or make physical contact with another person. The neutralization of an aversive event has been successfully completed when the event is no longer noxious to the sojourner.

The intercultural counselor can assist the sojourner to neutralize aversive events. The experienced intercultural counselor would know which events tend to be aversive in the host culture, which of these events are actually aversive to the counseled sojourner, and which events have been neutralized by other sojourners and how. When working within this type of social learning framework, the counselor should find extremely valuable his knowledge about the differences and similarities between the sojourner's home and host cultures.

In some instances the neutralization of aversive events results in the development of a reinforcing event; that is, the same event is changed from eliciting discomfort to eliciting satisfaction. For instance, preferences for food seem to be amenable to change. One Peace Corps training project in which I was involved provided a breakfast of kimchee and Korean soup (an aversive event for many trainees, but not sufficiently aversive to prevent them from eating breakfast), which in the course of 3 months became a reinforcing event for many of the trainees. The development of a new reinforcing event which was congruent with the expectations of the hosts (eating kimchee and soup for breakfast), along with the elimination of the aversiveness of the same event, was expected to contribute to the future adjustment of the volunteers.

Peace Corps volunteers in Korea have reported other aversive events that have been changed into reinforcing events. For instance, the experience resulting from physical contact between friends has changed from displeasure to pleasure, speaking Korean has changed from a begrudging effort to an enjoyable activity, and interacting with Koreans has changed from a fearful encounter to a delightful occurrence.

Some of the aversive events encountered by the Japanese tourist visiting Hawaii have been identified in recent newspaper articles (Cunningham, 1972; Kaser, 1973). Such events include bills that are 4 percent more than the quoted price because of an additional state tax; tipping for services; the sourness of fresh pineapple; the use of Western-style toilets, which require bodily contact; and lack of individual attention from retail store clerks. The identification of such events can also provide valuable insights into both the Japanese and American cultures.

METHODS FOR IMPROVING INTERCULTURAL ADJUSTMENT

There are numerous methods that have potential usefulness for preventing and alleviating intercultural difficulties (Wight & Hammons, 1970). For example, simply learning about the host culture from written materials, especially from papers that describe the experiences of previous sojourners, may aid the sojourner's adjustment to the host culture. Another method might be to talk with persons, both sojourners and host nationals, who have lived in the host culture. A more systematic approach would be to read a programmed instructional unit, if available, such as the Culture Assimilator described by Fiedler, Mitchell, and Triandis (1971).

Three methods which the intercultural counselor could use when working with intercultural problems are simulation of host culture situations, modeling of host culture behaviors, and desensitization by counterconditioning. These methods are sometimes associated with social learning theory, although they can also be used by counselors with other theoretical approaches.

Within the framework proposed in this chapter, the methods of simulation, modeling, and desensitization could be used to prevent the sojourner from encountering punishment in the host culture; that is, the methods could be used to prevent the removal of reinforcing events and to avoid or neutralize aversive events.

Simulation of Host Culture Situations

The simulation of host culture conditions can be used effectively for identifying aversive events. A series of simulated events, based on commonly experienced aversive events by sojourners in the host culture, could be presented to an individual sojourner to determine which of those events are actually aversive. The potentially aversive events would be based on the experiences of previous sojourners in the host culture, ensuring that the essential elements of common aversive events would be built into the simulated situation. The sojourner would experience each simulated situation, perhaps by role-playing, so that he could determine whether or not the event is aversive. If the simulation exercise were to occur prior to a sojourn, many aversive events could be identified and then avoided in the host culture.

Modeling of Host Culture Behaviors

Prior to a sojourner's departure, he or she should model host behaviors during the simulation of host culture situations. During this time the sojourner can learn how to avoid punishment and how to receive reinforcement by imitating the adjustment behaviors of appropriate models. Role-playing by the sojourner and the models is the procedure by which simulation commonly occurs in intercultural training projects. However, the behavior modeling can also occur as a result of observing films, video tapes, sound recordings, slides, and photographs of host culture situations. Such techniques would seem to be appropriate with either individuals or groups.

Perhaps the best models for the sojourner to imitate are those persons who have successfully adjusted to the host culture. The Peace Corps typically hires returned volunteers to work on training projects as technical instructors (teaching, for example, how to teach English in the host culture) and as intercultural instructors (providing information about the host culture from the perspective of a volunteer). Rather incidentally, the returned volunteer also may provide appropriate models for the trainees to observe and imitate. During his stay in the host country, the sojourner can observe and imitate the *in situ* behaviors of the effective sojourner.

Many Peace Corps training projects have called upon host nationals to teach the host language and to serve as models for the trainees. Sometimes less "modernized" host models have been sought so that their behaviors would more closely match the traditional behaviors of the host culture.

Many simple, but nevertheless important, acts can be learned from host models, such as the proper way to use chopsticks, the manner of signifying "yes," how to hail a taxi, how to buy a motion picture ticket, how to pay for a bus ticket, whether to tip a taxi driver, how much space to maintain between persons, the types of physical contact allowed, how to beckon someone, and many others. (Complex acts can also be learned from host models, such as the acceptable way of acting towards one's supervisor, how to greet a government official, how to eat a meal, and the reciprocal obligations between friends.) Obviously, however, the simple imitation of some host behaviors can result in unexpected aversive events. For instance, the sojourner who adopts the dress of the host culture may receive disapproval from both his fellow sojourners ("He has gone native.") and from the hosts ("Look at the tourist."). Thus, the expectation of his hosts and of his fellow sojourners may result in a rather narrow range of approved behaviors for the sojourner. In fact, those areas in which intercultural differences occur are potential sources of conflict for the sojourner—engendering approval from his hosts but disapproval from his fellow sojourners, or vice versa. For instance, a Korean male sojourner to the United States who begins to grow long sideburns and a beard would be risking disapproval from his fellow sojourners although he might receive approval from some Americans. And the middle-aged Japanese businessman in Hawaii who wears a bright red aloha shirt may find himself in a similar quandary—wearing the appropriate clothes for a tourist but not for a Japanese businessman.

Desensitization by Counterconditioning

Although there are various ways of desensitizing a sojourner to aversive events, the method of desensitization by counterconditioning is worthy of special mention because of its relatively simple procedure and its apparent effectiveness. My experience as a counselor of Peace Corps trainees also suggests that desensitization may be especially useful in preventing intercultural adjustment problems. Not only can desensitization of aversive events be used prior to the sojourner's departure but also during his stay in the host culture. Desensitization may help to eliminate or reduce the culture shock experience and perhaps could have prevented many of the premature returns of Peace Corps volunteers and other sojourners.

The sojourner, once he has arrived in the host culture, may find that the effects of aversive stimuli are so debilitating that his adjustment becomes worse in spite of his efforts. Assistance from an intercultural counselor may be especially helpful at this time. Without the assistance of a counselor, the sojourner is likely to label the hosts in general derogatory terms ("Americans are stupid!"), rather than specifying the situational elements of the aversive events that are hampering his adjustment. Such general labeling by the sojourner, along with attacking the hosts or withdrawing from them, may result in the passing of many months before the sojourner effectively adjusts to the host culture.

SUMMARY

Problems of intercultural adjustment may be viewed as a consequence of punishment encountered in the host culture. Punishment may occur as a result of the removal of a reinforcing event or the presentation of an aversive event. In attempting to prevent intercultural problems of adjustment, the sojourner should learn the stimulus cues of the host culture that are instrumental in attaining reinforcers and in avoiding punishers. To prevent the removal of reinforcing events when traveling to another culture, the sojourner should attempt to transfer those reinforcers that are compatible with the host culture, to modify those reinforcers that only partially transfer to the host culture, and to develop new reinforcing events that are congruent with the social structure of the host culture. To prevent encountering aversive events in the host culture, the sojourner should learn how to avoid certain aversive events and how to neutralize other aversive events. For some situations, the sojourner may be able to change host culture events that are initially aversive to ones that are reinforcing. The sojourner may learn to avoid many of the punishing events in the host culture by modeling his behavior after those persons from his home culture who have adjusted well to the host culture. The simulation of host culture conditions may help to identify many of the punishers that a sojourner will encounter. The use of desensitization by counterconditioning procedures may be particularly effective in decreasing the potency of aversive events in the host culture.

REFERENCES

Bandura, A. *Principles of behavior modification.* New York: Holt, Rinehart & Winston, 1969.

Brein, M., & David, K. H. Intercultural communication and the adjustment of the sojourner. *Psychological Bulletin,* 1971, *76,* 215–230.

Cautela, J. R. Reinforcement survey schedule: Evaluation and current applications. *Psychological Reports,* 1972, *30,* 683–690.

Cautela, J. R., & Kastenbaum, R. A reinforcement survey schedule for use in therapy, training, and research. *Psychological Reports*, 1967, *30*, 683–690.

Cunningham, J. F. Mistreatment may drive off Japan visitors, seminar told. *Honolulu Advertiser*, March 3, 1972, p. A-16.

David, K. H. Intercultural adjustment, cross-cultural training, and reinforcement theory. JSAS *Catalog of Selected Documents in Psychology*, 1973, *3*, 45. (Ms, No. 348)

David, K. H., & King, W. L. Review and analysis of problems of recent immigrants in Hawaii. JSAS *Catalog of Selected Documents in Psychology*, 1973, *3*, 46. (Ms. No. 349)

David, K. H., & Uhes, M. J. *Theoretical and practical considerations in developing a comprehensive reinforcement survey*. Unpublished paper, Center for Cross-Cultural Training and Research, University of Hawaii at Hilo, 1972.

Fiedler, F. E., Mitchell, T., & Triandis, H. C. The culture assimilator: An approach to cross-cultural training. *Journal of Applied Psychology*, 1971, *55*, 95–102.

Jones, R. J., & Popper, R. Characteristics of Peace Corps host countries and the behavior of volunteers. *Journal of Cross-Cultural Psychology*, 1972, *3*, 233–245.

Kaser, T. Visitors find patience necessary. *Honolulu Advertiser*, January 4, 1973, p. B-1.

Mischel, W. *Personality and assessment*. New York: John Wiley & Sons, 1968.

Wight, A. R., & Hammons, M. A. *Guidelines for Peace Corps cross-cultural training*, Part 2, *Specific methods and techniques* (Contract No. PC–23–1710). Washington, D. C.: Peace Corps, Office of Training Support, March 1970.

Wolpe, J., & Lang, P. A fear survey schedule for use in behavior therapy. *Behavior Research and Therapy*, 1964, *2*, 27–30.

8 Toward Research Evaluating Intercultural Counseling

NORMAN D. SUNDBERG

HOW DO YOU KNOW WHETHER OR NOT YOU ARE HELPING CLIENTS FROM OTHER CULTURES?

In this chapter, Norman Sundberg explores 14 hypotheses as sources for researching the effectiveness of intercultural counseling. Among the many variables related to such effectiveness, some of the more important are the participant's expectations about counseling, the counselor's communication skills, the client's intercultural skills, and the action or decision the client is considering.

There are a number of ways in which intercultural counseling can become more effective. First, there should be congruence between what the counselor and client expect from one another, this understanding to be arrived at through some sort of clearly defined agreement early in the counseling process. Second, the counselor needs the skill to interpret accurately any unclear and incomplete messages from the client; these messages provide the feedback to confirm the counselor's own understanding of the situation. Third, the counselor must help the client understand the environment around him, identifying appropriate alternatives and behaviors that would assist the client from within the client's own cultural viewpoint. Through all of these considerations, there is the strong possibility of the client's suffering alienation, marginality, and emotional "drifting" related to communication difficulties. The new culture often fails to support familiar habits or self-images. The counselor is likely to be used as a reality check or as an authority figure. One basic problem in all of these difficulties is that of establishing adequate criteria for measuring the persons, problems, and environments being researched.

Whose criteria do we use for evaluating outcomes of intercultural counseling or the intercultural training of counselors? This important issue relates both to the efficient delivery of counseling services to multicultural populations and to questions of professional ethics. All of the previous articles have described specific counseling behaviors and styles that provide the tools for a intercultural counselor. Sundberg draws out the implications for an ethical application of those tools in such a way that

139

the success or failure of counseling can be determined. Here again we are made aware of skills available through intercultural counseling that should improve the capabilities of counselors, even though they may not perceive themselves as working in a multicultural population.

The ordinary difficulties of any counseling relationship are magnified in the intercultural setting in such a way that otherwise tolerable weaknesses of a counselor working with persons from his or her own culture become grave burdens. As in previous articles, there is a practical emphasis in Sundberg's article that directs the counselor's attention toward suggestions that can be tried and rejected or assimilated into the counselor's own style, regardless of the client's cultural background.

> Every man is in certain respects
> a. like all other men,
> b. like some other men,
> c. like no other man.
> Kluckhohn and Murray, *Personality in Nature, Society and Culture*

At the heart of research on intercultural counseling is the problem of similarities and differences. One fact is that human beings around the world share many similarities, such as the ability to interbreed, the presence of physical environments, and the common experiences of birth, early helplessness, growing up, and growing old. Another fact is that human beings share many things with their groups of identification, though not with all mankind—knowledge of specific places, ways of socializing the young, language, and expectations about authority. Finally, each human being is unique, having one-of-a-kind fingerprints, a special history, and a particular life style.

The counselor meeting a client for the first time encounters all three aspects in one person—the universal, the group-specific, and the unique. The counselor also has these tripartite characteristics. Furthermore, the counseling pair also meets in a context, an interaction in a social and physical setting, which has a history and relation with similar contexts. Counseling itself is part of Western culture, though it probably has parallels in every society that has ever existed. "Culture is a great storehouse of ready-made solutions to problems which human animals are wont to encounter" (Kluckhohn & Murray, 1953, p. 54). Counseling, in a sense, is a cultural solution to the problem of problem-solving.

This intermixture of universality, group similarity, and uniqueness is not easily untangled and presents many difficulties for research on intercultural counseling and its effectiveness. Almost all research depends on comparisons—condition with condition, person with person. So research mostly concentrates on group phenomena and ignores both the universal and the unique. Seldom do most of us think about how much we share with others. Like newspaper reporters, social scientists tend to look for the unusual. Even statistical procedures are designed so that they prove differences rather than commonalities, and the bias of journals is against articles reporting support for the null hypothesis. It is difficult in cultural comparisons to strike a balance between the etic (universal) and emic (group-specific) approaches (Berry, 1969).

Dealing with uniqueness also has never been a strong point in personality research, despite Gordon Allport's long advocacy of that stance (1937). Fortunately, the behavior therapy movement has led to the appearance of individual case studies. In a review of psychotherapy research, Howard and Orlinsky (1972, p. 656) reported that there is an upswing of interest in single case research, though many single case designs have yet to be applied. Most of us in counseling are left between the two dangers of being overly concerned with cultural differences and being not concerned enough—between over-differentiation and under-differentiation.

The problem of understanding cultural differences and similarities is likely to increase. Despite occasional downturns in exchange programs and support for international study, increasing worldwide communication, interdependency, and mobility are making intercultural problem-solving more and more of a necessity. (My own experience illustrates this round-the-world mobility; I wrote the first draft of this paper while teaching in Spain, rewrote part of it for a different purpose while consulting in India, and finally finished it in the United States.) There seems to be no doubt about the increasing need to understand and assist sojourners, migrants, immigrants, and those in domestic intercultural contact.

Good research on intercultural counseling provides an important opportunity for one to develop more than just increased knowledge about counseling. A well-developed relationship in counseling provides possibilities for learning about the clients' home culture, the host culture, and the process of adaptation and to learn about these in an intensive fashion that would complement studies based on group data or anthropological field study. Despite the many pitfalls in intercultural research that have been delineated by Brislin, Lonner, and Thorndike (1973) and by other authors in this book, intercultural counseling still must be seen as an outstanding opportunity to study significant aspects of social science. Research, even if it remains on an exploratory, heuristic, and poorly controlled level, is dealing at least with the fundamental nexus of social problems—the point of contact between dissimilar peoples and the relationship between individual and society in an increasingly interactive and pluralistic world.

COUNSELING WITHIN AND ACROSS CULTURES

Though I speak in this chapter mainly about one-to-one counseling, I want to emphasize that counseling must be more broadly conceived. Counseling blends into advising in educational institutions and into psychotherapy in clinical institutions. It relates to indigenous helping relationships, and to the formal attempts to organize communities and institutions so that they can anticipate and alleviate distress and assist toward high levels of functioning. For present purposes, I will focus on the most common practice—the counseling interview in American colleges for educational-vocational and personal decision-making, clarification, and change—but the working agenda of counseling research and theory must also include what might be called "community counseling," particularly its preventive aspects.

Community counseling, or "counseling-in-the-large" (as opposed to the direct work with clients, or "counseling-in-the-small"), is the deliberate use of counseling knowledge and theory to enhance natural problem-solving in the community or assist other persons who are deeply involved in human interaction, such as college instructors, dormitory managers, community policemen and nurses, to handle personal disturbances and to promote individual development. Most community counseling consists of indirect services to individuals through consultation with direct caretakers (e.g., assisting teachers in student advising), training of non-professionals (e.g., preparing crisis intervention telephone interviewers), or teaching of general groups (e.g., career development classes), or programming (e.g., setting up orientation meetings or foreign student association activities). These community services include as a major element the prevention of behavioral disorders (Muñoz & Kelly, 1975) and the enhancement of the quality of life. The ultimate scope of research and evaluation in counseling then is very large indeed.

Here also I will focus on those aspects of one-to-one counseling that are most relevant to intercultural work. The crucial questions are these. Does the fact that the client and counselor differ in cultural background make any differences in the effectiveness of the counseling? What special problems may arise or what special opportunities exist for intercultural research? It would seem that the greatest value of doing research under intercultural conditions as opposed to the usual monocultural conditions lies in the possibility for studying the effects of similarity-diversity and for determining how general are our counseling theories and techniques. The variations in expectations, frames of reference, adaptation processes, and communication style offer excellent natural opportunities for experiments if we can record and analyze our observations effectively.

In the usual counseling-in-the-small situation the major components are the context, the client, the counselor, the mode of interaction, and the topic or problem. Intercultural considerations can affect any of the five. If one takes the first three, the following possibilities exist in order of frequency. (1) The client and counselor are from different backgrounds and are working in the cultural setting of the counselor—a student from Hong Kong, for example, seeing a Caucasian American counselor in an American college. (2) The client and counselor are different but are working in the homeland of the client—a student in India consulting a visiting American professor, or an American client seeing an immigrant Filipino psychologist in the United States. (Parenthetically, it may be noted that this situation is occurring more often in the United States as foreign-trained physicians and psychologists, mostly from Asia, are filling vacancies for medical personnel in American hospitals.) (3) The client and counselor differ from one another in culture and are interacting within a third setting—an Iranian student seeing a Hungarian refugee psychologist in an American counseling center. All three of these situations may be accompanied by a variation in mode of interaction: nondirective, information-giving, behavior-modifying, or psychoanalytic. Finally, the topic of discussion or action may vary—a financial problem, career planning, or male-female relations. Intercultural considerations come into play when the way in which the two individuals communicate and the nature and seriousness of the problem are interpreted.

All of the illustrations of cultural differences have been of people coming from contrasting geographical and language areas. This chapter emphasizes this kind of large difference, but obviously most of the same considerations would apply to within-country ethnic differences. Research on Black-white counseling problems in the United States is relevant to research on foreign students and vice-versa. Techniques and theory developed for one kind of difference may very well be tried with another.

SOME THEORETICAL CONSIDERATIONS

My bias is toward a systems-ecological point of view. I see the two participants in the one-to-one counseling session as each coming from a set of environments, which nurture certain behaviors and thoughts and discourage others. Typically the contrast-culture client comes from a current environment that supports him or her inadequately or conflicts in some way with a previous environment. As Tyler (1969) and Gilmore (1973) have shown, the three purposes of counseling are choice, change, and confusion-reduction. In systems terms applied to the usual counseling situation, the client (1) is faced with a decision to move from one environmental system to another or to plan for entry into a potential system, (2) is contemplating altering his personal system by acquiring different abilities or attitudes, or (3) is attempting to obtain more meaningful information to differentiate his or her personal world more accurately and usefully. An additional alternative is work to change the environment, as represented in one form by considerations of community counseling.

The boundary is an important system concept, one that determines what is external and what is internal to the system. Cultures differ, for instance, in who is included within family boundaries, who is to receive confidential information, and where certain activities are to take place. In-groups and out-groups vary from culture to culture, and what is considered a personal responsibility in one culture may not be in another. It takes more energy (and produces more emotional stress) to change from one system to another than to remain within the current system. Interactions tend to be particularly important at system boundaries or places of exchange geographically, temporally, and socially. Leaving one environment and moving to another—immigrating, going home, beginning a new job, or breaking a relationship with a boy- or girl friend—tend to increase anxiety. Yet the normal, relatively nonanxious organism, particularly in the young adult years, wishes to explore different environments and to seek different foods and "foods for thought." Travelers to a foreign land are likely to have more than the usual amount of curiosity and interest in new experience. The problem, as in the development of the young, is to provide novelty enough to be growth-producing but not overwhelming. The new environment becomes overwhelming when the supports for a person are insufficient or the stresses have become too great. The supports and stresses are mainly of three kinds for clients in intercultural or cross-ethnic situations: financial, physical, and social. Economic survival is a basic necessity, of course, and at borderline levels financial support makes the difference between access to many kinds of social systems and personal rewards. The physical supports include physiological assistance (health services, food), shelter, and safety. Social supports provide for the emotional and interpersonal needs of the client. Gilmore (1973) identified three major content areas of counseling: work, relationship, and aloneness (Freud's *Liebe und Arbeit*, plus Sartre's existential condition). The first two relate to support systems, and all three relate to the way the client deals with his personal system.

The personal system has two major aspects accessible to the counselor. First is that part that deals with the external world—the observable behavior of the individual, and second is that part that deals with the internal world—the self-talk of the individual. Behavior is relatively dominated by the environment and relates to the support systems and to the rewards and punishments of the various groups and physical contacts present in the client's daily orbit. The client's self-talk is, of course, only partially shared with the counselor. Cultural traditions as well as individual habits affect the kind and amount of sharing of internal thoughts. Prominent in the internal system are plans and expectations—the "possibility world" of the client, built up by affectively toned experiences and previous self-talk. The highly skilled counselor is able to communicate verbally and nonverbally and to work with the client on a behavioral as well as on a self-report level.

Of particular importance in intercultural counseling is effectiveness of communication. Communication is important in all counseling, but its effectiveness reaches a high problematic level when one or both of the actors sends messages poorly in the medium they are using—the spoken or nonspoken language. Messages are encoded and decoded in the two personal systems by means of "codebooks" that are only partially congruent. For instance, Schumacher, Banikiotes, and Banikiotes (1972) have shown that linguistic compatibility between Black students and Caucasian counselors in high school is quite low. Of particular importance are individual differences in cognitive differentiation as Triandis, Vassiliou, Vassiliou, Tanaka, and Shanmugam (1972) have pointed out in discussions of subjective culture—the way a group using a mutually understandable dialect perceives the social environment. Some groups differentiate and achieve fine degrees of meaning in areas that others differentiate very grossly. For instance, desert-dwelling Arabs have hundreds of words applying to camels, whereas Americans have hundreds of words applying to automobiles. In order for an Arab to talk about camels with an American or for an American to talk about automobiles with an Arab in some meaningful detail, much teaching and learning would be necessary. Similarly, some cultures and ethnic groups are very verbal about human relations and feelings, whereas others speak little about such things. If the two parties to a discussion live in cultures with different levels of differentiation about a particular topic, they are likely to become bewildered or bored with the discussion and to feel powerless and unsure of their own communications.

Triandis hypothesized that two individuals will interact effectively with each other if they overlap substantially in their subjective cultures and if they are matched so that they make similar differentiations. It is possible for both persons (client and counselor) to obtain highly congruent understandings which may be unrealistic and ineffective. Medicine men and quacks, no matter how respected and effective with psychosomatic disorders they may be, cannot treat glaucoma or smallpox as effectively as can modern physicians.

Another aspect of the systems theory is the crucial concept of feedback. The system, whether it be a dyad, a group, or an individual, regulates itself by information returned from its activities, even as a thermostat controls the furnace or an electronic missile homes in on its target. In counseling the counselor and client give each other verbal and nonverbal guidance about what is important and what is not important, and thus they establish relative mutuality of meanings. Cultures vary in the degree or manner with which feedback is given to another person. Japanese girls may not look males in the eye; for a Westerner accustomed to eye contact, this behavior can be disconcerting and may be misinterpreted.

Cultural differences may enter into the allowances made by the counselor for discrepancies between behavior and self-report on the part of the client. Promises to return for another appointment, punctuality, and all manner of contractual behavior will be violated or incompletely fulfilled (in the eyes of the Caucasian middle-class American) by people of different cultural and ethnic backgrounds. There are, of course, great individual differences between thought and action and in the carrying out of promises and plans, to which the counselor should also be sensitive.

HYPOTHESES FOR RESEARCH

The purpose of this section is to propose some hypotheses leading toward research. (Although I am calling them hypotheses, I would better term them "protohypotheses," since they are far from being clearly defined. One basic assumption to all of these hypotheses is that each of the human beings involved in the intercultural counseling dyad has the three components mentioned at the start of this chapter: universal human components which he or she shares with all human beings, group-related components of characteristics shared with certain other human beings, and unique components, which are particular to each individual.

Another basic assumption is that the kind and degree of shared components are important to the effectiveness of the counseling interaction. The relationship will vary in different content areas. For instance, the pair must share some way of communicating verbally or nonverbally, but beyond a certain level of command of the language it is unlikely that further knowledge adds much to effectiveness of counseling. Knowing 50,000 words of German may add little to a German dialogue beyond what would be said if one knew 20,000.

A third assumption is that the purpose of counseling or psychotherapy is to be found in systems away from the client-counselor interaction itself. It could be argued that it is sufficient that there be a rewarding experience in the dyadic session itself; the actors would not expect more than what happens at a good party and would leave the session with a sense of enjoyment. One could even argue that society should provide such opportunities for entertainment and pastimes, but such an objective is not what clients, counselors, or taxpayers expect from a counseling service. The purpose of the artificial counseling setting is to affect either the personal system of the client or the interactional systems of the client outside the counseling session. There should be transsituational effects.

The following is a series of five areas of important research in intercultural counseling. Each will present some relevant hypotheses.

Mutuality of Purposes and Expectations

The process of arriving at expectations for what is to be gained from counseling is a particularly important one in intercultural work. These intercultural expectations are on a continuum with those of clients of one's own culture, but a sense of intercultural difference will prepare the counselor to examine and to clarify for him- or herself and the client the expectations for this system of interaction and its relationship to the "outside world." The counselor's understanding of the kind of socialization for dependency and for openness in discussion of problems with a particular client will help to avoid cultural difficulties. One hypothesis arises:

a. The more similar the expectations of the intercultural client and of the counselor in regard to the goals of counseling, the more effective the counseling will be.

Not only in regard to goals but also in regard to the process and relationship to counseling do the client and the counselor have expectations that are implicit and explicit before their first meeting and that develop further as the counseling sessions progress. Socialization for dependency, customs of restricting personal communications to the family circle, and attitudes toward social hierarchy are learned. Another important variable is contained in predispositions toward liking or disliking whatever the counselor symbolizes in the culture-of-origin or the culture-of-residence (priest, healer, parental figure, scientist, or outcaste). Grey (1965) suggested, in discussing his experiences counseling in India, that counselors should be trained to cope with the client's expectations about authority and decision-making. Benfari (1969) found that primitive societies that foster a large degree of childhood dependence had person-oriented healers, whereas societies that socialize for low dependence did not. Tan (1967), in one of the few studies of intercultural expectancies, found that both American and foreign students tended to be more authoritarian than were graduate counselors in two American universities; those foreign students who had been in the United States longer were more similar to American students. In counseling, status-relationship, inclusion in communication, and friendliness require special understanding. Another hypothesis is as follows:

> b. Of special importance in arriving at common expectations toward intercultural counseling effectiveness is the degree of congruence between counselor and client in their orientations toward dependency, openness of communication, and other relationships inherent in counseling.

Common understanding of purposes is probably more important in some instances than in others. A counselor could help someone from another culture with a minor problem more easily than he or she could help someone from his or her own culture with a very serious problem. Minor problems are more likely to be alleviated by the simple supplying of information. This leads to another hypothesis:

> c. The more the aims and desires of the client can be appropriately simplified to appropriate objective behavior or by having common information (such as university course requirements), the more effective the intercultural counseling will be.

This hypothesis suggests that the intercultural counselor should be prepared to use multiple channels of communication. Brochures, printed explanations, graphic portrayals, and films of procedures for handling problems may be of much more value in intercultural counseling than in ordinary counseling. The counselor may also need to teach specific skills for handling specific situations. It should be noted, however, that the simplification and use of supplementary materials should be appropriate and not be used as an escape from facing crucial emotional issues.

Developing the Counselor's Intercultural Understanding and Communication Skills

In any system, but particularly in that of counseling, communication is important. A sensitivity to what the other person is trying to convey verbally and nonverbally and an ability to respond to that communication in turn are the cornerstones of much of counseling and psychotherapy. In the intercultural context, there is always some language problem. Early language learning seems to be particularly related to expression of feelings. Achebe (1960, p. 45) gave an interesting illustration in his novel about a young Nigerian who had just returned from college in London:

> Obi was beginning to feel sleepy and his thoughts turned more and more on the erotic. He said words in his mind that he could not say out loud even when he was alone. Strangely enough, all the words were in his mother tongue. He could say any English word, no matter how dirty, but some Ibo words simply

would not proceed from his mouth. It was no doubt his early training that operated this censorship, English words filtering through because they were learnt later in life.

In personal counseling it would seem particularly important for the counselor to know something of the early socialization of the client. Another hypothesis is as follows:

d. The more personal and emotion-laden the counseling becomes, the more the client will reply on words learned early in life, and the more helpful it will be for the counselor to be knowledgeable about socialization in the client's culture.

The counselor's learning could come about before or during the counseling sessions. Sometimes prior knowledge is an impediment, because the counselor may think he knows more than he does, and he may not individualize his approach. Learning from the client about his background is an important part of counseling. Of course, there are many advising and guidance situations where a large amount of knowledge of cultural background is not necessary; for example, if the focus is on a sharply defined financial or academic information problem, detailed examination may confuse the issue or alienate the client.

Counselor sensitivity—the ability to place one's self in the role of the client and to empathize with his or her feelings—is generally thought to be an extremely important variable. In intercultural work, the counselor must be sensitive to the meanings and connotations of language, both in the client's culture and in the contextual culture surrounding the interaction. Words carry different emotional charges and bring different images to persons of different cultures. Likewise, nonverbal aspects of communication enter into counseling. This may affect the understanding of feedback and reinforcement patterns. Americans often misinterpret as "no" the slight twist of the head which, in India, signifies "yes" or "agreed"; in bazaars they may even walk away thinking a haggling proposal has been rejected until the shopkeeper calls them back. Hall (1966) has pointed out that Arabs are much more likely than are northern Europeans to push and touch in public; i.e., to invade the "personal bubble" of strangers. Such information is of importance to both client and counselor in interpreting experience in a foreign culture. Within the counseling session itself, the study of nonverbal aspects of movement and use of space could prove to be an interesting contribution to a basic knowledge. Also, different cultures are likely to vary in free associations. For instance, one study (Shaffer, Sundberg, & Tyler, 1969) found that samples of adolescents in India listed many more words related to food than did Americans; another study (Bates, Sundberg, & Tyler, 1970) showed that Indians reveal much less aggressive and humorous content in drawings than do Americans. Johnson (1973) found that foreign students varied widely in the number and kind of adjectives they used to characterize Americans and other nationalities. The amount of feedback from clients to counselors or among group members in discussion groups is affected by culture. Ogowa and Weldon (1972) reported, for instance, that Japanese-Americans respond less to other speakers than do Caucasian-Americans, and they attributed the difference to the Japanese norm of *enryo*, or shyness and restraint. Despite all of the many problems inherent in intercultural communication, one must remember that some immigrants have been highly successful psychotherapists and counselors; for example, many of those psychologists and psychiatrists who fled the Nazis in the 1930s and 1940s. Underlying success is probably a refined sensitivity to other persons and what they are trying to say; such sensitivity might be measurable (Davitz, 1964; Sundberg, 1966). One likely way in which intercultural awarness and empathy in the counselor might be increased might be for him or her to study the arts of other places (Adinolfi, 1971), especially drama, films, newspapers, and novels.

An obvious hypothesis that arises from these considerations is as follows:

> e. The effectiveness of intercultural counseling will be enhanced by the counselor's general sensitivity to communications, both verbal and nonverbal, and by a knowledge of communication styles in other cultures.

Reviewing the research, H. C. Smith (1966, p. 177) stated that "most of what we have learned about people we have learned informally. The sensitive people are simply those who have learned the most. The most sensitive person is the most highly motivated, most open to new experiences, most ready to participate in learning about them, and most able to assess the adequacy of what he has learned." Communication sensitivity may be related to language-learning ability (Sundberg, 1966), to the sex of the counselor (i.e., women are reputedly more aware of interpersonal nuances), to knowledge and experience in at least one or two cultures other than one's own, to interest and motivation for understanding other cultures, to skill in paraphrasing and reflection of feeling in interviews, and, with specific clients, to some similarity of early experiences, socio-economic background, and occupational experiences. If the importance of many of these relationships proves to be true, then the use of peers and conationals for counseling should seriously be considered.

A related hypothesis relates to the background of the counselor. A biographical inventory and tests of knowledge might be used to measure relevant intercultural abilities. Carkhuff and Pierce (1967) have shown that the greater the similarity, the more the willingness for self-exploration. Training programs could be devised specifically as Carkhuff has stated (1972, p. 21) to "expand the response repertoire" of counselors interculturally and cross-ethnically. These considerations lead to this hypothesis:

f. Specific background and training in interactions similar to the counseling one and an understanding of the day-to-day living problems in other relevant cultures will enhance the effectiveness of intercultural counselors.

Though that hypothesis would seem intuitively to be correct, its actual testing will likely reveal many subtle problems. The quality of experience and training and not just the quantity is of great importance.

Developing the Client's Intercultural Attitudes and Skills

The other side of the coin in counseling is the preparation and development of the client so that he or she may participate effectively in the counseling interaction and the counseling program. Expectations and purposes have already been mentioned. The counselor must also give consideration to teaching specific skills to clients and to utilizing relevant attitudes and skills already present in the client's repertoire.

While it is advisable "to meet the client where he is," sometimes it simply is not possible to adapt the activities of a busy counseling service to the style of interaction to which the client is accustomed. The counselor may have to work with the client in developing an understanding of the counselor's point of view and in preparing for participation in the counseling process. With some clients, it may be necessary to explain the counseling process very carefully, with frequent checks on understanding through such techniques as paraphrasing and perception checks being used. For intensive counseling, the client may need to be taught to speak what is on his mind in a relaxed manner; in other words, to develop the skills required to play the counseling role. With lower-class clients, Strupp and Bloxom (1973) reported successful use of a role induction film for psychotherapy, and Heitler (1973) found an "anticipatory socialization interview" produced marked improvement in group therapy. The hypothesis which grows out of these considerations is as follows:

g. The less familiar the client is with the counseling process, the more the counselor or the counseling program will need to instruct the client in the skills of communication, decision-making, and transfer to outside situations.

Cultural Considerations of the Client's Areas of Action

So far we have been looking mainly at some of the characteristics of the two actors and their interaction. Now let us look briefly at off-stage characteristics, the environment in which counseling takes place—the experience and behavior in daily life of relevance to intercultural considerations, both in present settings and future ones. What is of most importance for understanding the context of intercultural counseling? Here I will select four factors which seem of great importance—cultural assumptions about choice and decision-making, the client's reference groups, the process of adapting to intercultural stress, and choice of the most significant arenas of action.

Early family influences, religious teaching, schools, and the surrounding mass media inculcate cultural values, many of which are implicit and unquestioned. Among these are a set of assumptions about choice, desirable alternatives, and decision-making. Cultures differ in the emphasis on self and parental responsibility in planning one's life. For instance, in India, as Sundberg, Sharma, Rohila, and Wodtli (1969) have demonstrated, the father is usually the unquestioned authority who makes the choices of his adolescent's future occupation and marriage. Assumptions about love and work, Freud's choices for the most important things in life, are frequently the concerns of counseling, and the counselor should be aware of cultural background factors of his client. Knowledge of the constraints and opportunities in Third-World countries is especially important if one is to assist a client in career planning. Beliefs about the timing of life's events also is of importance, not only in the long range, but in the immediate interaction. As mentioned before, the keeping of appointments and the degree of punctuality are subject to cultural influences, and the length of acquaintance time before one reveals what one wants to do in a meeting or makes important business agreements has been found to vary in cultures (Hall & Whyte, 1960). The following hypothesis expresses many of these considerations:

> h. The effectiveness of intercultural counseling will be increased by mutual knowledge of the values and assumptive frameworks of the culture of the client's origin in relation to the cultures of the present and future fields of action.

A caution needs to be inserted here about knowledge. Sometimes it can be a hindrance if it leads to "type-casting," or stereotyping, and misinterpretations. Knowledge may also help in understanding groups but not individuals. In general, however, a learning attitude toward intercultural phenomena, evidenced by knowledge, would seem important for intercultural work. Probably the learning attitude is closely related to the sensitivity mentioned in hypothesis e. Knowledge of other cultures and learning attitudes can be defined operationally by achievement and attitude tests.

Another significant element in understanding a client is acquaintance with and use of the reference groups that he or she considers to be important. With whom in the past and the present does he identify and to whom does he defer in judgment about his worth and status? Who will be important to him in the future? In traditional cultures, the family, the neighborhood, and the caste or clan are important. In modern urban settings, professional or work groups are more significant, and the nuclear family may be more important than the extended family. The study by Cottrell (1973) of cross-national marriages in India found that international life-styles had already been established by the couples before they married. These couples who lived mainly in urban settings judged themselves in reference to sophisticated standards rather than to the traditional Indian values that one might learn about from studying most books on Hinduism or Indian culture. Being highly selected, foreign students on an American campus are more likely to fit the modern and international setting than the traditional one (see Gordon, 1964, pp. 224–232). Many of them are more anxious to fit the reference group of Americans or of other students from their own country than home-country norms. Stecklein, Liu, Anderson, and Gunararatne (1971) found that foreign students are most likely to seek out other foreign students to help them solve personal problems, and Antler (1970) indicated that adjustment with conationals is more important than with Americans. The following hypothesis is relevant:

i. Intercultural counseling is enhanced by the knowledge and use of the intercultural reference groups most important to the client.

The counselor may find that he or she can use conationals of the client either as consultants, cocounselors, or peer counselors. The use of conationals may have its pitfalls, for these persons may impede the client's adaptation to the host culture and his or her independence, if these are goals of counseling; but, in spite of this, a well-chosen and trained conational can be very helpful. The importance of persons of similar background will also relate to the strength of identity of the client with his ethnic or cultural group. Jackson and Kirschner (1973) found that those who designated themselves Afro-Americans or Blacks more often preferred a counselor of African descent than did those who referred to themselves as Negro or colored.

How an individual adapts to another culture has long been of interest to anthropologists and psychologists. The over-used term culture shock signifies a difficult period of depression and anxiety that follows the initial enthusiasm of the first few weeks in a new and strange country. The newcomer is not yet able to control or predict the new system very well. In addition, he or she may be physically ill and may be unable to find familiar food. Students are often homesick. Professors and businessmen usually suffer a change of status in moving to a new country. (Sometimes, as when they are treated with more deference and have servants, they enjoy an increase in status.) Conway (1969) and Sundberg (1973) discussed different phases of sojourner satisfaction and their respective implications for advisors and institutions. Zain (1965), in a survey of foreign students, found a U-shaped adjustment curve, with a high initial adjustment for those in the United States less than 6 months and a high adjustment again among those in the United States for 3 years or more, but poorer adjustment in between. The counselor must be sensitive to basic physical needs and must assist the client in getting in touch with others who have successfully gone through the initial adjustment. Along the way there may be a challenge to home values and mores. The counselor must think through the ethical implications of challenging a foreign student's culture-related values. Male foreign students in America often mention their difficulty in understanding the availability of American girls and are confused by their revealing clothes and apparently provocative behavior, and by the portrayals of femininity on television and in the cinema. In this period of youth and young adulthood, identity and values are in the process of formation. Losing familiar supports, some young people become disoriented. Some, however, feel freer to try themselves out and experiment with new action patterns. Therefore, the following hypothesis is proposed:

> j. The effectiveness of intercultural counseling is increased by counselor awareness of the process of adaptation to the stress and confusion of moving from one culture to another (system boundary crossing) and by his or her consideration of the skills required to gain mastery over the new system.

It is likely that persons who have successfully made a transition from one environment to another—from a small town to a city, for example—will be better able to deal with culture shock. This problem of adaptation to a new environment applies also to reentry problems to one's own native land. Brislin and Van Buren (1974) have reported a program specifically aimed at training international sojourners to "worry" constructively and to expect problems when they return home. The counselor, in the role of community organizer, can do something about the orientation of students both for entry and return.

A major factor in counseling for the "arena of action" is whether or not the client intends to stay in the host culture. Sometimes the purpose of counseling is to help the client to make a choice between remaining or returning. There are probably a number of personality differences between remainers and returners, especially if these persons have come from high-contrast cultures such as those found in most of the Asian and African countries.

Most counseling will be oriented toward the short-range problems of the client. In a college situation, it is very likely that the arena of action will center on immediate problems dealing with language, academic work, and finances (Benson & Miller, 1966). Johnson's research (1971) with international clients indicated that these persons should be thought of as students first, not foreigners. They found international students' morale was high during vacations and low during examinations; they concluded that, contrary to popular belief, foreign students have the greatest difficulty in adapting to academic work, not to the American culture. The following hypothesis is proposed:

> k. Although the effective counseling situation requires a consideration of both the present living situation and the future arena of action, it must focus on the one of primary importance to the client.

Universality, Group-Communality, and Uniqueness in Intercultural Counseling.

Counseling as a social institution has arisen in America and Europe. Every culture probably has some method for handling the individual problems that are not easily solved by the normal social structure. Frank (1961), Kiev (1964), and Torrey (1972) found common elements between helping procedures in modern and premodern societies. DeVos and Hippler (1969, pp. 323–417) stated that indigenous practices are often as successful, if not more successful, than Western treatment of aberrant mental states. Counseling and similar processes produce a refuge from society. In interaction with the surrounding system, the client has lost out in the judgment of self (regarding sociocultural expectations) or in the judgment by society. He or she is out of step. The counselor provides the antithesis to mainstream society—offering a confidential, noncritical acceptance in which the client can talk about his weaknesses and dependence and about taboo topics such as hate, sex, and egotism. One foreign student advisor summed up his many years of experience with one word about the advisor's required virtue: patience. A counselor may need to spend more time and may find his or her work more difficult when working with clients from a culture different from the counselor's own. All of these ongoing considerations of commonality across clients and across theories lead to the following hypothesis:

> l. Despite great differences in cultural contexts, language, and in the implicit theory of counseling process, a majority of the important elements of inter-

cultural counseling are common across cultures and clients. These elements include such counselor characteristics as a tolerance for anxiety in the client, a manifest positive flexibility in response to the client, a reasonable confidence in one's information and belief system, and an interest in the client as a person.

Within the American culture there are several theorists and researchers who have pointed to commonality among different schools. Fiedler (1950), for instance, found that expert therapists from different schools, as compared to novices, held much in common, especially with regard to communication skills. Schofield (1964) pointed to the importance of the basic human dimension of nonjudgmental friendliness in psychotherapy. Gilmore (1973, p. 116) pointed out that Rogers, Tyler, Truax, and Carkhuff, using somewhat different terminology, all identified similar desirable characteristics in a counselor: empathic understanding, positive and nonpossessive acceptance, and sincerity. Behavior therapists also talk of the importance of positive attention and reinforcement of the client toward positive behaviors. It may be that an analysis of commonalities in different theories will also prove to lead to the discovery of commonalities across cultures in the helping process, but such universality remains to be carefully specified and measured.

Just as there are universal processes that will be shown by research, there are undoubtedly particular counseling techniques or tactics that may be especially useful within a given culture. Kiev (1969, 1972) and Torrey (1972) raised many questions about the transcultural applications of psychiatry; Draguns (1973) presented issues in the comparability of behavioral disorders. The use of charms and magic incantations to cure diseases would be ridiculous to most Westerners, but their use is very helpful in certain cultures. The difference between the universal and the culture-specific is likely to parallel the difference between abstract general laws of learning and problem-solving and the specific content, tactics, and symbols used in studies in different languages or with different species. Berry's (1969) suggestions for clarifying emic and etic cultural characteristics may be of help. The hypothesis can be stated:

> m. Culture-specific modes of counseling will be found that work more effec-
> tively with certain cultural and ethnic groups than with others.

Finally, an overriding caution in counseling is that the counselor should not treat the client as a "foreigner" or as a "stereotype" but as an individual person with his or her own unique background. The closer one gets to any group, the more one can distinguish individual differences.

The last hypothesis is particularly related to prolonged and personal counseling rather than to short information-giving contacts.

n. Intercultural counseling will be effective to the extent that the counselor shows an interest in the client as a special individual.

Fourteen hypotheses have been mentioned under five headings. As mentioned earlier, they are more properly called protohypotheses, since they must yet be sharpened and clearly defined and operations must be developed to measure the variables. It is hoped, however, that they will provide a move toward bringing cultural considerations into counseling theory-building and that the reader will be stimulated to carry the thinking further and to challenge these hypotheses through research. It remains to be seen whether some of these hypotheses are in themselves culture-bound. Research on intercultural counseling provides an important opportunity to develop knowledge both about counseling and cultural relations in general.

SIMILARITIES AND DIFFERENCES IN PERSONAL SYSTEMS

Throughout our discussion and in many of the hypotheses is the question of how one measures similarities between counselor and client, and how well each knows the cultures, values, and social environments of the other. One general hypothesis in psychotherapy and counseling is as follows: as the amount of shared client and counselor knowledge, background, and interests increases, the probable success of the process also increases. Several studies have shown that therapists work better with clients who are verbal and who have come from the same class as themselves.

Our topic of concern is a multivariate, patterned problem. A number of statistical methods would need to be considered for comparing people and situations, and the problem of getting large enough samples when there are so many variables is a serious one. (For methods of pattern comparison, see Bolz, 1972, pp. 161–260; Cronbach & Gleser, 1953; Wiggins, 1973.) The problem of establishing differences and similarities across cultures adds further complications (see reviews by Brislin, Lonner, & Thorndike, 1973; Triandis, Malpass, & Davidson, 1973). The problem of how similarities and dissimilarities should be measured is too large a topic for this paper. However, it seems reasonable to apply some of the procedures used in psychotherapy to compare therapists and clients. It might be possible to develop indexes of intercultural similarities in the manner of Bem (1974) when she measured cross-sex similarities. Members of two cultures could each respond to an inventory or another kind of instrument. A scale could be developed for each group separately; then the scales could be used to see to what extent a person identifies with each culture or takes a mixed position. A scale of cultural pluralism versus ethnocentricity would be useful.

Of highest priority, I would choose research on similarities of expectations in counseling, for this is close to the very reason for the existence of counseling. How are the participants matched as client and counselor, and/or what is the process by which people arrive at an agreement to work together? When purposes are clear, the need for extensive similarity in other ways is less essential. Analogies can be made with other "contract" situations. In cashing a check, it does not matter if the bank teller is foreign-born or local, white or black, young or old, male or female, as long as the request is understood and the money handed over. In an inquiry about location of classes or where to apply for a scholarship, the important thing is mutual understanding of the question and ability to deliver the answers. Much of intercultural advising and guidance has this practical aspect, and counseling shares this feature to some extent. A training program for intercultural counselors should not ignore the importance of imparting realistic financial, academic, and procedural information, even though many "sophisticated" counselors prefer to become immersed in the more personal and "juicy" aspects of social relations, emotions, and strange customs.

In this regard, college programs and personnel probably should make role distinctions clear. Students coming from traditional cultures are especially unlikely to "open up" to someone they perceive as being in an evaluative position. Clear distinctions between services offered in the foreign student advising office and the university counseling center may help some foreign students to establish proper expectations.

For convenience, contact expectations can be divided into three kinds: (a) short-contact, information-oriented advising and counseling (usually of only a few minutes duration, although there may be several meetings), (b) moderate length counseling (typically two to four sessions), and (c) long, personal counseling (typically 10 or more sessions). The number of sessions relates to the usual college counseling experience and will vary a great deal. Intensive contacts are likely to require a longer series of meetings. Both participants must have similar expectations of counseling sessions—of whatever length—if such sessions are to be effective. But a similarity of copersonal features, such as a knowledge of culture and values, is likely to be helpful in direct proportion to the intensiveness of contact. If the two participants are to "experience life together," they need to share a lot.

There are, however, some obvious physical and behavioral features that might influence the occurrence and nature of the first contact. For instance, a sojourner in a strange land is much more likely to speak first to someone who appears to have come from his country. Americans in

India unsure of their situation are more likely to talk with other Americans. Some Afro-Americans prefer going to Black counselors, at least initially. Some research on testing indicates that Black interviewees are more open with Black interviewers than with Caucasians (Ledvinka, 1971). Grantham (1973) found that disadvantaged Blacks preferred Black counselors and explored themselves in greater depth with female counselors. Vontress (1971) saw the establishment of a common group membership as being a very significant for rapport. Carkhuff's review (1972), while in general agreement with the conclusions just presented, shows that effectiveness in Black-Caucasian relationships depends on the interpersonal skills of the helpers; and, among some, race is not an issue. Another possibility to explore and evaluate is a channeling operation whereby first contacts are from the potential client's culture (perhaps specially selected and trained foreign students); these persons could assess the client's needs and refer him to someone in whom they have confidence. Thus, the counselor would have a kind of seal-of-approval from a member of the counselee's cultural group. But, aside from some individual preferences for first contact, the compatability of the counseling pair is likely to be of more importance, the longer and more intensive the contact. The increasing use of peer-counseling and indigenous paraprofessionals is a reflection of the belief in the importance of personal similarity. Training programs in which individuals live and work in the ghettoes or other cultural situations may also help to produce a similarity of "cognitive maps." Some research indicates that matching interviewers with interviewees can be helpful (Berzins, Ross, & Cohen, 1970; Persons & Marks, 1970).

But the question remains—similarity in regard to what? For most moderate-term and long-term counseling, what actually is important? Compatability and similarity may be based on many different variables—sex, socioeconomic status, education, handicaps, experience with drugs, and leisure-time interests—in addition to ethnic similarity. One experienced counselor who read an early draft of this paper said "I'm still reeling from the assertion 'You have to be one to counsel one' from Blacks, Chicanos, gays, and women. Must you be a schizophrenic to help a schizophrenic or a criminal to help a criminal?" The influences that make for compatibility need to be better understood. More research in which clients and counselors are compared as to their orientations to counseling is needed. (For some work in therapist orientations, see Spilken, Jacobs, Muller, & Knitzer, 1969; Sundland & Barker, 1962.) Of relevance here, too, is the question about whether international student clients should be treated as students first, or as foreigners. As mentioned earlier, the former alternative seems to be more important in the eyes of several researchers.

The intercultural counselor needs to beware of overemphasizing the exotic (just as the clinical assessor faces the danger of overemphasizing pathology).

PROBLEMS OF CRITERIA AND PROGRAMS OF EVALUATION

Most of the hypotheses in this paper refer to the effectiveness of counseling. Thousands of pages have been written about the measurement of outcomes of dyadic or small-group counseling and psychotherapy and thousands of additional pages have been published about evaluation of programs that are relevant to counseling-in-the-large, or community counseling. (For overviews of evaluation programs, see Bergin, 1971, pp. 217–270; Howard & Orlinsky, 1972; Sundberg, Tyler, & Taplin, 1973.) Therefore, there is no need to recount here the many kinds of criteria that might be used, such as client reports of satisfaction, counselor ratings, Q sorts, tests, changes in activities, and grade-point averages. Here we need to look at some intercultural aspects of measurement of effectiveness.

The problem is that many of the measuring instruments are affected by cultural differences. Multiple-choice tests are often difficult even for Europeans, whose cultures are closer than the cultures of Africa or Asia. Foreign student advisors are plagued by the meaning of the Graduate Record Examination or other entrance examinations that have been taken in a distant country. Similarly, the norms and scores of other tests are subject to question. If a foreign student achieves a bona-fide increase in achievement test scores after being counseled, then this is one form of positive evidence; but, on the other hand, it would be difficult to interpret lack of change. Well-developed English ability tests like the Test of English as a Foreign Language are useful for admissions and possibly could be used as criteria for improvement, if the ability to speak English is one of the problems with which counseling is concerned. The norms and language of tests of personality, values, attitudes, and interests are almost all based on American populations; where norms are available for other countries, there is a question as to what extent they apply to highly selected foreign students. For research purposes—with proper qualifications, of course—any of the tests can be used; but, for practical purposes, their results should be expected to be very "mushy" and dubious. At best most tests might be used as a form of interview to assess progress during counseling.

Probably the best kinds of criteria to evaluate the effectiveness of intercultural counseling would be those especially designed for that purpose and would employ several judges to check on perceptions of change or benefit. The instruments used in behavioral assessment and the self-anchoring kind of measurement devised by Cantril seem promising. Also nonobstrusive measures, such as indexes of campus participation, grade-average improvement, and observation of dormitory behavior, may be appropriate for certain studies.

The criteria for effectiveness of counseling mentioned so far have been short-range. Long-range criteria are more difficult to obtain. To obtain such criteria, researchers would need to follow up their former clients in later situations away from the counseling setting. Seldom found in counseling research are 5- and 10-year follow-ups. The rare example is Campbell's study (1965), which showed that counseled subjects, as compared with noncounseled controls, continued to be slightly superior on most measures of success even after 25 years. Such a study would be difficult to reproduce with a mobile intercultural sample.

A large sample research being made into the effectiveness of intercultural counseling is unlikely. Even a rather sizable number of international students in America, when classified by the important factors that affect them such as sex, country of origin, year in college, and whether or not they sought counseling, produces extremely small numbers in experimental cells.

There seem to be three directions to go. One way is to retain the goal of obtaining a large sample but also to broaden the notion of intercultural status to include the category of marginal students compared with mainstream students. Marginal students might include all those with unusual characteristics and backgrounds, such as minority members, handicapped students, and students who speak poor English. In such a sampling, foreign students might occupy positions on continua, their position being based on such factors as communication ability, knowledge of mainstream social customs, and ability to cope with problem situations. The continua might then be related to the larger problems of counseling effectiveness and process.

Another direction would involve the study of individuals—one at a time. Allport, Skinner, and other psychologists have found it very productive of ideas to conduct intensive studies of personal documents, performances, and reports of experience. Case histories with attention being paid to the evaluation of effectiveness of treatment with individuals (Blank, 1965) would be instructive. Chassan (1967), Davidson and Costello (1969), and Dukes (1967) have suggested ways in which research can be conducted with an n of one. Leitenberg's review (1973) of the major single-case studies is probably the most useful for present purposes. The object of the controlled case study is to demonstrate that changes in behavior co-vary with changes in counseling. The most common designs now are those used with behavior therapy. A baseline of observed behavior is established, then a period of intervention follows, and then the client and counselor see if the recorded behavior has changed. In order to prove that the intervention made a difference, the counselor withdraws treatment for a period of time and then returns to the original intervention. For a behavior problem such as the inability to study, a client may be asked to keep a record of the number of half-hours spent studying each day. The intervention may be the positive reward of a 5-minute break after each half-hour in which the student may obtain a personally preferred drink. The application need not be limited to the usual behavioral approaches. Similar research programs can be used with free associations and other verbal behavior. The history of psychology shows examples of outstanding single case research, e.g., Stratton's use of inserting lenses to test visual adaptation, the Kelloggs' study of a chimpanzee they raised in their home, and Mary Cover Jones' reconditioning of Peter's fears. Such intensive study, one by one, of the individuals involved in intercultural counseling would gradually build up a shared knowledge, the basic objective of all science.

A third way in which intercultural research may be performed is to recruit persons with special cultural backgrounds for experiments that mimic the counseling situation. Studies of dyadic interaction by analogs, role-playing, and simulation of real-life problem-solving may shed light on the dynamics of counseling. Research should be conducted on foreign students' problems at an early point, thereby preventing the later need for counseling; this active seeking of intercultural problems may be needed since many foreign students tend to be reluctant to come for counseling.

Centers for the systematic collection of intercultural case data would help a great deal in the development of a knowledge base. What is needed is an organized way in which subjects who represent major problems, major countries with high-contrast cultures (such as India, Hong Kong, Iran, and Nigeria, as compared with Western countries), and major cross-ethnic problems may be sampled, so that over time there might be a comparison across methods used in intensive individual studies. It would be important to conduct parallel studies testing the same processes within different cultural or ethnic communities. This research would check within-cultural utility of principles. The intercultural comparisons would be at the level of theories, not at the level of individual and group differences alone. Lonner (1975) stated that the best research is multimethod, multiinvestigator, multicultural, longitudinal, and theory-related. Such a complex investigation would require close coordination and a high degree of commitment, and these factors might be provided by a center on intercultural human development.

COMMUNITY COUNSELING

Counseling-in-the-large, as mentioned before, involves indirect approaches to helping individuals. It is related to community psychology and community mental health. Glasscote and Fishman (1973) described mental health programs on American campuses. In intercultural work, the campus advisor and counselor needs to be aware of difficulties or gaps with the regular campus programs and facilities and, in addition, he or she should develop activities and opportunities directly related to the foreign student. If psychotherapy is, as Schofield (1964) cleverly says, the purchase of friendship, then the increase of friendly activity toward students from other countries may take the place of counseling in a more formalized setting. Friendship families and other community-related programs no doubt increase the effectiveness of the college experience. Reisman and Yamakoski (1974) have shown, however, that a simplistic equivalence of friendship and counseling behavior is not reasonable; their subjects did not want empathic, noninformative communications from friends.

Studies of these programs and their value could be instituted to help to determine the best ways to orient foreign students, relate them to the community, and organize their fellow countrymen for mutual support. Zain's study (1965) led him to conclude that orientation programs are of extreme importance in disseminating realistic information about the academic processes, which are the students' main problems. Mills (1967) found in a survey that foreign students tend to overrate their knowledge of English and their academic preparation, as compared with American administrators' ratings of them. Administrators also believed foreign students need more advising than do American students, and they favored special orientation programs.

Kelly (1970, pp. 183–207), in an article on programs and research for interventions in a community, outlined ways of studying three aspects of this problem. (1) The effectiveness of mental health consultation as a radiating process would involve sequential assessment of key persons in a community and of the students themselves. (2) The effectiveness of programs to bring about organizational change in meeting personal crises, for instance, would be the focus of another concern. (3) Creative planning and community development techniques applicable to the foreign student situations should also be evaluated. The programs aimed at prevention of distress and failure seem to be particularly important for experimentation. Muñoz and Kelly (1975), in providing a good introduction to the prevention of psychological problems, pay considerable attention to cross-ethnic problems.

How Widely Applicable is Counseling?

Another way of looking at the intercultural counseling problem is to raise the question about its utility in different cultures and settings. We already know from many accounts about psychotherapy that there are serious questions about its ethnocentric application to other societies. Let us take India as a specific example. A prominent psychiatrist in India is reported to have said that it took him 5 years in the West to learn its ways of psychotherapy and then it took him 5 years back in India to unlearn what he had learned abroad. For instance, there are great differences between India and the United States in regard to decision-making—a very important aspect of counseling young people. Compared with American teenagers and college students, Indians seem to have many fewer choices (Sundberg & Tyler, 1968). There are several reasons for this. (1) Often for economic survival in India a person must take whatever work he can get, and the opportunities are few. (2) The extended family system exercises strong control over the young person; he cannot make his mind up independently about occupation or marriage or many other things. (3) The traditional "groupisms" of India, as exemplified by the significance of religion, caste, language, and political and social alignments, prevent the individual from choosing freely. (4) The limitations on geographical mobility based on family loyalties and traditions as well as on economic constraints prevent a person from having distant opportunities. (5) The sheer absence of objects of attraction, of television in most places, and the paucity of recreation and other things to do reduces alternatives for choice. Finally, (6) the lack of physical activity and weakened energy characteristic of a person who is affected by poor nutrition and a debilitating climate might limit such a person's options. Sundberg et al. (1969) demonstrated that adolescents' views of decision-making in India were much more restricted by family considerations than they are in America. Tyler, Sundberg, Rohila, and Greene (1968) concluded that the degree of external structure, as it exists in educational arrangements in three countries, may be inversely related to the aspect of personal decision in vocational choice-making. If the school system splits children into different streams at an early age, the children are less likely to develop cognitively complex structures of life possibilities.

In addition, the counseling interaction itself is affected by certain cultural factors in India. The concept of privacy and openness is not the same as in America. One can talk in the family about certain "family matters," but one does not bring them up with outsiders, such as counselors. Family cohesiveness and dominance over personal life requires consideration of family in any decision. The traditional authoritarianism throughout society makes clients more dependent upon a counselor and more expecting that he play a strong and decisive role. Being nondirective might mean rejection and lack of interest or inadequacy to the Indian client. All of these factors, combined with differences in customs and content, make the transfer of counseling to India a serious problem.

An intercultural element to counseling in India—that is, an Indian counselor working with a Thai student or an American visiting professor counseling an Indian student—further complicates the problems.

One of the important tasks for future research is the study of "folk counseling" and "natural" systems of problem-solving in various countries (Kiev, 1964; Torrey, 1972). The person who would teach or counsel in another country would do well to find out as much as he or she can about the living situations of the prospective clients and how they handle personal problems. It might be that the best thing the visitor could do would be to help clarify these processes and work with the community to enhance and supplement them appropriately, rather than to superimpose imported counseling concepts and practices.

THE ETHICS AND PROPRIETY OF INTERCULTURAL RESEARCH

Psychologists and other social scientists are becoming aware that their research choices, processes, and reports are not produced in a vacuum. They impinge on subjects' feelings, pride, and way of life. Ethnic groups in the United States and several foreign countries have pointed out the unilateral exploitation and the invasion of privacy of some social science research. The American Psychological Association (1973) has established ethical guidelines for the conduct of research on human subjects, with particular attention being paid to the arrangement of subjects' informed consent for the data collection before it is carried out.

Beyond the concern for ethical treatment of individual subjects, there is still a problem of the propriety of the way research is carried out in intercultural settings. Questions arise. Is the research going to be of benefit to the subject? If not, is there some way of recompensing him for his time and effort? How can the researcher best give feedback to the subject, perhaps to improve his self-knowledge and understanding of the cultures involved? If the research is done in a foreign country, of what benefit is it to the institutions involved? Is it desirable to share authorship with a citizen of the host country, both to give credit and gain credence? Is it necessary to have multinational colleagues to help interpret results? If the researcher is studying unusual groups in a society, will he or she be introducing procedures and ideas that will have a detrimental effect on their culture? These and many other professional political and administrative considerations need to be included in an intercultural counseling study.

Still, in spite of all of the caveats and complications, intercultural counseling is an exciting and promising area of study. It brings to psychology and other social sciences many opportunities for important learning —how different peoples might understand each other better, how one culture is viewed by another, and new ways of observing our basic human commonalities, similarities, and uniqueness.

The author wishes to thank the following friends who read early drafts of the chapter: Gerald Fry, Kenneth Ghent, Walter Lonner, Margaret Mann, Thomas Mills, Ricardo Muñoz, Pritam Rohila, Saul Toobert, and Leona Tyler.

REFERENCES

Achebe, C. *No longer at ease.* New York: Ivan Obolensky, 1960.
Adinolfi, A. A. Relevance of person perception research to clinical psychology. *Journal of Consulting and Clinical Psychology*, 1971, *37*, 167–176.
Allport, G. W. *Personality: A psychological interpretation.* New York: Holt, 1937.
American Psychological Association. *Ethical principles in the conduct of research with human participants.* Washington, D.C.: American Psychological Association, 1973.
Antler, L. Correlates of home and host country acquaintanceship among foreign medical residents in the United States. *Journal of Social Psychology*, 1970, *80*, 49–57.
Bates, B. C., Sundberg, N. D., & Tyler, L. E. Divergent problem solving: A comparison of adolescents in India and America. *International Journal of Psychology*, 1970, *5*, 231–244.
Bem, S. L. The measurement of psychological androgyny. *Journal of Consulting and Clinical Psychology*, 1974, *42*, 155–162.
Benfari, R. C. Relationship between early dependence training and patient-therapist dyad. *Psychological Reports*, 1969, *25*, 552–554.
Benson, A. G., & Miller, R. E. *A preliminary report on uses of the Michigan International Student Problem Inventory in research, orientation and counseling, developing a balanced program and evaluating potential for academic success of/for foreign students.* Unpublished paper, Michigan State University, International Programs Office, May 1966.
Bergin, A. E. The evaluation of therapeutic outcomes. In A. E. Bergin and S. L. Garfield (Eds.), *Handbook of psychotherapy and behavior change.* New York: John Wiley & Sons, 1971.
Berry, J. W. On cross-cultural comparability. *International Journal of Psychology*, 1969, *4*, 119–128.
Berzins, J. I. Ross, W. F., & Cohen, D. I. Relation of the A-B distinction and trust-distrust sets to addict patients' self-disclosure in brief interviews. *Journal of Consulting and Clinical Psychology*, 1970, *34*, 289–296.
Blank, L. *Psychological evaluation in psychotherapy: Ten case histories.* Chicago: Aldine Publishing Co., 1965.
Bolz, C. R. Personality types. In R. M. Dreger (Ed.), *Multivariate personality research.* Baton Rouge: Claitor's Publishing Division, 1972.
Brislin, R. W., Lonner, W. J., & Thorndike, R. M. *Cross-cultural research methods.* New York: John Wiley & Sons, 1973.
Brislin, R. W., & Van Buren, H. Can they go home again? *Exchange*, 1974, *9* (4), 19–24.
Campbell, D. P. *The results of counseling: Twenty-five years later.* Philadelphia: W. B. Saunders Co., 1965.

Carkhuff, R. R. Black and white in helping. *Professional Psychology*, 1972, *3*, 18–22.

Carkhuff, R. R., & Pierce, R. Differential effects of therapist race and social class upon patient depth of self-exploration in the initial clinical interview. *Journal of Consulting Psychology*, 1967, *31*, 632–634.

Chassan, J. B. *Research design in clinical psychology and psychiatry.* New York: Appleton-Century-Crofts, 1967.

Conway, R. M. *The psychological effects of cross-cultural experience.* Louvain, Belgium: Université Catholique de Louvain, 1969.

Cottrell, A. B. Cross-national marriage as an extension of international life style: A study of Indian-Western couples. *Journal of Marriage and the Family*, 1973, *35*, 739–741.

Cronbach, L. J., & Gleser, G. C. Assessing similarity between profiles. *Psychological Bulletin*, 1953, *50*, 456–473.

Davidson, P. O., & Costello, C. G. (Eds.), *N = 1: Experimental studies of single cases.* New York: Van Nostrand Reinhold Co., 1969.

Davitz, J. R. (Ed.). *The communication of emotional meaning.* New York: McGraw-Hill Book Co., 1964.

DeVos, G. A., & Hippler, A. A. Cultural psychology: Comparative studies of human behavior. In G. Lindzey & E. Aronson (Eds.), *Handbook of social psychology*, Vol. 4, *Group psychology and phenomena of interaction* (2nd ed.). Reading, Massachusetts: Addison-Wesley, 1969.

Draguns, J. G. Comparison of psychopathology across cultures: Issues, findings, directions. *Journal of Cross-Cultural Psychology*, 1973, *4*, 9–47.

Dukes, W. F. $N = 1$. *Psychological Bulletin*, 1965, *64*, 74–79.

Fiedler, F. E. A comparison of therapeutic relationships in psychoanalytic, nondirective and Adlerian therapy. *Journal of Consulting Psychology*, 1950, *14*, 436–445.

Frank, J. D. *Persuasion and healing: A comparative study of psychotherapy.* Baltimore: Johns Hopkins University Press, 1961.

Gilmore, S. K. *The counselor-in-training.* New York: Appleton-Century-Crofts, 1973.

Glasscote, R., & Fishman, M. E. *Mental health on the campus.* Washington, D.C.: American Psychiatric Association and National Association for Mental Health, 1973.

Gordon, M. *Assimilation in American life.* New York: Oxford University Press, 1964.

Grantham, R. J. Effects of counselor sex, race and language style on Black students in initial interviews. *Journal of Counseling Psychology*, 1973, *20*, 553–559.

Grey, A. L. The counseling process and its cultural setting. *Journal of Vocational and Educational Guidance*, 1965, *11*, 104–114.

Hall, E. T. *The hidden dimension.* Garden City, New York: Doubleday & Co., 1966.

Hall, E. T., & Whyte, W. F. Intercultural communication: A guide to men of action. *Human organization*, 1960, *19*, 5–12. (Reprinted in A. G. Smith [Ed.], *Communication and culture.* New York: Holt, Rinehart & Winston, 1966.)

Heitler, J. B. Preparation of lower-class patients for expressive group psychotherapy. *Journal of Consulting and Clinical Psychology*, 1973, *41*, 351–360.

Howard, K. I., & Orlinsky, D. E. Psychotherapeutic processes. In P. H. Mussen & M. R. Rosenzweig (Eds.), *Annual Review of Psychology*, 1972, *23*, 615–668.

Jackson, G. G., & Kirschner, S. A. Racial self-designation and preference for a counselor. *Journal of Counseling Psychology*, 1973, *20*, 560–564.

Johnson, D. C. Problems of foreign students. *International Educational and Cultural Exchange*, 1971, *7*, 61–68.

Johnson, D. C. Ourselves and others: Comparative stereotypes. *International Educational and Cultural Exchange*, 1973, *9* (2–3), 24–28.

Kelly, J. G. The quest for valid preventive interventions. In C. D. Spielberger (Ed.), *Current topics in clinical and community psychology* (Vol. 2). New York: Academic Press, 1970.

Kiev, A. (Ed.), *Magic, faith and healing: Studies in primitive psychiatry today.* New York: Macmillan Co., Free Press, 1964.

Kiev, A. Transcultural psychiatry: Research problems and perspectives. In S. C. Plog & R. B. Edgerton (Eds.), *Changing perspectives in mental health.* New York: Holt, Rinehart & Winston, 1969.

Kiev, A. *Transcultural psychiatry.* New York: Macmillan Co., Free Press, 1972.

Kluckhohn, C., & Murray. H. A. Personality formation: The determinants. In C. Kluckhohn, H. A. Murray, & D. M. Schneider (Eds.), *Personality in nature, society and culture.* New York: Random House, Alfred A. Knopf, 1953.

Ledvinka, J. Race of interviewer and the language elaboration of Black interviewees. *Journal of Social Issues,* 1971, *27,* 185–197.

Leitenberg, H. The use of single-case methodology in psychotherapy research. *Journal of Abnormal Psychology,* 1973, *82,* 87–101.

Lonner, W. J. An analysis of the prepublication evaluation of cross-cultural manuscripts: Implications for future research. In R. W. Brislin, S. Bochner, & W. J. Lonner (Eds.), *Cross-cultural perspectives on learning.* New York: John Wiley & Sons, Halsted, 1975.

Mills, T. J. *Identification of the academic problems confronting foreign graduate students at the University of Oregon, 1966–67.* Unpublished Master of Science thesis, University of Oregon, 1967.

Muñoz, R. F., & Kelly, J. G. *The prevention of mental disorders.* Homewood, Illinois: General Learning Systems, 1975.

Ogowa, D. M., & Weldon, T. A. Cross-cultural analysis of feedback behavior within Japanese American and Caucasian American small groups. *Journal of Communication,* 1972, *22,* 189–195.

Persons, R. W., & Marks, P. A. Self-disclosure with recidivists: Optimum interviewer-interviewee matching. *Journal of Abnormal Psychology,* 1970, *76,* 387–391.

Reisman, J. M., & Yamakoski, T. Psychotherapy and friendship: An analysis of the communication of friends. *Journal of Counseling Psychology,* 1974, *21,* 269–273.

Schofield, W. *Psychotherapy: The purchase of friendship.* Englewood Cliffs, New Jersey: Prentice-Hall, 1964.

Schumacher, L. C., Banikiotes, P. G., & Banikiotes, F. G. Language compatibility and minority group counseling. *Journal of Counseling Psychology,* 1972, *19,* 255–256.

Shaffer, M., Sundberg, N. D., & Tyler, L. E. Content differences on word listing by American, Dutch and Indian adolescents. *Journal of Social Psychology,* 1969, *79,* 139–140.

Smith, H. C. *Sensitivity to people.* New York: McGraw-Hill Book Co., 1966.

Spilken, A. Z., Jacobs, M. A., Muller, J. J., & Knitzer, J. Personality characteristics of therapists: Description of relevant variables and examination of conscious preferences. *Journal of Consulting and Clinical Psychology,* 1969, *33,* 317–326.

Stecklein, J. E., Liu, H. C., Anderson, J. F., & Gunararatne, S. A. *Attitudes of foreign students toward educational experiences at the University of Minnesota.* Minneapolis: University of Minnesota, Bureau of Institutional Research, 1971.

Strupp, H. H., & Bloxom, A. L. Preparing lower-class patients for group psychotherapy: Development and evaluation of a role-induction film. *Journal of Consulting and Clinical Psychology,* 1973, *41,* 373–384.

Sundberg, N. D. A method for studying sensitivity to implied meanings. *Gawein,* 1966, *15,* 1–8.

Sundberg, N. D. Cross-cultural advising and counseling. *Student Services Review*, 1973, *7*, 6–12.

Sundberg, N. D., Sharma, V., Rohila, P. K., & Wodtli, T. Family cohesiveness and autonomy of adolescents in India and the United States. *Journal of Marriage and the Family*, 1969, *31*, 403–407.

Sundberg, N. D., & Tyler, L. E. Adolescent views of life possibilities in India, the Netherlands and the United States, *Student Services Review*, 1968, *3* (1), 8–13.

Sundberg, N. D., Tyler, L. E., & Taplin, J. R. *Clinical psychology: Expanding horizons* (2nd ed.). New York: Appleton-Century-Crofts, 1973.

Sundland, D. M., & Barker, E. N. The orientation of psychotherapists. *Journal of Consulting Psychology*, 1962, *26*, 291–212.

Tan, H. Intercultural study of counseling expectancies. *Journal of Consulting Psychology*, 1967, *14*, 122–130.

Torrey, E. F. *The mind game: Witchdoctors and psychiatrists.* New York: Emerson Hall Publishers, 1972.

Triandis, H. C., Vassiliou, V., Vassiliou, G., Tanaka, Y., & Shanmugam, A. V. (Eds.). *The analysis of subjective culture.* New York: John Wiley & Sons, 1972.

Triandis, H. C., Malpass, R. S., & Davidson, A. R. Psychology and culture. In P. H. Mussen & M. R. Rosenzweig (Eds.), *Annual Review of Psychology*, 1973, *24*, 355–378.

Tyler, L. E. *The work of the counselor* (3rd ed.). New York: Appleton-Century-Crofts, 1969.

Tyler, L. E., Sundberg, N. D., Rohila, P. K., & Greene, M. M. Patterns of choices in Dutch, American and Indian adolescents. *Journal of Counseling Psychology*, 1968, *15*, 522–529.

Vontress, C. E. Racial differences: Impediments to rapport. *Journal of Counseling Psychology*, 1971, *18*, 7–13.

Wiggins, J. S. *Personality and prediction: Principles of personality assessment.* Reading, Massachusetts: Addison-Wesley Publishing Co., 1973.

Zain, E. K. *A study of the academic and personal-social difficulties encountered by a selected group of foreign students at the University of Oregon.* Unpublished doctoral dissertation, University of Oregon, 1965.

9 The Use of Western-Based Tests in Intercultural Counseling

WALTER J. LONNER

HOW DO YOU MEASURE WHETHER OR NOT CLIENTS FROM OTHER CULTURES NEED COUNSELING?

There is now ample evidence that great caution must be used when Western-based psychological tests are employed in conjunction with the counseling of students from cultures outside the Euro-American sphere of cultural influence. These cautions have been voiced for standardized intelligence tests and personality tests, but the pitfalls are even more ominous for projective tests.

The issues, in addition to the ever-present translation problem, revolve around three key areas: (1) the construct/criterion controversy; (2) the issue of verbal versus nonverbal stimuli in tests; and (3) the use of norms on populations other than those for which the tests were standardized.

The construct-criterion controversy deals with the viewing of psychological constructs as being purely culture-bound (emic) or relatively pancultural (etic). A case can be made that constructs and criteria may be interchangeable, depending upon the nature of the phenomena being investigated through psychological tests. The verbal versus nonverbal issue stems from the popular, but incorrect, view that nonverbal stimuli are more "culture-fair" than are verbal stimuli. Various intercultural studies have shown that nonverbal stimuli may, in fact, be interpreted as being more variable than verbal stimuli. The use of test norms on populations for which there are no existing norms is related to the construct-criterion controversy. Generally stated, norms developed in one culture should not be used in another unless a case can be established that the norms show invariance across cultures.

To the extent that tests from one culture cannot accommodate all relevant resources from another culture are their interpretations subject to error. Once again, we are confronted with the necessity for considering the client's cultural environment as being part of his totality. Available tests have been notoriously inefficient, if not downright inaccurate, beyond a fairly narrow cultural range, that range in which the test was developed and normed. To the extent that decisions are based on inefficient or inaccurate scores, any test can lend itself to an interpretation that is both unfair to the client and unethical for the counselor.

Lonner's chapter provides practical guidelines for counselors who use test data in intercultural counseling. He identifies the problems confronting intercultural interpretations and highlights the issues essential to the decision about whether or not to use tests at all with a multicultural population. As Lonner points out, a test is a poor representation of a person and exhibits only a part of that person's resources. When that partial picture is itself distorted, test data can in fact be more damaging than no data at all. Lonner's contribution to this collection of articles is to demonstrate how effectively, through the undisputed authority of test data, a racial-ethnic-cultural bias has infiltrated the respectable and sophisticated systems of counseling and mental health care in our society.

A probably widely underestimated problem in the counseling of students from various cultural and ethnic groups is that of how to determine the extent to which Western-based (that is, normed or developed in the West) psychometric devices can be used or misused by professional counselors. The focus of this chapter primarily is on tests, inventories, checklists, and other instruments that are typically to be found in the offices of personnel workers whose task it is to deal with personal adjustment problems of students, foreign and otherwise. These problems include initial and long-term personal adjustment, academic goals and aspirations, and so forth. While not minimizing their importance, I will make little specific mention of such nationwide testing programs as the Graduate Record Exams or the College Entrance Examination Boards, since such purely academic-oriented instruments perform quite a different function than do clinical or psychological assessment instruments. Moreover, those who administer such academic- and achievement-type testing programs to foreign and Third-World students no doubt sensibly and wisely take into consideration such matters as differentials in previous schooling, language competencies, and expected levels of preparation before the student returns to his home country or subcultural group. Most of the points raised in this chapter, however, may be validly generalized to certain problems associated with the use of such purely academic-type tests.

The points raised herein will have varied applicability to that diverse cadre of students known by that somewhat ethnocentric catchall term, the "foreign student." Clearly some foreign students, for example, those from Canada or Great Britain, more closely approximate the modal American student than do students from a variety of subcultures within the United States. One must acknowledge the very strong possibility that the non-American student, regardless of country of origin, systematically does not represent the modal citizen of his country. Rather, he or she may be a cultural elitist and quite cosmopolitan, and he or she may know more about the United States and its history than does the typical student from Schenectady or Omaha.

Nevertheless, there are several issues that must be recognized by counselors whenever a psychological instrument is used to elicit information from students who hail from cultures or subcultures that have not been systematically included in initial stages of instrument construction.

ISSUES IN INTERCULTURAL TESTING THAT ARE APPLICABLE TO FOREIGN STUDENT ASSESSMENT AND COUNSELING

In recent years there have appeared several books and journal articles that have addressed themselves to problems of intercultural assessment. These writings are primarily counteroffensives against the unwitting naiveté represented by countless and somewhat pardonable attempts to develop culture-fair tests or to use tests with gross incautiousness among members from other cultures without some basic methodological and perhaps ethical issues being considered. Four recent books contain nearly all the problems and cautions to be summarized here. The book by Triandis, Vassiliou, Vassiliou, Tanaka, and Shanmugam (1972) contains monographs dealing with various ways that extensions of Osgood's semantic differential can be used in the analysis of the ways in which people evaluate and perceive their unique subjective cultures. For example, Triandis pinpointed both antecedents and consequents of behavioral dispositions. He and his colleagues also assessed the manner in which different cultural roles affect the behavior of those from other cultures. More recently, Triandis (1975) has given a different treatment of his basic rationale. There he talks about isomorphic-versus-nonisomorphic behavior, and how behavioral scientists in various applied settings may benefit from the work that has been done with various "cultural assimilators." Cultural assimilators are training devices aimed to help others become more familiar with "other culture" roles, values, behavioral intentions, and so forth. To my knowledge, no foreign student office has used cultural assimilator data in an effort to aid in intercultural communication, so that this may be a fertile research area for many foreign student advisors and others who wish to deal with such communication problems in a systematic and empirical manner. Another book, by Manaster and Havighurst (1972), summarizes a potpourri of problems associated with the use of scales to measure values and personality. A third treatment, by Cronbach and Drenth (1972), consists of a collection of papers resulting from a 1971 Istanbul conference, which addressed the varied problems of adapting "mental" tests (i.e., intelligence or ability tests) for use in other cultures. Finally, the volume by Brislin, Lonner, and

Thorndike (1973) discusses a wide range of methodological problems in intercultural psychology. It includes several chapters of direct relevance to the assessment of personological variables in intercultural counseling.

None of the above books have explicitly analyzed testing problems that one may encounter when dealing with adult foreign students. Hence, this chapter is a synthesis of the major intercultural testing problems and has been designed both to supplement and complement the other chapters of this book, all or most of them being nonmeasurement oriented.

I believe that the following issues are most important.

1. The construct versus criterion controversy
2. The nature of the test stimuli—verbal versus nonverbal
3. The exporting of norms
4. Response sets
5. The tendency to infer deficits from test score differences
6. The cultural isomorphism of Western-based tests and the motives for taking them

THE CONSTRUCT VERSUS CRITERION CONTROVERSY

Blatantly distinguished, constructs examined interculturally may be viewed as potentially pancultural psychological shorthand for the "givens" that psychologists infer to characterize humans (intelligence, anxiety, submissiveness, dependency, etc.); criteria, on the other hand, are usually the points of evidence or proof in empirical research. Criteria usually involve measurable levels of performance or functioning that may be suggestive of the magnitude of the underlying construct being assessed or scaled. Conveniently, psychological tests have often been dichotomized as being either construct-related (theoretical) or criterion-related (atheoretical). Since some researchers do not believe that constructs can be assumed to exist everywhere (owing to indigenous thought or value systems, for example), the use of construct-related tests could result in the artificial attribution of a construct to an individual who does not have it in his or her value system. In the jargon of intercultural psychology, this is called "imposing an etic," or assuming a construct to be valid everywhere, rather than evaluating "emically," or from within a particular cultural group, to determine the nature and possibility of the construct(s) actually being present within a cultural group and thus shared by individual members of the group (see Berry, 1969). Using similar rationale, the same researchers may maintain that criteria are likewise not transferrable. Thus, the conservative solution would be to develop instruments based on locally (within culture) conceived constructs, with locally valid criteria to "prove" the existence of the construct being used. Berry (1972) has called this approach "radical cultural relativism," as opposed to its extreme, which may be called universal construct ubiquity. Obviously, the "radical" extreme would lead to a dilemma and would render comparisons across cultures impossible; every group of people would have its own noninterchangeable set of constructs and attendant criteria. Carried to an existential extreme, this line of thought would mean that every person would have his or her own sets of constructs and criteria, a belief that will be familiar to adherents of the counseling orientation of phenomenological theorists like Carl Rogers and George Kelly. More technically, this may mean that what we are dealing with are ipsative (nonnormative) scales, wherein the one and only reference point for the measurement of the construct is "locked in" each culture separately. Thus, the "metric" used within one cultural group would be noncomparable with another group's metric. The same would hold for individual persons within one culture.

A more reasonable way to view the problem and its ultimate solution is to assume that there is high extensional agreement among behavioral scientists (as well as in a client-counselor dyad) as to what a construct is, but that those criteria that document its particular cultural manifestation may vary. Example: A counselor and his foreign or minority-member client may agree that "shyness" (extensionally validated by both as at least a personality adjective) is one of the client's characteristics. The counselor, knowing what the overt manifestations and social or personal ramifications (criteria) are for shyness in his culture, may falsely attribute these criteria to his client; although, for the client (and unknown to or overlooked by the counselor), shyness may be based on criteria that still reside overseas or in a Navajo village. The word shyness would be agreed upon; its culturally determined referents would not necessarily be. Such differentials are probably used extensively in many intercultural counseling encounters as a ploy, or as a "foot-in-the-door," one leading to more effective learning of feeling or affect on the part of both the client and the counselor.

It is largely because of this particular issue that criteria-based tests such as the Minnesota Multiphasic Personality Inventory (MMPI) are thought to be inappropriate for intercultural use, whereas construct-related tests are generally considered to be more acceptable. In this context, the "healthy man's MMPI," the California Psychological Inventory, would be an example of a construct-related test, because its items are cast in "folk concepts"—recurring themes of social interaction that may exist everywhere, and, hence, are easily understood and easy to translate. But elsewhere (Brislin, Lonner, & Thorndike, 1973), the point has been made that constructs and criteria may essentially "merge" across cultures to the extent that the world is shrinking into a homogeneous mass. Nevertheless, this notion of "merging" is only an idea, and it would be safest at present to assume that constructs and criteria are not equivalent. Unless and until firmly proven otherwise, the client's interpretation of the construct should prevail, not that of the counselor.

THE NATURE OF STIMULI: VERBAL VERSUS NONVERBAL

It has long been assumed, probably incorrectly, that tests employing the use of nonverbal stimuli are relatively unambiguous and, hence, more appropriate for intercultural use. Many tests, for example, use figural analogies, mazes, and other formats which assume that abilities, intelligence and even personality can be assessed more fairly across cultural groups if the linguistic dimension can be transcended. This assumption has resulted in the wholesale and often grossly inexact use of projective tests interculturally, such tests having their own methodological problems (Abel, 1973; Lindzey, 1961; Spain, 1972) and in the equally widespread use of such tests as Raven's Progressive Matrices and Cattell's Culture-Fair Intelligence Test, both of which are saturated with nonverbal content.

Much research on cultural and ecological influences on perceptual and cognitive style has amply demonstrated that different modes of perception can influence the way in which these stimuli are interpreted, a classic example being the work of Hudson (1960), which ushered in a great amount of intercultural work on topics such as two- and three-dimensional perception. These rather esoteric, experimental psychological studies have minimal relevance for the counseling of foreign students, but they do give us sufficient evidence to suggest that a great deal of caution be used when nonverbal stimuli are utilized to cut across cultural boundaries for measurement purposes.

Nor should it be assumed that verbal stimuli—words, phrases, and sentences found in personality and intelligence tests—have the same meanings to persons everywhere, even if they can read English very well. Western-based tests and inventories, particularly those developed in the United States, are liberally endowed with subtle idioms. Before rather technical advances in translation procedures became available (Brislin, 1970), many tests were translated literally, word-for-word, without adequate attention being paid to accuracies in meaning in the context of the idioms and meanings of other languages.

THE EXPORTATION OF NORMS

It should be immediately apparent that test norms based on one cultural group should not be considered valid for other cultural groups. This issue is related to the construct-criterion issue raised earlier. Norms, of course, include the use of percentile ranks based on the proportion of students who meet various levels of criterion performance. Unless there is strong evidence for the invariability of such performance, one must "decenter" the various rankings and adjust the levels of performance on the basis of other factors. For example, a foreign student's score placing him at the 50th percentile could, with adjustment for language, place him at the 75th percentile. A useful example of how psychometric adjustments of test scores can lead to better "culture-fairness" has been given by Thorndike (1971). The basis of these adjustments was briefly explained in this way (Brislin, Lonner, & Thorndike, 1973):

> "Fairness" [may be approximated or developed] by setting levels of test performance that will qualify applicants or students from diverse cultural groups in proportion to the percentage of those in the groups who reach a specified level of criterion performance. Neither mean test scores nor mean criterion values alone would be used as indicators of "superior" or "inferior" performance. Different regression lines for each group as the lines relate to the same levels of criterion performance across groups would be instrumental in guiding one's use of the world "fairness."

Nor should comparisons with national norms be considered valid unless invariance across cultures can be established. Without some common reference point—an external and neutral level of criterion performance, for example—sets of norms developed independently in two or more countries are just that—independent measures. Numerous researchers have used "norms of convenience" in comparative research, especially in the area of personality measurement. Good examples of this questionable procedure include numerous attempts to compare the MMPI data extracted from a small number of subjects from a foreign country or ethnic group with the anchoring United States data and norms. If scores are very nearly identical, the intercultural extension of one set of norms may be valid. But the more that one set of scores or norms departs from the pattern of the second set of scores or norms, the less confidence one can have in interpreting the significance of the differences. Segall, Campbell, and Herskovits (1966), in their well-known investigation of visual illusions, were confident that their comparisons of perceptual-ecological processes affecting illusion susceptibility were making sense because they found such small differences between groups of subjects. When these small differences occurred, they were generally in line with ecological hypotheses. Had the differences been widely discrepant, a failure to communicate with the subjects (about the nature of the task, clarity of the directions, and so on) would have been the more plausible reason for score differentials. Thus, the closer norms or scores across cultures "fit," the more likely those norms are comparable, since frequent cross-norm points of articulation could not be due to statistical error or the failure to communicate.

An example may help to explain how these articulating scores can build confidence in the use of a particular test among diverse groups of foreign students. The United States' Strong Vocational Interest Blank (SVIB), used in both translated (German) and untranslated forms for possible extensions to other countries, yielded few significant occupational scale differences among subjects from nine Western nations (Lonner & Adams, 1972). Since a very large number of interest scale differences were possible, the essential uniformity of profiles across all countries suggests strongly that the inventory is doing about the same job of measuring interests in all the countries sampled. Had there been many significant differences, two conclusions could have been drawn: (1) the scales yielding the significant differences were obviously not comparable across countries, and (2) that being the case, a number of the concordant scales may have "articulated" across countries purely by chance. Thus, not knowing which, if any, of the scales may have accurately measured interests across two or more countries, the entire array of cross-national profiles would have had to be dismissed as being too dangerous to try to salvage for valid interpretative purposes.

RESPONSE SETS

In the psychological testing literature there is a whole grab bag of response sets (sometimes referred to as response styles) that could affect test scores. The response set of *acquiesence* generally refers to the tendency of a subject to agree (or its reverse, to disagree) with extremes, usually on attitude statements. Some foreign students taking tests may tend to say "yes" out of politeness, for instance. The stereotype of the Oriental student's disposition comes to mind as one quick example of this phenomenon. The response set of *social desirability* refers to the tendency of subjects to answer in the direction they consider to be the more socially favorable alternative. Other response sets include *evasiveness* (unwillingness to commit oneself) and *carelessness* (the making of inconsistent judgments). A brief summary of response sets and the types of instruments in which each can most liberally be found has been given in Fiske (1971), and a recent analysis of "extreme response style" interculturally has been provided by Chun, Campbell, and Yoo (1974).

Unless a psychological test or other data-gathering device has a built-in sensor to help detect the presence of response sets, it may be an important factor in the final score. Any given group of foreign students will likely contain an assortment of cultural values and general culture-originating personality factors that predispose these students to respond in ways that appear unique to a United States psychologist or counselor. For example, people who have been conditioned not to take a middle-of-the-road position will likely respond infrequently to the? in a Yes-?-No response format. Such dispositions could lead to distorted or inflated responses, especially if the test has not been normed on the culture of which the student is a member. Thus, a critical step to be taken before unusual or bizarre profiles or scores are interpreted would be to ascertain whether or not response sets have influenced the results. If they are even slightly suspect, the safest alternative would be to ignore altogether the results rather than to try to bend interpretations around them.

Consistently extreme response sets, then, would invalidate test scores in terms of uniculture norms. However, there may be times when the response sets themselves could be helpful in assessing particular aspects of a student's personality or attitudinal dispositions. For example, it may be of significant interest to discuss with the client his or her reasons for responding in unexpected ways, and these stated reasons may give clues to imp rtant ways in which the client approaches life situations.

THE TENDENCY TO INFER DEFICITS FROM TEST SCORE DIFFERENCES

Only recently has there been growing concern about the tendency to overinterpret test score or other differences, a situation in which the tester generally is seeking to account for lower (pathological or less intelligent) scores (for a general review of culture and thinking and other cognitive processes, see Cole & Bruner, 1971; Cole & Scribner, 1974). Typical personality tests are usually constructed so as to scale both the positive and the negative sides of personality dimensions (peaks and valleys of a personality profile). Hence, any tendency to overinterpret these tests may be to make high scores even higher and low scores even worse. The story is different with intelligence and ability tests. When a member of another culture does not do too well on standard intelligence tests or on the tasks requiring mental gymnastics that psychologists have invented, then reasons for the differences advanced by interpreters may fall into an artificially imposed deficit column. Cole (1975), who is most concerned about such inferences being drawn from our briefcase of psychological tricks, gives an excellent example of this. His remarks stem from his reaction to the many findings of recent vintage that many people throughout the world fail on tasks designed to measure whether or not the Piagetian notion of "conservation" (e.g., a tall beaker contains more water than a series of short beakers) has been reached.

> Are we to believe that aborigine adults [who may earlier have failed to convince the researcher that they can "conserve" water] will store water in tall thin

cans in order to have more water? . . . Do they think they lose water when they pour it from a bucket into a barrel? I am tempted to believe that they would have disappeared long ago were this the case.

The same point is valid for the more standard ability tests that may be imposed on foreign students. Unless compelling corroborating evidence from varied external sources suggests that test scores are valid, no inferences suggestive of deficits in ability or in personality should be drawn. A test is a most incomplete representation of a person. However, I do accept Draguns' comments in chapter 1 about this simplistic statement as being valid. A test is a poor representation of a person, but it is, nevertheless, better than nothing at all. One may argue that reasonably good tests given under optimal conditions to foreign students are in fact more reliable initial representations of behavioral predispositions than are initial interviews or other information of a highly subjective nature.

The Cultural Isomorphism of Western-Based Tests and the Motives for Taking Them

By the time a youngster from Mainstreet, U.S.A., has reached college, he has taken dozens of tests designed to measure his personality, abilities, achievement, intelligence, and potential for success in college. These tests, especially those of maximum performance, are isomorphic to the competitive, technological, and success-oriented West; that is, they are part of the system and presage what is to come in the academic and business world. Not only are most students from other countries not familiar with psychological tests, they may be a parody of whatever may be isomorphic to measures of academic performance or promise in their own countries. For instance, the typical European, who may never have seen a multiple-choice test, is often apalled by their ubiquity in the United States. Are we in the United States seriously to expect students from over 100 different countries to succumb to our devices without some incredulity or anxiety? Can we expect them to don our modes and motives, accepting our psychometric yardsticks with ease?

In the context of determining levels of intellectual functioning among United States subcultural groups, psychologists generally concede that the primary source of tested differences in intelligence lies in the subject's level of motivation. (See Labov, 1970, for an excellent example of how a researcher can elicit good responses from minority-group children by examining which factors in a testing or interview situation are important to the subject.) When a member of a minority group sees no likely payoff for taking assorted tests, why should he bother? In a similar vein, Pedersen (1971) has found evidence in the literature suggesting that a foreign student's motivation to learn English is correlated with his desire to integrate with the American community or to remain in the United States after his education. A "payoff" is what drives the student to English proficiency.

The analog source of variability between United States and foreign college students likely can be accounted for by two dimensions—a familiarity-unfamiliarity dimension and a differential culture/test isomorphism dimension.

ATTEMPTS TO RESOLVE ONE OR MORE OF THE ISSUES

There have been numerous attempts to decenter the Euro-American bias in many psychological assessment instruments. By devising tests that contain stimuli—both verbal and nonverbal—that cut across cultural lines, or by adequately norming existing tests on subjects from many cultures, testers may be able to make more valid comparisons of test scores across cultures. But realistically, the problems may never be fully resolved. Nevertheless, those who wish to examine these problems in more complete detail are invited to consult the recent books, mentioned earlier, that address themselves to these problems and to related methodological concerns. These books have surveyed in considerably more depth than I have in this chapter the various problems of testing, adaptation, and interpretation.

Brislin, Lonner, and Thorndike (1973) have described numerous interculturally viable tests and inventories, and have cited ample intercultural attempts at validating or using each of these measures. For example, the D-48 Test is a possible new way to cut across cultural and linguistic lines in measuring intelligence. The D-48 has an aura of legitimacy for the simple reason that the stimuli it employs, dominoes (hence the title, 48 Dominoes), are held to be invariant both across cultures and across time because the basic domino format has been around for at least 3,000 years. Domino (1968), who reported on the use of the various tests with foreign students from 21 countries, has presented evidence that of four "culture-fair" intelligence tests employed, the D-48 correlated best with grades and was easiest to administer. (It should be mentioned that George Domino, the author of the article, has a completely coincidental nominal connection with the Domino test!) With test construction logic similar to the logic used in the construction of the D-48, the Perceptual Acuity Test (Gough & McGurk, 1967) is held to be a reasonable tactic for comparative purposes since it capitalizes on various types of visual illusions, precedents in the intercultural study of illusions being abundant.

In the personality-interests-values domain of tests and inventories, there are pathetically few instruments that can lay claim to possible invariant stimuli, invariant constructs, or invariant norms. Aside from projectives—the "right arm of the clinician"—which virtually defy adequate standardization for comparative purposes, there are only a few serious contenders for possible intercultural consumption. One is Gough's California Psychological Inventory with its built-in "folk concepts" mentioned earlier, and another is Cattell's factor analytically derived 16 PF (personality factors), with its 16 bipolar personality dimensions which have been assigned, somewhat pretentiously, "universal indices." An old timer making a serious effort for ultimate and legitimate inter-cultural export is the MMPI. Its chief current protagonist, James N. Butcher of the University of Minnesota, is becoming quite active in promoting its more valid or helpful intercultural uses and is currently writing a book on this topic. Articles by Glatt (1969), Gynther (1972), Kadri (1971), and a book of profiles (Lanyon, 1968) are representative current examples of some of the extensions and problems of the MMPI in its applicability for use beyond a Caucasian American population.

Two additional instruments, which have recently come to my attention, represent approaches worthy of mention in the context of the use of tests as aids in the counseling of foreign students. The first is an instrument called ACCENT (American Cross-Cultural Ethnic Nomenclature Test). Developed by Howard Lyman (see Lyman, 1970, for a very brief report), ACCENT is a maximum-performance-type test which contains both traditional (white-biased) and Black-biased items. The logic behind the test is that Black students should score higher on Black-biased items, and that white students should score higher on white-biased items—un-impeachable logic! In a preliminary tryout of the test, this pattern was indeed found, the mean differences for each set of items (white or Black) differentiating between the races at $p. < .001$. ACCENT has a competitor known as the BITCH test (an acronym for either Black Intelligence Test Counterbalanced for Honkies, or Black Intelligence Test of Cultural Homogeneity—alternate titles for use presumably depending upon how serious an image one wishes to project). Both ACCENT and BITCH have definite research possibilities, and one can imagine parallel tests popping up for all separate ethnic groups. Readers have probably seen such variants of these devices. One is the Chitling Test, which basically uses the same idea as the BITCH (just when is Booker T. Washington's birthday?). Such a proliferation of totally ethnic-based devices would, however, prove only what we intuitively know—that every ethnic group has its own slang, idioms, heroes, and cultural legacies. This point can be proven ad infinitum, but valid intercultural test comparisons could never be made without the items common to all such tests first being identified.

The Porter-Haller Michigan International Student Problem Inventory (MISPI) has been developed along the lines of the Mooney Problem

Check List. The MISPI contains 132 items depicting possible problems that foreign students may have (e.g., concern about religious beliefs, learning English, costs of an automobile, not being able to find dates). The items are a result of hundreds of interviews with foreign students who sojourned to the United States. Porter (1966) gave little information regarding the validity and reliability of the MISPI and gave no information at all about the minimum level of English proficiency that would be required by foreign students before they could understand the inventory.

Where do we go from here, if anywhere? At the Istanbul conference on mental tests and cultural adaptation (reported to Cronbach & Drenth, 1972), one speaker was quoted as saying, "Everything that has been said in this conference has demonstrated that it is meaningless to make comparisons in different cultural environments of even so-called culture-free tests." In the initial version of this chapter, I asked the following question: "Will any wrap-up statement resulting from this symposium bear any resemblance to that indictment?" Well, such a question was not directly asserted, but it is still quite a legitimate one.

At the same symposium, I offered an introductory apology. It went something like this: "I do not know how many foreign students in the United States take (or are required to take) psychological tests, especially in this antitest era. Further, I do not know how many professionals working with foreign students actually rely on tests to any extent, or what their level of test interpretation competence is if they do. I only know that I can offer some humble opinions and summaries of cross-cultural testing problems in the hope that someone may find a few beneficial tidbits within these few pages." The apology remains, as does the hope.

REFERENCES

Abel, T. M. *Psychological testing in cultural contexts.* New Haven, Connecticut: College and University Press, 1973.

Berry, J. W. On cross-cultural comparability. *International Journal of Psychology*, 1969, *4*, 119–128.

Berry, J. W. Radical cultural relativism and the concept of intelligence. In L. J. Cronbach & P. J. D. Drenth (Eds.), *Mental tests and cultural adaptation.* The Hague: Mouton, 1972.

Brislin, R. W. Back-translation for cross-cultural research. *Journal of Cross-Cultural Psychology*, 1970, *1*, 185–216.

Brislin, R. W., Lonner, W. J., & Thorndike, R. M. *Cross-cultural research methods.* New York: John Wiley & Sons, 1973.

Chun, K., Campbell, J., & Yoo, J. Expreme response style in cross-cultural research: A reminder. *Journal of Cross-Cultural Psychology*, 1974, *5*, 465–480.

Cole, M. An ethnographic psychology of cognition. In R. W. Brislin, S. Bochner, & W. J.

Lonner (Eds.), *Cross-cultural perspectives on learning.* New York: John Wiley & Sons, Halsted, 1975.

Cole, M., & Bruner, J. S. Cultural differences and inferences about psychological processes. *American Psychologist,* 1971, *26,* 867–876.

Cole, M., & Scribner, S. *Culture and thought: A psychological introduction.* New York: John Wiley & Sons, 1974.

Cronbach, L. J., & Drenth, P. J. D. (Eds.), *Mental tests and cultural adaptation.* The Hague: Mouton, 1972.

Domino, G. Culture-free tests and the academic achievement of foreign students. *Journal of consulting and clinical psychology,* 1968, *32,* 102.

Fiske, D. W. *Measuring the concepts of personality.* Chicago: Aldine Atherton, 1971.

Glatt, K. M. An evaluation of the French, Spanish, and German translations of the MMPI. *Acta Psychologica,* 1969, *29,* 65–84.

Gough, H. G., & McGurk, E. A group test of perceptual acuity. *Perceptual and Motor Skills,* 1967, *24,* 1107–1115.

Gynther, M. White norms and Black MMPIs: A prescription for discrimination? *Psychological Bulletin,* 1972, *78,* 386–402.

Hudson, W. Pictorial depth perception in subcultural groups in Africa. *Journal of Social Psychology,* 1960, *52,* 183–208.

Kadri, Z. N. The use of the MMPI for personality study of Singapore students. *British Journal of Social and Clinical Psychology,* 1971, *10,* 90–91.

Labov, W. The logic of non-standard English. In F. Williams (Ed.), *Language and poverty.* Chicago, Markham Publishing Co., 1970.

Lanyon, R. I. *A handbook of MMPI group profiles.* Minneapolis: University of Minnesota Press, 1968.

Lindzey, G. *Projective techniques and cross-cultural research.* New York: Appleton-Century-Crofts, 1961.

Lonner, W. J., & Adams, J. L. Interest patterns of psychologists in nine Western nations. *Journal of Applied Psychology,* 1972, *56,* 146–151.

Lyman, H. B. A first report on ACCENT. Educational Testing Service's *International Newsletter,* July 1970, p. 10.

Manaster, G. J., & Havighurst, R. J. *Cross-national research: Social-psychological methods and problems.* Boston: Houghton-Mifflin Co., 1972.

Pedersen, P. *A proposal for the use of multi-lingual resources in education of non-English speaking foreign students through non-degree, problem-oriented curricula offerings in one or more foreign languages.* Paper presented at the NAFSA-CBIE International Conference, University of British Columbia, May 1971.

Porter, J. W. *Manual: Michigan International Student Problem Inventory.* East Lansing, Michigan: International Programs, Michigan State University, 1966.

Segall, M., Campbell, D. T., & Herskovits, M. *The influence of culture on visual perception.* Indianapolis: Bobbs-Merrill Co., 1966.

Spain, D. H. On the use of projective techniques for psychological anthropology. In F. L. K. Hsu (Ed.), *Psychological anthropology* (new ed.). Cambridge, Massachusetts: Schenkman Publishing Co., 1972.

Thorndike, R. L. Concepts of culture-fairness. *Journal of Educational Measurement,* 1971, *8,* 63–70.

Triandis, H. C. Culture training, cognitive complexity and interpersonal attitudes. In R. W. Brislin, S. Bochner, and W. J. Lonner (Eds.), *Cross-cultural perspectives on learning.* New York: John Wiley & Sons, Halsted, 1975.

Triandis, H. C., Vassiliou, V., Vassiliou, G., Tanaka, Y., & Shanmugam, A. V. *The analysis of subjective culture.* New York: John Wiley & Sons, 1972.

10 Intercultural Psychotherapy: Issues, Questions, and Reflections

JULIAN WOHL

CAN WE EXPORT WESTERN PSYCHOTHERAPY TO NON-WESTERN CULTURES?

The author of this chapter does not distinguish between psychotherapy and counseling as they affect intercultural issues. Although attempts have been made to establish differences between the two disciplines, such attempts almost invariably have been based upon contextual or tangential features rather than upon fundamental ones. These tangential features include distinctions with respect to the degree of psychopathology (counselors, it is said, work with normal persons who have problems, whereas psychotherapists deal with the seriously disturbed or mentally ill), with respect to the place where the activity is performed (educational centers versus medical clinics), and with respect to the depth, intensity, frequency, and length of the process (counselors are supposed to be on the superficial end of such dimensions as compared to therapists who are often perilously close to the deep end).

Jurisdictional disputes, professional allegiances, and training variations among the helping professions do exist. But none of these allegations and arguments touch the heart of the matter. The fact is that there exists no satisfactory distinction between the process of psychotherapy and the process of personalistic counseling. The two-person situation, consisting of a trained, socially defined expert and a client, both of whom have agreed to meet regularly to discuss the client's difficulties for the purpose of reducing those difficulties, alleviating his unnecessary distress, and improving his effectiveness in living may, with equal justification, be called psychotherapy, counseling, or psychotherapeutic counseling.

Dr. Wohl's paper is part of a larger project in which he has been engaged periodically for a dozen years. Stemming from his teaching and research in Burma and restimulated by similar activity in Thailand, the paper focuses both theoretically and generally upon Southeast Asian universities and their students, while practically and specifically it looks toward the development of psychotherapeutic counseling services for these students.

The first step in this effort was a consideration, by an examination of the question of universals in psychotherapy, of the general issue of transferring psychotherapy to non-Western societies. If our forms of psychological helping are to be exported, it would be helpful to know that psychotherapy itself is found in non-Western realms and that similarities exist between what we do and what they do. A second step was to look at an array of reports of intercultural psychotherapy in an effort to develop an appreciation of the complex interweaving of clinical problems with cultural phenomena. It is these two aspects that have been drawn upon for this presentation. Just to complete the story, the third part (now underway) will be a study of the problems and situations that university students in the target area confront. This should lead ultimately to the development of a proposal for a practical effort to develop services for these students.

In the summer of 1961, a month or so after leaving the Veterans Administration clinic in which I had been a staff clinical psychologist, I found myself in Rangoon facing an obviously (from my cultural view) tense university student. He had been referred by his teacher and supervisor, an American anthropologist who had done research in the young man's home district, far up-country from the University of Rangoon. The young man told me in limited but understandable English that he was very nervous and felt considerable distress in the abdominal region. His belief that his discomfort was due to some demonic spiritual power that he had offended was consistent with Burmese folk conceptions of psychological disturbance (Spiro, 1967), but it surprised me because of his status as a university student of anthropology. In my ignorance I thought that university students, especially those in cultural anthropology, would not hold such "prescientific" beliefs. When I asked about his belief in the light of his knowledge of anthropology, I was even more surprised by his calmly indicating that he knew "primitive people" (his term) believed that spirits caused such distress and, since he was of this class of people, he of course held this belief. At this point the intricate complexity of the relationship between culture on the one side and psychopathology and psychotherapy on the other became real for me. It was very fortunate for both of us that I was not called upon to pursue his therapeutic needs much further.

For a year then, and another 7 years later in Thailand, plus the years between and subsequently, I alternated between complete hopelessness and very slight optimism over the idea of transferring Western ways in counseling and psychotherapy to Southeast Asian populations. Unlike some of the efforts described in the literature, my target population was clear; not the much-researched "villager," or the Asian student in the United States, who is the focus of the work of Alexander, Workneh,

Klein, and Miller (chapter 5), but the university student in his own milieu. It might be useful if the reader, in reacting to this paper, keeps as a reference point the fact that the patient or client who is ultimately the object of intercultural therapy in the author's mind is a university student in his own country, whose ability to speak English is very limited, whose Westernization is relatively superficial (Wohl & Silverstein, 1966; Wohl & Tapingkae, 1970), and whose problems lie generally toward the milder end of a psychopathology continuum. I am thinking primarily of the many students who do function, although with excessive tension, as well of those few who experience severe disruption of functioning.

Of Universals and Essences

The application of Western psychotherapy and counseling to non-Western societies is predicated upon the assumption and the hope that there exist some qualities or aspects of this generic treatment that make sense and will be effective in those foreign domains. One could, of course, with equal justification, make the identical assertion in reverse—that the application to the West of Eastern, or South of Sahara, or, more generally, non-Western therapies for the mind or soul assumes or hopes for the existence of something universal in the therapy technique beyond its area of origin.

But in the great historic struggles for power and riches, the West has won, for now at least, and the colonial tradition, along with the scientific and technological gap between the haves and have nots of this world, led to the West applying its approaches to the East and not the other way around. One could argue with Torrey (1972) that the alleged scientifically superior basis for Western psychotherapy provides a difference more in verbal mystique than in efficacy of treatment. And it is also possible to suggest that the West has better reason to create superior therapies for bifurcated souls, since it has developed modes of thought and ways of life which are more effective in creating mental miseries.

But all of that is beside the point, which is that the balance of payments in psychotherapy favors the West; we are in the position of being the exporter of our psychotherapies to the importing rest of the world. Anthropologists and intercultural psychiatric and psychologic students inform us that, in all societies which have been observed, procedures and practices are found that are the functional equivalents of our therapies. We have, however, no prior grounds for the belief that our forms are workable in those other societies. One critic (Torrey, 1972) has suggested, but not satisfactorily documented, that efforts at performing psychotherapy across substantial cultural barriers either have failed or were exceedingly difficult.

Intercultural psychotherapy is not itself a clear, unambiguous concept. It can have at least two meanings, each of which may require some degree of differential treatment. Although the literature generally fails to make distinctions, an exception to this trend is Sundberg's exposition (chapter 8). In one sense, intercultural therapy refers to the practitioner from one cultural context who, for one reason or another, finds himself in a situation where he is applying his form of psychotherapy to a member of a different culture. This may take place in the patient's cultural setting, in the therapist's cultural setting, or in a third cultural setting. A special, but not necessarily rare, cultural interface situation has been described in which members of Western culture have lived for some time in a non-Western culture and have associated to a great extent with Westernized members of the non-Western culture (Useem, Useem, & Donoghue, 1963). This "third culture" situation is one variation of intercultural psychotherapy in which the Western practitioner plies his trade upon a non-Western clientele. In its other major meaning, intercultural psychotherapy has reference to the more abstract situation in which the practice, rather than the practitioner, is exported. This, of course, is of far greater practical significance, for the lone practitioner in a foreign cultural realm usually has but a small impact. He either stays long enough to adapt to the local scene or, more likely, is present for a short time, perhaps a year or two, as a teacher or scholar, and his practice is secondary to training or research activity. The essential long-term concern is with the transferring of a body of theory and practice from its place of origin and growth to a significantly different cultural climate. Ultimately, the practice must be performed by local persons who have been trained in the foreign approaches.

Torrey and a number of other scholars who recognize the historical geographic, cultural, political, and ideological parameters that restrict the applicability of our kinds of therapy have noted that the sheer existence of therapy is not culture-bound. Humans seem always to have nonphysical troubles that require them to seek help, and they have always created institutions to satisfy this need.

In his exhaustive study of the "cure of souls" in religious and philosophic traditions, J. T. McNeill defined this activity as "the sustaining and curative treatment of persons in those matters that reach beyond the requirements of animal life" (1965, p. vii). He noted that the healing function includes a caring and a concern on the part of the healer (p. vii). In other times and in other societies these caring activities were not and are not the specialized, discrete functions that they are in the Western world today. McNeill observed that the separation of mental healing from its source in religious and philosophic thought and its conversion to a specialized scientific discipline are relatively recent developments.

Theological distinctions among various churches and religions tend to obscure their common function of soul healing. To this group of "physicians of the soul," referred to by McNeill as a "spiritual elite" (p. 330), must be added the modern psychotherapists of all persuasions who, despite their chronic squabbling, are joined in this specialized brotherhood and together enjoy its special status. He could have added that this spiritual elite must also span the variations among the modern psychotherapies.

Although the partisans of each cult may believe that theirs is the best way to cure or care for the troubled people who consult them, collectively they comprise what Meadows (1968) referred to as the "mediatorial elite." In discussing ancient Greece, Meadows noted that "therapy was an act of mediation between the sufferer and the superordinate world of powers and values . . . the mediatorial role of the priesthood was that of the cure of souls, whether by divination, exorcism, absolution, expiation, orgiastic dance, ritual mysteries, teaching, revealing, directing" (1968, p. 497), all of which are techniques used in psychotherapeutic practice throughout the world today. All cultures, he added, have members who play this mediatorial role. And one is tempted to add that, while all practitioners in all cultures have successes and failures, the existence of the "mediatorial elite" is not dependent, even in the scientific West, upon its ability to demonstrate understanding of causes, ability to predict outcome of intervention as against nonintervention, or upon the empirical measures of efficacy of treatment; rather, it is dependent on its socially sanctioned (licensed, "degreed") role as healer. Limitations on the general exportability of our therapies have been considered by Lesse (1969) who focused upon psychoanalytic therapies that emphasize or value individual autonomy and self-awareness. He suggests that for nonentrepreneurial societies or for societies in which the larger social group is favored over the individual, adaptation may be impaired by a therapy that too highly values self-determination and individuality. Although Lesse questioned the casual exportation of all of our therapies and noted ideological and sociopolitical hindrances to indiscriminate application of all therapies to all cultures, he did not question the idea that some of our psychotherapy is exportable to some of the world some of the time.

The fact that activities or functions which we today and here refer to as psychotherapy appear to have been universally performed can indeed provide some hope to those who assert that Western psychotherapy can be useful in non-Western societies. But the specific form a psychotherapeutic function takes must be compatible with the cultural ethos; in its essential nature it cannot violate the "world view" of the culture, and its system of "yes, yes's" and "no, no's." In his self-styled "Eastern interpretation" of Western psychotherapy, Pande (1968) argued that fundamental processes of therapy are provided with a cultural cosmetic to achieve this compatability. He looked at Western concepts in psychotherapy in the manner of an anthropologist examining the strange rituals of some exotic group and found a covert collusion between patient and therapist. Under a cover of manifest content couched in the language of science and medicine is the latent fact that therapy provides a special, close, love relationship. To allow that we deliver and derive emotional gratification in therapy is not consistent with our valued conception of psychotherapy as a scientific, intellectual, objective, healing process, and, therefore, we are forced to conceal this fact from ourselves.

Pande's ethnocentric and ahistoric implication that psychotherapy is a peculiarly Western response to deficiencies in Western culture is not compatible with our knowledge of the universal existence of psychotherapeutic activity. Problems in living or mental illness or intolerable deviancy or whatever else we choose to call such problems apparently exist universally, and all cultures create social institutions in response. They also create their own criteria for circumstances that warrant intervention. In his extensive social and historical study, Rosen (1968) emphasized how the diagnosis or categorization of psychological disorder is a function both of the extent to which a person's actions are disturbed and of the standards set by the social group performing the evaluation. In our own time we are seeing this relativity extend even to the notion of mental illness itself, as criticism of the euphemism mounts on scientific, legal, and social grounds (Kittrie, 1973; Szasz, 1961).

In the conclusion to his survey of non-Western approaches to mind healing, Kiev (1964) suggested that we ought to "strip [psychotherapies] to ... bare essentials and find new rationalizations for them" (p. 459). While this seems a sensible course for one to follow, and the literature does show a trend to this direction, two difficulties or questions suggest themselves. The first has to do with the word rationalization which, in the technical, clinical sense that Kiev may (or may not) be using it, refers to intellectual activity applied after the fact to justify an action which the actor senses to be essentially irrational or generally inconsistent with his or her sense of self, self-evaluation, or standards. Rather than being a reasonable cover for an unreasonable act, rationalization may mean here that we should seek out the underlying essentials of psychotherapy—that which is universal in this universally found practice—and should understand the nature of that universality. The second question is raised by the "stripping" metaphor. After the layers of superficiality have been removed, it is possible that nothing will remain. Perhaps there are no essentials, no universals beyond that of the existence of psychotherapy and its practitioners. An acknowledgment of the emperor's lack of clothes at this point would mean that the game is over so, although this may be a logical conclusion, it is one that cannot be accepted yet as empirical fact.

The universality of therapy itself has been paired with an acknowledgment of possible "limits of cultural plasticity of psychotherapy" by Draguns and Phillips (1972, p. 19) in a brief survey of the topic. They suggested that an amalgamation of suitable foreign methods with indigenous ones might be more suitable than an attempt to replace local with Western systems of mental health services.

These observers have been joined by several others in noting that the idea of utilizing indigenous methods and locally sanctioned healers is not universally cheered by the mental health professionals (Bolman, 1968; Carstairs, 1973). In his extensive survey, Bolman emphasized the difficulty in exporting psychotherapy but argued that the knowledge to be derived from doing so is worth the effort. In emphasizing the research advantage, he seems to minimize both the therapeutic justification and the advantage to the recipient society of such an effort. The disparity between "what is offered and what is needed" (p. 1238) is greatest with respect to underdeveloped countries, and he sees the problem of cultural fit to be critical, this being a point made by a number of writers in this field.

The search for a residue of common, universal, essential features in psychotherapy has been arduously pursued in recent years by a number of scholars. Since one frequent argument for the promulgation of intercultural psychotherapy, in the mildly imperialistic sense in which it is conventionally understood, is found in the idea that some universal, basic, or common characteristics can be identified, a closer examination of the literature of this discipline is appropriate.

Of the three major contributors to the discussion of universals in psychotherapy, only one, Torrey (1972), approached non-Western materials in any depth; of the others, Frank (1963, 1971) made some use of them but not extensively so, and Strupp (1973a, 1973b) generally was not concerned with them. The common interest of all is the identification of aspects of the psychotherapeutic venture that might extend beyond the limits set by culture and society, time and place, as well as of theories of therapy or personality held by the therapist.

A major effort in this direction was the publication of *Persuasion and Healing* (1963), in which Jerome Frank looked at psychotherapy as being one among many methods for getting someone to change his mind or mend his ways. Since there is perhaps nothing in human affairs as ubiquitous as attempts to achieve those ends, he obviously hit upon a useful approach from the interculturalist's point of view. Frank also made much of the placebo effect, the phenomenon that occurs when sick people get better when given a medicine that chemically can have no possible effect upon their condition. He looked at the placebo effect as being a manifestation of a suggestion reaction due to the interaction of personal influence of the healer with certain characteristics of the patient and of the social context in which the healing occurs. Frank's definition of psychotherapy offers the advantages of being broad enough in scope to minimize minor distinctions among variously titled helping methods and of being comprehensive enough to provide a basis for the idea of pancultural, or universal, features, as well as for examination and comparison of psychotherapy across cultures.

For Frank, psychotherapy encompasses several interactive sets of forces. These are: (1) a sociocultural context that provides criteria, definition, value, healing capacity, and social recognition to (2) certain individuals possessed of healing powers and to whom all concerned believe it right and proper for the (3) sufferer to present himself to obtain relief for certain classes of difficulties. Arrangements are made for some (4) regularized, even ritualistic, contacts between therapist and patient, which occur in an atmosphere heavy with hope, faith, and concern for change to occur in the patient's condition. He sees these social forces as being instrumental in promoting a placebo effect, a concept which in later work seems to be replaced by the idea of nonspecific aspects of psychotherapeutic healing.

In an important essay a decade later, Frank (1971) returned to the search for nonspecific, general or universal factors in therapy; this essay was abundant with strong but plausible assertions, supported more by his professional standing than by the power of his documentation. He now finds his nonspecificity anchored in the interpersonal relationship between therapist and client. Playing upon the earlier theme of Carl Rogers (1957), Frank agreed that a special human relationship is necessary for psychotherapy but it alone is not sufficient for healing. There is required in addition an array of common features made possible by the relationship itself, including a belief and thought system, shared by patient and therapist, which gives a basis for comprehending disturbance and its therapy, modifying the patient's knowledge, enhancing the patient's idea that he will be helped, providing meaningful success experiences, and facilitating the patient's emotional experiencing.

In achieving this recognition of the overriding importance in a therapeutic relationship as the nonspecific factor, Frank provided an excellent introduction to the work of Strupp (1973a, 1973b), who has dealt with this problem in great detail.

Strupp, one of the major synthesizers in the field of psychotherapy, articulated clearly two themes which have emerged in its recent history. One of these is an emphasis upon the healing aura hovering around the therapeutic relationship and a denigration of techniques. It has been stated most effectively and continually in the work of Carl Rogers (see, for example, Rogers, 1957), as well as most forcefully by the followers of the "humanistic" approaches. The second theme is the emphasis upon technical skill and therapeutic techniques combined with a disregard for the "relationship." Until relatively recently, behavioral and psycho-analytic approaches have been accused of disregarding the relationship itself. Greenson (1967) provided clear evidence that this is no longer true (if it ever was) of psychoanalysis, whereas Strupp (1973a) reminded us that Freud did not consider human relationship variables as being of no consequence, but rather took for granted that therapists were humane and concerned.

Strupp has sought to identify the specific features of therapeutic influence, originally with the hope that it would be possible to devise specific techniques for individual persons and their unique symptoms. He relinquished this mechanical conception when he wrote that "we are beginning to recognize and take seriously the extraordinary complexity of the therapeutic influence" (1973a, p. 275). With what seems to be great reluctance, he acknowledged that generally "the search for highly specific techniques . . . is probably futile" (p. 313). His final position is that the therapeutic influence is composed of two fundamental factors. One consists of the nonspecific, basic or general effect, which inheres in the interpersonal relationship; the other consists of specific techniques employed by the therapist. The techniques, however, are operative only in and through the medium of the relationship and all effects can be attributed, at least in part, to the human qualities of the therapist, such qualities being "interest, understanding, respect, dedication, empathy, etc. . . . which instill trust" (1973a, p. 283). He underscored this by asserting "the equivalence of therapeutic techniques," all of which can achieve results, and are "anchored in, and potentiated by . . . the establish-ment and maintenance of a proper helping relationship" (1973a, p. 283), the core of which is the "emotional experience" made possible by the therapeutic relationship.

Probably few people experienced in personal counseling or psycho-therapy would take issue with this position. We are now saying that at least one, universal, fundamental feature of psychotherapy is an emotion-ally special interpersonal relationship that is created and managed in such a way that personal change is fostered in the client.

Despite this universality, it is possible, and even probable, that the constituent elements of the "good human relationship" are different in one culture than they are in another. Certainly the different specific techniques used, such as interpretation, advice-giving, or reassurance, will be culturally appropriate in various cultures; but the question needs also to be raised as to the extent to which our American conception of the good therapeutic relationship is universally valid. And even if it is, even if in all cultures most people respond well to "acceptance," "respect," "interest," "concern," "wish to help," and the other components, we still must ask whether the outsider can deliver, create, express, and communicate these factors in terms understandable and acceptable to the client.

Aside from these "internal" aspects of therapy, there are others that are usually taken for granted when both parties share the same culture to a significant extent. These are generally external in the sense that they refer to the social context in which therapy goes on. Frank (1963) emphasized the requirement that patient and therapist share the acceptance of the social trappings and the framework of meaning within which disorder and treatment are understood and confronted. Strupp followed him in recognizing the necessity for a rational system that both parties can use to make sense out of therapeutic events. Is it possible for two people of different cultures to achieve a reasonable degree of agreement and understanding on this superstructure?

Of these authors who have focused upon the issue of common features of psychotherapy, only Torrey (1972) has approached the problem in a truly anthropological, intercultural manner. He too wished to develop a better understanding of psychotherapy, but argued that to do so one should examine the professional activities of those individuals who perform the social functions that we recognize as being psychotherapeutic in as wide a range of cultural settings as possible. By first identifying the social function, the therapist is better able to consider similarities in performance, techniques, and other aspects, thereby pursuing the same end sought by Frank and Strupp—that of identifying universal or common features of all psychotherapy.

In his preface, Torrey stated that his work would "focus on the healer, or the therapist." It would attempt to show how much of the therapist's effectiveness comes through his or her sharing of a common world view with the patient, through certain personality characteristics, and through expectations that the patient has of him or her. It would then show how another source of therapeutic effectiveness, the techniques of therapy, are "basically the same whether they are used by a witchdoctor or a psychiatrist" (1972, p. xiv). If this preface was written like most others —after, rather than before, the book itself—it might stand better as a summary of what he attempted, rather than as a prediction. While his allusion to quantification is hyperbole, as are several of his more sweeping assertions, he does, all in all, forcefully develop the thesis in this work.

Torrey found four universals of psychotherapy: (1) a world view shared by healer and sufferer, (2) a close personal relationship, (3) the patient's expectations of being helped, and (4) specific techniques. Of these, Torrey most easily disposes of the issue of techniques by arguing that the techniques used in the West are found worldwide and that there are essentially no culturally unique techniques. He also includes a great variety of specific physical methods such as drugs and shock; social influence methods such as confession, suggestion, hypnosis; psychoanalytic techniques such as dream analysis and free association; various group and environmental manipulation approaches; and conditioning.

Of particular interest to devotees of this last approach might be the practice used in Western Nigeria to treat enuresis in male children. A toad is tied by a string to the penis. The toad croaks as the child wets him and the child is awakened. Perhaps Frank was correct when he stated, "in psychotherapy ... it appears there is nothing new under the sun" (1971, p. 355).

It is interesting to note that Torrey said nothing in his discussion of techniques about working with transference, the untangling of the distortions of the interpersonal relationship, which for most psychoanalytic clinicians is the bedrock of psychotherapy (Freud, 1958; Greenson, 1967; Strupp, 1973a). Setting this question aside, however, the universality of techniques and of an interpersonal relationship that creates trust and hope and enhances expectations of good results in the patient, seems to support the belief that psychotherapy is feasible across significant cultural gaps.

It is primarily because of Torrey's first principle, the shared-world view, that one has to question the possibility that any substantial intercultural psychotherapy can occur.

The idea that psychotherapy is dependent upon communication between patient and therapist is old; however, it also is of the greatest importance and worth reemphasizing, as Torrey does. The essence of the psychotherapeutic process is human communication. Furthermore, much of the activity in therapy consists of communication about communication. Psychotherapy is a process in which effort is directed toward clarifying meanings and making conscious and explicit what is indirect, subtle, and unwitting in the client's communication. Participants in a conversation, be it a therapeutic one or of any other variety, are able to communicate to the extent that they employ a common referential symbol system. They achieve agreement on what they are discussing and on the manner in which they are to discuss their subject matter. On this point, see also the discussion in Alexander et al. (chapter 5), which focuses on the therapist's difficulty in understanding the meanings being communicated by a patient who uses signals in a way that is novel for the therapist. The patient, of course, has the same problem.

Although the area in which communication demands greatest precision —analysis of resistance and transference—is excluded from Torrey's coverage, another fundamental aspect of psychoanalytic therapy is included as a universal feature. To support his emphasis on "naming," Torrey noted that psychoanalysis involves giving meaning to the apparently meaningless, thus creating order and comprehensibility out of chaos and confusion. He cited Ezriel (1956) and Mendel (1968), the latter also emphasizing that the meaning assigned need not be "correct to bring about change in the patient" (p. 402). This point delineates naming (including interpretation and its variants) to be a general, rather than a specific, technique factor. Mendel's article is a discussion and commentary upon another article by Frank on hope as a nonspecific variable. In his commentary Mendel added to hope an assignment of meaning, transference, countertransference, and learning as universal elements of any psychotherapeutic process. But all of these are contingent upon, or are aspects of, the therapeutic relationship. Says Strupp with pith and eloquence, "change . . . is forged in the crucible of the patient-therapist relationship" (1973a, p. 310).

Ultimately, communication in a special kind of human relationship is fundamental to achieve the effects that will be seen as psychotherapeutic. If communication is to develop within a tolerable limit of error, the framework of understanding within which it occurs requires the sharing of a set of assumptions about the world and its working, about the nature of man and his relation to natural events and supernatural influences, and about the physical and social circumstances within which this healing function goes on, which Torrey terms a "world view." To use another of his expressions, a good degree of "cognitive congruence" is required between the participants with respect to the whole complex of signals and symbols, words and gestures, which function as part of the ground to which communication in the psychotherapeutic relationship serves as figure.

The therapeutic relationship can tolerate some disparity between the partners and, indeed, this always exists. Part of the therapeutic work is mutual learning about the gaps and the negotiation of them; but if the gap between the participants is too great, there is no basis of understanding and the "noise" becomes too loud to permit a working alliance (Greenson, 1967). For example, the gap may occur because of "personal qualities of the healer." It is possible that the much researched "holy trinity" of warmth, empathy, and genuineness might appear in a Burmese context to be evidence of weakness and incompetence. Or perhaps client-centered or psychoanalytic positions, with egalitarianism, mutuality, and shared problem-solving as part of their value orientations, may not mesh effectively with the hierarchically ordered Thai society. In chapter 3, Vontress deals with subcultural questions, pointing up such barriers to achieving a working relationship; whereas in chapter 5, Alexander et al. indicate how a fundamental therapeutic stance of the therapist, such as non-directiveness, can be misinterpreted as lack of interest.

Thus, while the fact of a special human relationship is common to all psychotherapy, the particular expression of such a relationship and the distinct qualities required of the therapist to create the necessary hope, trust, and faith on the client's part may not universally be those about which Western therapists have achieved a consensus. Furthermore, it is quite possible that the sounds and gestures that are intended to convey certain meanings may actually convey other meanings which do not create the desired attitudes in the patient.

One inference that can be drawn from this survey is that if one uses high-level, broad-spectrum concepts and definitions, then common or basic features of therapy can be universally located historically and contemporaneously. The most fundamental cultural universal is the very existence of psychotherapeutic practice. Beyond this are other broad dimensions of agreement. First is the existence of social support, a cultural context that is generally known and understood and by which the healer and his or her activities are defined. There are societal rules, which govern or regulate the healing rituals with respect to their social and physical environmental aspects. Second are the sets of variables internal to the process of therapy. Included here are concepts dealing with the personal qualities of the therapist and of the therapeutic relationship. Third are the so-called technique variables, those characteristics traditionally seen as being most directly involved in the change-inducing process, but which are now seen as being dependent for their power upon the existence of a working therapeutic relationship. Techniques seem to be the most clearly finite in number and universal in appearance.

Yet without a fitting external, societal context and without therapist and relationship suitability, the magical power of technique is lost. Not only must these sets of variables coexist, they must be harmoniously related to each other. The physical setting, social rules, therapist's style, the relationship the therapist tries to establish, and the techniques he or she uses must be such as to fit in with the general expectations of the patient concerning what a healer will do and how he will do it.

Finally, all of these fundamentals in their concrete manifestations require that communication occur between the participants. They must be able to achieve an understanding of what the other is about, and, to do this, must achieve, "real communication," which, as Torrey observed, "presupposes not only a shared language but a shared world view as well" (1972, p. 13). All of this should give pause to those of us who argue the case for cultural transferability of psychotherapy. The problems can be seen in better relief when some of the reports of those who have attempted to engage in intercultural psychotherapy are examined.

Less than Meets the Eye

This section presents a selective, evaluative survey of some reports of intercultural psychotherapy. The articles were chosen because they focus upon the encounter of psychotherapeutic issues with cultural contexts. In all cases they involve a Western or Western-trained therapist applying his art to a member of a social body upon which Western psychotherapeutics are a foreign graft. The sociocultural sources of patients are American Indian, Chinese, Cuban and Afro-Cuban, Tahitian, Indian, Japanese, and Malaysian.

In what he believes to be the "first study devoted specifically to the technical problems of a culturally oriented individual psychotherapy," Devereux (1951, p. 422) summarized his experiences in psychoanalytic psychotherapy with Plains Indians (1951, 1953). He concluded that three major features—transference, dream utilization, and therapeutic goals —require a significant appreciation of the patient's cultural background. To understand and interpret appropriately transference communications, the cultural context of the patient's family life must be understood by the therapist; to understand dreams in therapy, the cultural framework of dream interpretation must be understood; and, for Devereux, the greatest problem was "rooted in the therapist's own conception of health" (1951, p. 420). He apparently had a very difficult time with this issue and found his solution by saying that the therapist must want to return "the patient to himself." The goal of therapy, as Devereux stated it, provides some understanding of his dilemma for he says that the "patient must be helped to handle the realities of the reservation, which is his predicted future environment" (1951, p. 421).

This question of therapeutic goals in this form is a general issue which can appear in the context of therapy with any member of a restricted, oppressed, or discriminated-against group. Devereux's solution was an acceptance of the current social situation, a political act which would tend to reinforce that situation. The problem in these cases was especially poignant because his patients were well acculturated to the degree that they considered their "Indian heritage peripheral" (1951, p. 411). Today's "radical therapists" would resolve the dilemma of goal selection in the direction of supporting or promoting social change. But whatever direction is taken, political implications of psychotherapeutic activity are apparent. In certain societies this could be an especially sensitive question, one which would require careful consideration before an attempt should be made to embark on any major, programmatic importation of foreign therapies.

The fact that these patients were all well educated and considered themselves partly removed from their heritage underscores the significance of the fact that the understanding and handling of psychotherapeutic fundamentals involves cultural problems. The gap here between the therapist and the patient is less than the unmodified term "Plains Indian" might suggest. Is therapy possible here only to the extent that patients are acculturated and can share the therapist's world view to a considerable degree?

The author of these papers is an anthropologist and he noted that his professional interest in culture as such was an obstacle to therapy at those times when he became too interested in cultural features at the expense of clinical involvement with the patients (1953). Anthropological preoccupation is a real danger in any intercultural endeavor. There is always a tendency to use the subject as an informant who will provide a window to the culture; but in psychotherapy more than in other fields such involvement can become an impediment to the purpose of the interaction.

Bishop and Winokur (1956) reported therapy that took place in the United States between a Japanese male physician and an American female psychiatrist. The authors asserted that, in general, knowledge of the cultural background increases the therapist's understanding of the patient's problems and also helps in goal selection, the problem that greatly bothered Devereux. Such knowledge can help avoid "guiding him into patterns" that, although acceptable in the therapist's culture, would create trouble "when the patient returns to his own group" (p. 369). The authors admit to a seduction of the prospective patient into therapy by a 3-week warm-up period in which the therapist became a friend of the patient, expressing interest in and knowledge of Japan and of the patient's current activities in an American hospital.

Without going further into this apparently successful treatment, I believe that therapeutic procedure, at least in the initiation of therapy, was significantly modified in this case, and that the East-West cultural gap was narrower than it might have seemed at first glance. The authors reinforced this point by saying that "there was practically no difficulty with language," and that the patient "has lived so long in a cosmopolitan society and had associated extensively with Americans" (p. 372).

Abel (1956) in an oft-referred-to article advocated the understanding of cultural facts in order to improve the therapist's ability to understand the patient's meanings and to present formulations in a useful manner. The argument is supported by clinical illustrations—vignettes of her own and others' experiences with cultural differences. Although the points she makes about the advantage of cultural understanding by the therapist are valuable, it must be noted that all of her material refers to therapy in the United States with indigenous or immigrant subcultural groups, largely European in origin. Her own work with a Chinese patient was done in English, and his degree of acculturation was considerable, as Abel reported in a later article (1962).

The kind of intercultural therapy she discussed is a predecessor to the wave of interest that began in the 1960s in problems associated with therapy provided by middle-class, mainstream, Americanized helpers working with the people who are educationally and economically impoverished and discriminated-against members of ethnic minorities. This subcultural domain and the associated "culture of poverty" do reflect intercultural issues, and the subcultural and the true intercultural domains can instruct each other, but not all of the issues are the same. The cultural gulf between therapist and patient in the instances she describes was not as wide as the term intercultural, as used in this chapter, would suggest.

The paper by Abel reflects psychotherapeutic interests and issues existing within the cosmopolitan climate of New York City in the thirties and forties with its marvelous heterogeneity of national and ethnic groups, varying in extent of assimilation, but all tending toward Americanization. Intercultural therapy in this chapter is concerned with members of a foreign population who will stay foreign, so to speak, and be treated in their own lands, not ours. In chapter 3, Vontress also warns of the importance of noting variations in degree of cultural assimilation among members of the same cultural group.

The paper by Bustamente (1957) is similar to that of Abel in its focus upon patients within one society who are being treated by a therapist of different cultural or subcultural background, and it makes the same reasonable points as does Abel's paper. "A psychotherapist must be able to assess the cultural background of his patient, and have a thorough knowledge of his own culture as well, to be effective with polycultural patients" (p. 811). By "polycultural," he meant his patients who shared or participated in Cuban, European, and Afro-Cuban traditions.

Eric Berne (1960) presented data from 15 cases, all of whom he interviewed; 12 of these were chronic, severely psychotic people seen in a mental hospital, and three were acutely disturbed people seen in a general hospital in Tahiti. Berne (1960) appeared to be the lone dissenter, vehemently opposing the idea that cultural issues play a part in psychotherapy. The article displays a remarkable lack of sophistication about "culture," and shows no comprehension of its subtle workings. As a skilled interviewer, he uses cultural phenomena but, like the boy who speaks prose, is unaware that he does so. His grandiose assertion of the universality of "psychotherapeutic maneuvers," and the statement that "principles learned in the treatment of young women in Connecticut or California were just as effective in the South Pacific" (p. 1080) are simply not supported in any way by the case material he presented, material which is not psychotherapy, but brief diagnostic interviews (with the help of an interpreter) in French. Although this article is frequently cited in intercultural literature, it appears usually without suitable evaluative comment. I have included it here primarily to note it as a quaint relic of a preanthropological era.

Information-gathering (research) rather than therapy is the interview function discussed by Carstairs (1961), whose conclusions derive from work done with villagers in India. He noted that a clinician engaged in research may be obligated to employ his therapeutic skill, even though his interest lies in research. The act of drawing forth information may open up problems for the informant which the clinician cannot ignore.

The article contains a number of useful suggestions and observations which help develop some issues in intercultural psychotherapy. Carstairs is insistent that interviewing be done in the native language of the informant or in the one that he or she normally uses. The use of an interpreter is not adequate, because this interferes with the establishment of a relationship. Carstairs also pointed out that as an outsider one is not expected by the members of the culture to have a full knowledge of cultural facts. This position of acknowledged ignorance can be used to promote openness and clarity of communication because it provides a good justification for asking people to explain themselves. He warned against premature interpretations, formulations, or diagnoses. "It is only after a gradual process of feeling one's way into the accepted values and expectations of the group that one learns to recognize behavior which *they* regard as abnormal. . . . " (p. 545). Here again appear the problems of how to define the goals of psychotherapy and how to establish conceptions of just what is to be defined as the patient's problem or symptom.

The authors I have discussed here are highly conscious of the danger of imposing culturally foreign criteria. But the literature seems to include no author who is willing to assert categorically that the definition of a symptom, problem, or trouble is the prerogative of the sufferer. All of these carefully, consciously, culturally sensitive writers are not at all concerned about imposing standards upon the patient. Their concern is only that any bias they impose be from the patient's culture—whether the patient agrees or not.

The same problem of goal-setting has been raised by Hsu and Tseng (1972). They make the same point that Devereux made—that goals need to fit the cultural realities or what is culturally possible for the patient. They emphasize that the therapist needs to know the patient's cultural context very well so that he or she can engage in this goal-oriented activity. And indeed if the therapist is to set goals and judge what goals are suitable he must have this knowledge. But he could also make the mistakes of Carstairs' (1961) culturally ignorant explorer who centers his interest upon the patient's background and makes the patient explain the culture to him. Ultimately then, perhaps the sufferer can define his suffering and what must be done to terminate it.

In addition to continuing the preoccupation with goal-setting, Hsu and Tseng confronted a fundamental issue in the process of psychotherapy, the issue that there still remains a communication problem beyond the basic knowledge of a common language. Verbal localisms, facial expressions and special cultural nuances of symbols distort communication even when words and sentences are understood literally.

Metaphoric communication can be used to emphasize this problem. Communication in therapy constantly employs metaphor, and metaphor presents an almost impassible cultural barrier. A sad, yet humorous, example of this occurred not long ago in connection with a patient admitted to a large Midwestern mental hospital. One of the allegations made about him upon admission was that he had a delusion that there was a radio in his stomach. Inquiry about this strange belief revealed that the admitting physician, a recent immigrant to the United States whose knowledge of English was very limited, interpreted literally the patient's complaint about the constant loud playing of a neighbor's radio in which the patient said, "I got a belly full."

Hsu and Tseng also pointed out that, beyond the problems of language and communication, there can be other complications in the relationship, particularly that of the danger of mutual projection of cultural stereotypes. This was also noted with respect to subcultural differences by Thomas, (1962). These authors concluded by offering a collection of therapeutic aphorisms, highly desirable as criteria for excellence in performance but probably greatly limited in actual fulfilment. These include: awareness of the importance of culture in a general sense; knowledge of the patient's culture specifically; mutual acknowledgment and discussion by patient and therapist of differences as they appear;

search for the meaning of a patient's history; and provision of a good relationship. These praiseworthy features of therapy could be used as standards applicable to any psychotherapy. But apart from intercultural therapy with the relatively intelligent, educated, and culturally aware patients in this survey, it seems unrealistic to expect these criteria to be more realizable in intercultural therapeutic ventures than in intracultural efforts.

An informative paper by Kinzie (1972) supports both doubts and hopes about intercultural psychotherapy. His presentation utilized both "true" intercultural literature and the literature on social class and subcultural differences to argue for the need to take into account cultural influences in intercultural psychotherapeutic efforts. Both seem especially relevant for the Western practitioner approaching the polyethnic society of western Malaysia. From this scholarship and his clinical experience, he provided a list of "approaches and techniques . . . found to be useful in overcoming the difficulties in cross-cultural therapy" (p. 255). These include almost all of the items generally appearing in this literature, such as cultural self-awareness, awareness of the culture of the patient, open attitude by a therapist, continual mutual checking on adequacy of communication, and readiness of therapist to suit his own style and actions to the patient's conception of a healer. With respect to the issue of language, Kinzie suggested that, because language difficulties make fine and subtle communication impossible, "thoughts and feelings often have to be expressed directly" (p. 225). He advocated also the use of an interpreter where necessary; although recognizing that this seriously complicates the situation, he felt that it has proven worthwhile.

On the topic of goals in therapy, Kinzie approaches more closely than any other author the position suggested earlier in this paper that goals "will be primarily determined by the patient himself and by his culture" (p. 226). He noted that perhaps after therapy the patient may well have achieved a broader perspective of himself in his cultural context and have a better recognition of his choices. The positive point here is that the therapist must recognize the danger of foreign cultural values being imposed as goals or criteria for successful therapy and must combine this knowledge with the therapeutic position that such criteria are determined by the patient and his cultural framework. The therapist need not worry about what criteria to set as much as he needs to guard against setting foreign ones or making any other inappropriate interventions. If Devereux had focused on helping the patient to see his own directions and inclinations more clearly, and help him sort out his "realities," he might have been less concerned with the goal of survival on the reservation and been less an uncomfortable cultural colonialist and more a genuine anthropological psychotherapist.

The paper by Kinzie provides three case examples, uniquely qualified to exemplify another issue discussed in this paper and adapted from Torrey (1972), whose point was that intercultural therapy is possible only if the cultural gap between patient and therapist, especially the language and world-view aspect of it, is not overly wide. The first case was a rural and uneducated woman who could see her "problem in magical and medical terms" (p. 227), and not in concepts of family and interpersonal stress. She was treated with medication which brought relief. The second patient who had a moderate degree of Western (English-language) background asked for hypnosis and advice on his interpersonal inadequacy. He was treated with a hodgepodge of behavioral and medical methods which produced little change until he was able to discuss his feelings openly. From that point on he improved because of the relationship rather than because of techniques. The third patient was apparently at home in the European world, had already some experience in marital therapy, and was able to involve himself immediately in a cathartic-supportive, self-exploratory relationship. The author pointed out that "because of his previous experience, this patient quickly became involved in therapy" (p. 228).

In two of the three case examples of successful intervention, the patient shared conceptions with the therapist about the usefulness of Western psychological methods of helping, whereas in one these methods were not attempted. This is really not a very substantial demonstration of intercultural psychotherapeutics. One could just as well argue that the first case suggests the utility of working with traditional healers to make them more effective, or the futility of trying to impose Western therapeutic approaches where they are incomprehensible or unknown to the recipients.

These three cases demonstrate a continuum of readiness to accept psychotherapy which seems to correlate with the patient having had previous experiences of a kind that tend to reduce the cultural gap between the Western therapy and the patient's expectations. Furthermore, it is plausible to suggest that, had the therapist been less quick to fire a shotgun of manipulative techniques at the second patient, a therapeutic relationship might more readily have developed.

One criticism commonly made of the traditional (now something of a pejorative expression) Western psychotherapist is that he prefers and is able to work only with the young, intelligent, sophisticated, verbal, middle-class individual who has a similar world view to himself. It is striking that the same statement might be applied to the successful psychotherapy described in the foregoing studies. In almost all cases, patients have deviated from their cultural background in ways that make them more like the desirable American patients and less like other people in their own culture. If psychotherapy is to be aimed at this population, perhaps one problem is less cultural and more clinical; we must account for those who have the same level of cultural sophistication as do those people who have accepted therapy but who do not themselves accept it. Cultural provincialism after all is not limited to Americans. Among equally educated people of any culture there are degrees of awareness and openness—of tolerance or acceptance of novelty and of foreignness. It may be that one variable not being accorded sufficient respect in our fascination with cultural problems and our desire to understand culturally based resistance to novel forms of helping is the individual personality of the sufferer. It should be recognized in intercultural therapy as in any other that one significant set of variables in therapy is the individual motivation, style, anxiety, and defenses of the recipient, as discussed by Draguns in chapter 1.

This literature suggests that intercultural psychotherapy is possible if the patient's expectations, based upon some aspects of cultural, subcultural, or intercultural experiences, are such as to make him or her at least minimally receptive to Western psychotherapy. The clinical examples presented are generally of people who are inclined toward accepting Western psychotherapy, whose world views are, even if fundamentally different, open enough to permit some new scenery to be examined. Yet, paradoxically, these cases have been used to argue for the feasibility of applying Western psychotherapy to non-Western cultures, and even then always with the stipulation that some highly idealistic standards of therapist quality and competence be met. One could with at least equal justification suggest that if the therapist must be the paragon of therapeutic skill that is suggested by this literature in order to deal with patients who only marginally fulfill a criterion of intercultural candidacy, then the enterprise has very limited value.

The real test of intercultural psychotherapy, the carry-over to a foreign cultural environment of our ways of doing psychotherapy, will come in the effort to work with non-Westernized patients only minimally familiar with Western ways. By this selection criterion, such people will probably be so minimally able to use English that therapeutic communication will have to go on in their usual language, either with an interpreter or a therapist—be he foreign or domestic—who is very much at home in that language. If that end is to be achieved in any practical way, those members of the local culture must be found who are able to identify with Western culture sufficiently to develop a real understanding of its psychotherapies and who are sufficiently flexible and understanding enough of their own cultures as to be able to sense how these therapies can be made to work within their cultures. This means that the occasional Westerner engaging in intercultural therapy is at best doing therapy to learn the culture so that he can better do research or perform training and consultive functions for the direct deliverer of service. In such an instance, the correct model for understanding and solving the problems, issues, and difficulties in planting Western psychotherapy in non-Western lands lies outside of the domain so far considered here.

One place to look would be in the literature and experience of individuals who are concerned with more general psychological and cultural aspects of technical assistance programs. Psychological knowledge has been fruitfully used to deepen understanding of some instances of that special kind of teaching-learning relationship (Morrill, 1972; Rapaport, 1964).

Another frame of reference is the field of community mental health, in which the foreign expert is not the deliverer of services but a consultant resource person, a tool of those who directly deliver services. An interesting example of this reported by Kinzie, Teoh, and Tan (1974), although something less than a complete success, is suggestive of a potentially valuable method. Both of these approaches might well be looked to as a source of paradigms by those of us who wish to apply our therapeutic approaches to personal difficulties of people in other cultures.

I would like to add, also, that after this chapter was completed I received a copy of a forthcoming article by Draguns (1975), which deals with many of the issues in this chapter, especially those in the first section. Although there is overlap, our perspectives and emphases differ, and the papers complement each other. Unfortunately, it was not possible at this writing to give due appreciation to this work.

A substantially shorter version of this paper was presented in a symposium on Psychopathology in Cross-Cultural Perspective on 7 August 1974 at the Second International Conference of the Association for Cross-Cultural Psychology, held at Kingston, Ontario, Canada.

REFERENCES

Abel, T. Cultural patterns as they affect psychotherapeutic procedures. *American Journal of Psychotherapy*, 1956, *10*, 728–740.

Abel, T. The dreams of a Chinese patient. In W. Muensterberger & S. Axelrad (Eds.), *The*

psychoanalytic study of society (Vol. 2). New York: International University
Press, 1962.

Alexander, A., Workneh, F., Klein, M., and Miller, M. Psychotherapy and the foreign
student. In P. Pedersen, W. Lonner, & J. Draguns (Eds.), Counseling across
cultures, Honolulu; University Press of Hawaii, 1976.

Berne, E. The cultural problem: Psychopathology in Tahiti. *American Journal of Psychiatry*,
1960, *116*, 1076–1081.

Bishop, M., & Winokur, G. Cross-cultural psychotherapy. *Journal of Nervous and Mental
Disease*, 1956, *123*, 369–375.

Bolman, W. Cross-cultural psychotherapy. *American Journal of Psychiatry*, March 9, 1968,
124, 1237–1244.

Bustamente, J. Importance of cultural patterns in psychotherapy. *American Journal of
Psychotherapy*, 1957, *11*, 803–812.

Carstairs, G. Cross-cultural psychiatric interviewing. In B. Kaplan (Ed.), *Studying personality cross-culturally.* New York: Harper & Row, 1961.

Carstairs, G. Psychiatric problems of developing countries. *British Journal of Psychiatry*,
1973, *123*, 271–277.

Devereux, G. Three technical problems in psychotherapy of Plains Indian patients. *American
Journal of Psychotherapy*, 1951, *5*, 411–423.

Devereux, G. Cultural factors in psychoanalytic therapy. *Journal of the American Psychoanalytic Association*, 1953, *1*(4) 629–635.

Draguns, J. Resocialization into culture: The complexities of taking a worldwide view of
psychotherapy. In R. Brislin, S. Bochner, & W. Lonner (Eds.), *Cross-cultural
perspectives on learning.* New York: John Wiley & Sons, Halsted, 1975.

Draguns, J. Counseling across cultures: Common themes and distinct approaches. In P.
Pedersen, W. Lonner, & J. Draguns (Eds.), *Counseling across cultures.* Honolulu:
University Press of Hawaii, 1976.

Draguns, J., & Phillips, L. *Culture and psychopathology: The quest for a relationship.* Morristown, New Jersey: General Learning Press, 1972.

Ezriel, H. Experimentation within the psychoanalytic session. *British Journal of Philos-
ophy and Science*, 1956, *7*, 29–48.

Frank, J. *Persuasion and healing.* New York: Schocken Books, 1963.

Frank, J. Therapeutic factors in psychotherapy. *American Journal of Psychotherapy*, 1971,
25, 359–361.

Freud, S. The dynamics of the transference. In *Standard edition of the complete psychological works of Sigmund Freud* (Vol. 12). London: Hogarth Press, 1958. (Originally published in 1912.)

Greenson, R. *The technique and practice of psychoanalysis* (Vol. 1). New York: International
Universities Press, 1967.

Hsu, Jing, & Tseng, Wen-shing. Intercultural psychotherapy. *Archives of General Psychiatry*, 1972, *27*, 700–706.

Kiev, A. (Ed.). *Magic, faith and healing.* New York: Macmillan Co., Free Press, 1964.

Kinzie, J. Cross-cultural psychotherapy: The Malaysian experience. *American Journal of
Psychotherapy*, 1972, *26*, 220–231.

Kinzie, J., Teoh, J., & Tan, E. Community psychiatry in Malaysia. *American Journal of
Psychiatry*, May 5, 1974, *13*, 573–577.

Kittrie, N. N. *The right to be different.* Baltimore: Penguin Books, 1973.

Lesse, S. Obsolescence in psychotherapy: A psychosocial view. *American Journal of Psychotherapy*, 1969, *23*, 381–395.

McNeill, J. T. *A history of the cure of souls.* New York: Harper & Row, Torchbook, 1965.

Meadows, P. The cure of souls and the winds of change. *Psychoanalytic Review*, 1968, *55* (3), 491–504.

Mendel, W. The non-specifics of psychotherapy. *International Journal of Psychiatry*, 1968, *5*, 400–402.

Morrill, R. Consultation or control: The cross-cultural advisor-advisee relationship. *Psychiatry*, 1972, *35* (3), 264–280.

Pande, S. The mystique of Western psychotherapy: An Eastern interpretation. *Journal of Nervous and Mental Diseases*, 1968, *146*, 425–432.

Rapaport, R. Some notes on para-technical factors in cross-cultural consultation. *Human Organization*, 1964, *23*, 5–10.

Rogers. C. The necessary and sufficient condition of therapeutic personality change. *Journal of Consulting Psychology*, 1957, *21*, 95–103.

Rosen, G. *Madness in society*. Chicago: University of Chicago Press, 1968.

Spiro, M. *Burmese supernaturalism*. Englewood Cliffs, New Jersey: Prentice-Hall, 1967.

Strupp, H. Toward a reformulation of the psychotherapeutic influence. *International Journal of Psychiatry*, 1973, *11*, 263–327. (a)

Strupp, H. On the basic ingredients of psychotherapy. *Journal of Consulting and Clinical Psychology*, August 1, 1973, *41*, 1–8. (b)

Sundberg, N. Toward research evaluating intercultural counseling. In P. Pedersen, W. Lonner, & J. Draguns (Eds.), *Counseling across cultures*. Honolulu: University Press of Hawaii, 1976.

Szasz, T. S. *The myth of mental illness*. New York: Harper & Row, 1961.

Thomas A. Pseudo-transference reactions due to cultural stereotyping. *American Journal of Orthopsychiatry*, 1962, *32*, 894–900.

Torrey, E. F. *The mind game: Witch doctors and psychiatrists*. New York: Emerson Hall, Publishers, 1972.

Useem, J., Useem, R., & Donoghue, J. Men in the middle of the third culture: The roles of American and non-Western people in cross-cultural administration. *Human Organization*, 1963, *22* (3), 169–179.

Vontress, C. E. Racial and ethnic barriers in counseling. In P. Pedersen, W. Lonner, & J. Draguns (Eds.). *Counseling across cultures*. Honolulu: University Press of Hawaii, 1976.

Wohl, J., & Silverstein, J. The Burmese university student: An approach to personality and subculture. *The Public Opinion Quarterly*, 1966, *30* (summer), 237–248.

Wohl, J., & Tapingkae, A. Values of Thai university students. *International Journal of Psychology*, 1970, *7* (1), 23–31.

11 Psychotherapy in Intercultural Perspective: Some Personal Reflections

RONALD M. WINTROB

WHAT DOES IT FEEL LIKE TO WORK AS A THERAPIST IN A FOREIGN CULTURE?

Ronald Wintrob's paper presents a personalized account of a psychotherapist who, finding himself immersed in another culture, has to mediate his own cultural adaptation. His approach is distinctively different from that of the authors of previous chapters, who have dealt with the problems of intercultural counseling as phenomena for academic study. Wintrob's personal account expresses the frustration and stress felt by a psychotherapist who has to apply many essentially Western techniques to a non-Western culture. The theory and the practice of intercultural counseling are notably separate in the kinds of demands they make on a counselor. It will be useful to participate vicariously in the struggle described by Wintrob, applying his insights to other intercultural situations.

Wintrob speaks of the difficulties inherent in coping with cultural shock, having to depend on unreliable helpers, understanding the interpersonal dynamics of a foreign culture, and following the problems of psychotherapy into otherwise diverse fields of politics, economics, and religion in its applications. To some extent, Wintrob deals with problems in intercultural counseling as they apply to a specific context, especially when he talks about setting up a program of counseling services. It is therefore fitting and appropriate that this be the last chapter of our volume.

After I completed my medical degree in Toronto, I went to New York for a year as a rotating intern at the 3,000-bed Kings County Hospital. I experienced a kind of medical culture shock. There were major differences in the racial, ethnic, and even social-class characteristics of the patients, as compared with my familiar environment of the Toronto teaching hospitals. There were also less striking but significant differences in social status and social interaction among the attending physicians, house staff,

208

and nurses. I had trouble communicating—with patients and with staff. I was anxious and my self-esteem was shaken.

Yes, the old story of the greening of another young doctor. And I did the common thing to cope with my discomfort. I increased my "professional efficiency" by increasing my social and emotional distance. That kind of defensive distancing can be adaptive: you feel so much less in conflict and so much more in control. (And, of course, a vast number of physicians function in just that way with their patients—and often enough with their own families at home.) It can be adaptive, but at the price of diminishing your expressivity and your ability to establish and maintain rapport; in short, at the price of your sensitivity, the very quality you need to be effective in intercultural counseling.

I mention my stressful beginning as an intern because, perhaps naively, I had been quite unprepared for it. After all, there was no reason to expect disorienting differences between two cities 600 miles apart. I mention it because I *did* experience what I think of as cultural dysadaptation (Wintrob, 1969); that is, relatively minor changes in a person's familiar environment and emotional support system can and do provoke dysadaptation responses. And it is evident that you cannot function effectively as a psychotherapist when you are preoccupied with your own anxieties.

Since my internship in New York I have conducted psychotherapy in several countries, including a 2-year period in Liberia. In those settings in which I functioned primarily in a treatment role, as well as in those in which I undertook research with Cree Indians in Canada, physicians in Peru, and Puerto Ricans in Connecticut, I again experienced—in varying degrees—that complex of feelings of cultural dysadaptation that had painfully impinged on my awareness when I was an intern in New York.

In reflecting on my own experiences as a psychotherapist in the context of cultural differences between my patients and me, I wish to illustrate some of the theoretical and practical issues in intercultural counseling that have been discussed by the contributors to this volume. It is my hope that my case example, as it were, will dramatize some of the complexities, self-deceptions, and gratifications inherent in intercultural counseling.

My reflections on intercultural psychotherapy begin with my sense of cultural dysadaptation, because I share with the contributors to this volume the conviction that a helpful transaction between patient and therapist can be achieved only when the therapist is as carefully attuned to his own feelings as he is to those of the patient. Such self-understanding is never an automatic process, but one that is greatly influenced in intercultural psychotherapy by the extent of the therapist's sense of strangeness in an unfamiliar setting, of his positive and negative feelings about the people with and for whom he is working, as well as those whom he is treating. The therapist needs to consider carefully the quality and degree of his identification with the "foreigners" he is interacting with—in his own culture no less than in a distant one. The tendency to react to and be motivated by stereotypes is hard to avoid. Cultural stereotyping affects relatively sophisticated cultural relativists such as anthropologists and psychologists, just as it does other people (Nash & Wintrob, 1972).

I can illustrate this cultural stereotyping tendency from my own experience. Living in Liberia was a difficult, stressful experience for me. Being the only psychiatrist in the country and charged with developing and running the country's mental health services, I found clinical demands to be extraordinarily heavy both for my associates and myself. I increasingly felt constrained and constricted by high-level government officials—inhibited from carrying out the program we had discussed and formally agreed upon. At that time in Liberia (the mid-1960s) most upper-level government officials defined themselves as Americo-Liberians, descendants of those liberated American slaves who settled along that part of the West African coast during the first half of the 19th century and who founded the first Black African republic in 1847. Americo-Liberians distinguished themselves (until recently) from "tribal" Liberians. Most of the patients and staff with whom I worked were tribal Liberians. And, as I sensed increasing resistance from Americo-Liberian officialdom, I increasingly dichotomized my feelings about the patients, forming a progressively stronger positive identification with tribal patients. I was well aware that my splitting of the images of the two groups of Liberians interfered with my ability to sympathize with and accurately evaluate the interpersonal conflicts of Americo-Liberian patients. It forced me to monitor my own reactions with particular care, to recognize and separate my conflicts from those of the patient, to separate stereotype from individual.

I would also point out that it is relatively rare that a therapist in our country is required to function in close proximity to national policymaking and the political process. In many developing countries, that role is thrust on the therapist because of his administrative responsibilities for program development. It may be seductive in the sense of being an "ego-trip" and may distort his capacity to draw accurate inferences from clinical data. This was another aspect of the especially careful self-monitoring I had to do in Liberia, since a number of my patients were among the senior decision-makers of the country. My point is that ideological neutrality of a therapist is neither necessary nor desirable; but it is essential that the therapist not distort the patient's communications by introducing ideological inferences not intended by the patient. It is of course equally essential that each patient be considered and treated as an individual and not as a representative of a group, class, race, or ideology. To accomplish that, the therapist must be acutely sensitive to his own values and commitments.

Reflecting in another way my own biases and commitments, I devoted major effect in Liberia to developing counseling services for students. It is widely recognized in Liberia that higher education is the sine qua non to good jobs, and the competition is intense. Anxiety states among students are common. It was easy for me to empathize with their struggles and identify with their aspirations, and (I thought) my work was politically uncomplicated. Leaving aside the issue of the politics of treating particular patient populations—an issue of considerable importance in some countries—I want to indicate here that I was not really aware of the extent to which I had sublimated my conflicting feelings about Liberians until I prepared my first clinical paper in Liberia. It was titled "A Study in Disillusionment" and described the dysadaptation reactions of Liberian students who had returned from advanced training abroad (Wintrob, 1967).

In the Liberian case I have discussed the risks of distortion due to the therapist's negative feelings because I feel it is important material from which to learn, material that is all too rarely discussed by therapists. But the same risk of misinterpretation of clinical data also comes from positive overidentification with a group. To some extent this was the case with me in my treatment of students and tribal Liberians. It was a much more striking feature of my approach to Cree Indian patients in Quebec. Undoubtedly influenced by my perceptions of the powerless status of tribal Liberians, and by the anthropologist's well-known proclivity to identify with the people he studies, I knew that I would constantly have to check and recheck my tendency to interpret the conflicts of Cree students as the intrapsychic sequelae of prejudice and Cree political powerlessness. I would have to reevaluate my reactions to the clinical data because the content far more often related to interpersonal, intra-Cree concerns than it did to the concerns of the Cree as a Canadian minority subject to discrimination. Of course the two themes often interdigitated in the expression of Cree students' conflicts, and much of my therapeutic effort was devoted to understanding precisely that interdigitation. That fact did not diminish the necessity of carefully monitoring my own feelings so that I did not incorrectly infer discrimination in a discussion of, for example, a Cree student breaking up with his white girlfriend.

More recently, several colleagues and I have been studying how certain groups of people in Connecticut explain mental illness. We have been particularly concerned with supernatural explanations of emotional disorders—with hexing and rootwork explanations among Blacks and spiritism and witchcraft beliefs among the Spanish-speaking (Gaviria

& Wintrob, 1975; Wintrob, 1973). This research, growing out of our psychotherapeutic contact with people who share these supernatural explanations of their symptoms, caused us to review our feelings about who is the appropriate therapist for such people. It was apparent that a majority of both patients and community informants felt that the treatment methods of community healers were more effective than psychiatric treatment, largely because of the closer "fit" between healers' explanations of illness and the community residents' explanations of illness. Accordingly, healers' treatment procedures were more understandable to patients and their families, involved a much greater degree of family and community support for the victim of the illness, and were felt to produce better results.

This example from Connecticut could be repeated in any part of this country and many other countries, as Pedersen suggests in chapter 2. Our experience in Connecticut caused us, and I hope will also cause the reader, to remember that one of the strongest biases we have as therapists is our commitment to what we choose to consider rational, scientific explanation. It was an assault on the sense of professional identity and self-esteem of some of my colleagues to have the fact forced on them that their scientific world view was neither welcomed nor accepted by a large part of the population they felt they were there to help. I have little doubt I would have felt the same way had I not been sharply sensitized to that issue in Liberia and elsewhere. Therapists who want to work in an intercultural context need to remind themselves regularly, as I again had cause to do in Connecticut, that we are least anxious and probably most effective as psychotherapists when we treat people whose world view corresponds with our own.

That is not to say we should not attempt to do psychotherapy with people who diverge—even diverge sharply—from our world view; just that we should carefully assess the objectives and limitations of the therapy we undertake, and just as carefully explain those objectives and limitations to the people who ask for our help.

We should recognize too that the fact of the therapist being an outsider to a given social group, class, or subculture may be the very reason he has been asked to fill the helping role. One of the few Black psychotherapists in our area, for example, has been told repeatedly by Caucasian patients who have come to him for treatment that they feel more secure about his maintaining objectivity and preserving confidentiality because of his being Black and having what they assume to be a quite different background, both of upbringing and experience. (He adds that many of these patients like to use ghetto talk with him "to establish their liberal credentials.") I had similar experiences with Americo-Liberians, who were understandably very concerned that a breach of confidentiality could have serious repercussions for themselves, their families, and others within the relatively closed society in which they lived.

This is the kind of situation that comes up time and again in the intercultural context of psychotherapy, one that makes this kind of undertaking an interpersonal transaction of great complexity and of equally great challenge. In my view, it is an unparalleled challenge to the therapist to understand him- or herself. I agree with Vontress in chapter 3, who believes that living in another culture is most important to doing effective counseling with minorities—not primarily because one gets to know another culture but because one is forced to undergo one's own cultureshock and subsequent self-analysis.

REFERENCES

Gaviria, M., & Wintrob, R. M. The foreign medical graduate who returns home after postgraduate training in U.S.A.: A Peruvian case study. *Journal of Medical Education,* 1975, *50,* 167–175.

Nash, D., & Wintrob, R. M. The emergence of self-consciousness in ethnography. *Current Anthropology,* 1972, *13,* 527–542.

Wintrob, R. M. A study of disillusionment: Depressive reactions of Liberian students returning from advanced training abroad. *American Journal of Psychiatry,* 1967, *123,* 1593–1598.

Wintrob, R. M. An inward focus: Psychological stress in fieldwork experience. In F. Henry & S. Saberwal (Eds.), *Stress and response in fieldwork.* New York: Holt, Rinehart & Winston, 1969.

Wintrob, R. M. The influence of others: Witchcraft and rootwork as explanations of behavior disturbances. *Journal of Nervous and Mental Disease,* 1973, *156,* 318–326.

Author Index

215

Subject Index

Adaptation, modes of personal, 7–8
African students, 89
Alloplasticity, 6–7
American(s), 8, 9, 10, 32, 33, 43, 44, 83–84, 85–89, 91, 92, 93, 101–104, 105, 108, 109, 118, 120, 125, 126, 129, 130, 132, 136, 137, 143, 145, 146, 147, 148, 149, 150, 153, 154, 156, 158–159, 160, 163, 165, 171, 181, 198, 199, 204; Afro-, 44, 53, 58, 153, 159; Anglo-, 49; Asian-, 31; Chinese-, 31, 48; counseling center, 143; counselor(s), 33, 143; five systems of mainstream values, 24; identity, 109; Indians, 10, 44, 65–66, 67, 69, 78, 197; Japanese-, 31, 55, 56, 58, 128, 150; Jewish-, 44, 58; Mexican-, 30, 44, 49, 51, 58, 59; "real," 43; self-perception, 108; uniformity of language among, 101
American counseling techniques, 3; and assumptions, 4; as widely accepted in certain restricted areas, 5
American Cross-Cultural Ethnic Nomenclature Test, 181
American Psychological Association, 165; conference in Vail, Colorado, 17, 35
Anthropologist(s), 19, 72, 198, 211; American, 185, 186
Appalachian people, 12, 47, 50, 52, 54–55, 61
Arab(s), 145, 149
Arapaho Indians, 72
Arapaho-Shoshone Indian values, 74
Asia, 33, 143, 160
Asian(s), 32, 33; students, 33, 87, 88, 89, 185–186
Autoplasticity, 6–7
Aversive events experienced by sojourners: avoidance of, 131–133; identification of, 130–131; neutralizing of, 133–134
Aversive Survey Schedule, 131

Behavioral approaches in psychotherapy, 192
Behaviorism, 114
Behavior modification, 117; as universally valid, 5, 10
Behavior therapy, 161–162
Bilaterality of the client-counselor relationship, 5–6
Black(s), 10, 25, 29, 48, 51, 53, 59, 61, 153, 158, 211; -biased items on tests, 181; children, 61; clients, 26, 29; counselors, 159; fear of losing "blackness," 61; ghetto, 10, 60; lower-class, 52, 55; nuances of culture, 48; power, 44; psychologist, 42; psychotherapists, 212; slave heritage of, 44; southern, 49; students, 145
Black Intelligence Test of Cultural Homogeneity, 181
Blacky Pictures Test, 74
Bureau of Indian Affairs, 69, 75
Burmese, 196; folk conceptions of, 185

California Psychological Inventory, 174
Canada, 171
Case histories, use of, in evaluating counseling effectiveness, 161–162
Cattell Culture-Fair Intelligence Test, 175
Caucasian(s), 25, 49, 53, 73, 146, 159; Anglo-, 49, 74; counselee, 48, 212; counselor(s), 29, 47, 52, 53, 56, 58, 60, 145; establishment, 48; middle-class society, 29; student values, 72; with Southern accents, 57
Centrifugal versus centripedal pull in intercultural work, 3
Characteristics needed by the intercultural counselor, 11–12
Cherokee Indians, 73, 75
Chickasaw Indians, 75
Chinese, 128, 197, 199; adjustment of, 82; family, 31; students, 32, 48
Chitling Test, 181
Choctaw Indians, 51, 75

221

About the Authors

A. A. Alexander is a professor of psychiatry at the University of Wisconsin Medical School and research associate of the Wisconsin Psychiatric Institute, Madison, Wisconsin. Since 1967, he and his collaborators have been studying the psychological and psychiatric responses involved in intercultural adaptation.

Kenneth H. David has done extensive research with the Peace Corps Training Center in Hawaii and is now a member of the Office of Human Resources, Honolulu, Hawaii. He has taught psychology in the United States and in Asia, has been active in numerous international professional organizations, and has published more than 20 articles dealing with intercultural psychology, learning theory, and other topics in social psychology.

Juris G. Draguns, professor of psychology on the faculty of The Pennsylvania State University, has published numerous articles on intercultural psychopathology. He has acted as a consultant and taught extensively in Europe. His articles are useful to counselors seeking to pursue the topic of intercultural counseling into the various ways in which cultural differences affect psychopathological disturbances.

Marjorie H. Klein researched the problems of Scandinavian students while she was a doctoral student at Harvard University (Social Relations Department). In 1963, she joined the University of Wisconsin Department of Psychiatry as a National Institute of Mental Health postdoctoral fellow. In 1967, with Ford Foundation support, she began researching foreign student adaptation. She was appointed assistant professor at the University of Wisconsin in 1972. Her research presently is divided into studying the ways in which foreign students adjust to American campuses and into developing methods by which the results of psychotherapy can be measured objectively.

Walter J. Lonner is a professor in the Department of Psychology at Western Washington State College, Bellingham. He has published many articles or chapters on intercultural research and learning methods. As founding editor of the *Journal of Cross-Cultural Psychology,* he has been in a position to review and evaluate much of the significant literature on intercultural topics. His own background in counseling psychology further recommends his contribution to this book.

Milton H. Miller is professor and head, Department of Psychiatry, Health Sciences Center, University of British Columbia, Vancouver, British Columbia. He began his research on intercultural adaptation at the University of Wisconsin and is continuing it in Canada, where he is one of the founders of the Pacific Rim Educational Program.

Paul Pedersen taught and counseled students in Indonesia and Malaysia for 5 years before coming to the International Student Advisors Office at the University of Minnesota as a counseling psychologist and as an associate professor in the Department of Psycho-Educational Studies. He is developing a program designed to train counselors to work in multicultural populations and has written a number of articles and professional papers dealing with such training.

Edward C. Stewart, presently director of intercultural research, Washington International Center, Washington, D.C., brings a wealth of knowledge from his experience in counseling and training Peace Corps volunteers. He has worked in the United States with students from foreign countries who have come to study in American schools. He brings the perspective of the psychology of communication to the problems of intercultural counseling. In addition to his university teaching experience, he has been active as an international consultant for public and private agencies. Through the Human Resources Research Office and elsewhere, he has also published some of the most frequently quoted materials on intercultural training.

Norman D. Sundberg is a professor in the Department of Psychology and the Wallace School of Community Service and Public Affairs at the University of Oregon. As a counseling and clinical psychologist, he has adapted his counseling style in recent years to teach in both European and Asian university programs. He has written a number of articles and materials on clinical psychology. He has consulted on multicultural programs and has led extensive research projects in which adolescent choice situations were compared against personality in India, the Netherlands, and the United States.

Joseph E. Trimble, research scientist, Social Change Study Center, Battelle Human Affairs Research Centers, Seattle, Washington, is perhaps one of the more active psychologists involved in articulating the problems of transcultural communication among American Indians. He has directed more than two dozen extensive multicultural research projects on problems of ethnicity, has consulted for numerous government and private agencies, and has published numerous articles on intergroup relationships, with an emphasis on social psychology.

Clemmont E. Vontress is professor of education at The George Washington University, Washington, D.C., and is best known for his more than 50 articles, chapters, and papers on the ways in which ethnicity affects the counseling process. He has been active in the leadership of several national organizations and is one of the best known blacks in the field of counseling psychology. He has acted as a consultant to university programs, government agencies, and other organizations on problems relating to intercultural counseling.

Ronald M. Wintrob, associate professor of psychiatry and anthropology at the University of Connecticut, has been a leader in the field of transcultural psychiatry, both in the United States and abroad. Through the American Psychiatric Association, he has been active in promoting courses on cultural sensitivity in medical schools and among mental health professionals. He has taught in Montreal, Canada, and in Liberia.

Julian Wohl, a clinical psychologist, is professor of psychology at the University of Toledo where he served as chairman of the Department of Psychology for 6 years. Most of his professional activity now is divided between psychoanalytic psychotherapy, and universities and their students in Southeast Asia. He has published several papers on each of these subjects. He held Fulbright lectureships at Rangoon University in Burma and at Chiang Mai University in Thailand.

Fikré Workneh was trained as a psychiatrist at the University of Wisconsin and is now assistant professor of psychiatry at the medical school of The University of Addis Ababa, Ethiopia. His interests range from the problems of foreign students and medical graduates to that of developing the psychiatric services of his homeland.